MON
ROC
ROC **W9-CIK-953**

Double Standards in Medical Research in Developing Countries

Ruth Macklin

CAMBRIDGE
UNIVERSITY PRESS

338773

AUG 1 0 2006

PUBLISHED BY THE PRESS SYNDICATE OF THE UNIVERSITY OF CAMBRIDGE
The Pitt Building, Trumpington Street, Cambridge, United Kingdom

CAMBRIDGE UNIVERSITY PRESS
The Edinburgh Building, Cambridge, CB2 2RU, UK
40 West 20th Street, New York, NY 10011–4211, USA
477 Williamstown Road, Port Melbourne, VIC 3207, Australia
Ruiz de Alarcón 13, 28014 Madrid, Spain
Dock House, The Waterfront, Cape Town 8001, South Africa

http://www.cambridge.org

© Ruth Macklin 2004

This book is in copyright. Subject to statutory exception
and to the provisions of relevant collective licensing agreements,
no reproduction of any part may take place without
the written permission of Cambridge University Press.

First published 2004

Printed in the United Kingdom at the University Press, Cambridge

Typeface Plantin 10/12 pt.   *System* LATEX 2ε   [TB]

A catalogue record for this book is available from the British Library

Library of Congress Cataloging in Publication data
Macklin, Ruth, 1938–
Double standards in medical research in developing countries / Ruth Macklin.
    p.   cm. – (Cambridge law, medicine, and ethics; 2)
Includes bibliographical references and index.
ISBN 0 521 83388 4 – ISBN 0 521 54170 0 (pbk.)
1. Medical care – Research – Developing countries.   2. Medical ethics – Developing
countries.   3. Public health – Research – Developing countries.   I. Title.   II. Series.
RA441.M33   2004   174.2′8 – dc22   2003065532

ISBN 0 521 83388 4 hardback
ISBN 0 521 54170 0 paperback

The publisher has used its best endeavours to ensure that the URLs for external websites
referred to in this book are correct and active at the time of going to press. However, the
publisher has no responsibility for the websites and can make no guarantee that a site will
remain live or that the content is or will remain appropriate.

Contents

Acknowledgments

The author is grateful to the many people – some identified in endnotes, others unnamed – whose words and ideas were invaluable resources for this book. Special thanks go to the individuals and organizations who granted permission to quote their comments on drafts of the 2002 *CIOMS International Ethical Guidelines for Biomedical Research Involving Human Subjects*. I profited greatly from numerous conversations with Reidar Lie, who corrected some errors and provided much food for thought. I benefited from my collaborative work with Alice Page while serving as Senior Consultant to the National Bioethics Advisory Commission on its international project and after the project's completion. Colleagues on the professional staff of the World Health Organization, the Joint United Nations Program on HIV/AIDS (UNAIDS), and CIOMS made possible my participation in meetings, workshops, and review of research that provided essential information for this book. I am especially indebted in this regard to David Griffin, José Esparza, Peter Piot, and Juhana Idänpään-Heikkilä. I also benefited from and am grateful to the anonymous reviewers of the proposal I submitted for this book to Cambridge University Press.

Work on the book was begun during a month's residency at the Rockefeller Foundation's Bellagio Study and Conference Center in Italy. There can be no better setting for reflection and productive work, and I am most grateful for the opportunity my residency there provided for organizing the book and completing the initial chapters. Several colleagues who were at Bellagio during my stay helped to shape my thinking on critical issues.

Last but not least, I thank the following people at CUP with whom I worked from beginning to end: Finola O'Sullivan, Nikki Burton, Alison Powell, and Diane Ilott. I am grateful to the General Editor, Alexander McCall Smith, for including this book in the new Cambridge University Press Series.

1 International research contested: controversies and debates

At an international meeting devoted to ethics in research, one participant from a developing country remarked: "It is important to specify that research should be conducted in developing countries only when it cannot reasonably be carried out in developed countries. Research should not be carried out in developing countries solely for economic reasons."

A participant from the United States replied: "It's proving useful to conduct studies on allergy and depression in developing countries. The people who do the studies do them well. Do people want to discourage that sort of thing? It's going on now, with consent of the countries."[1]

These comments illustrate two responses to a question that has given rise to international debate and controversy: Should medical research be conducted in Third World countries when it could equally well be carried out in the United States or Western Europe? According to one view, the answer is a probable "no":

We fear . . . a major increase in studies that could easily be done in an industrialized country, but where the participants are denied optimal medical care and the products are not made available afterward. The benefits to the pharmaceutical industry are obvious: potentially lower costs, less red tape, larger pools of "naïve" subjects and lower ethical requirements.[2]

This position considers populations in developing countries to be vulnerable, and therefore it is inappropriate to involve them in research when the same studies could be done in an industrialized country.

An opposing view maintains that requiring research to be conducted in industrialized countries before initiating a similar study in a developing country is an unacceptable form of paternalism. It treats developing country decision-makers, researchers, and research subjects like children, incapable of knowing their own interests and protecting those interests in the way the rights and welfare of research subjects are protected in industrialized countries.

A great deal of research is conducted in both industrialized and developing countries when the same health problem exists in both places.

Spokespersons from developing countries are among those who encourage this trend, arguing that their countries are capable of protecting their own citizens from harm or exploitation at the hands of local and foreign researchers alike. If the population in these countries has to wait for drug trials to be completed in industrialized countries before the medications can be tested and approved by their own regulatory authorities, the delay can result in untreated diseases and loss of lives.

Yet another question looms large: are developing countries and their citizens able to afford the cost of drugs that are the products of successful research once they are approved for sale? Will the treatments, in fact, become available when research is concluded? According to one view, all that is required is to conduct research according to the highest ethical standards. Researchers and sponsors have no further obligations. Once the research is over, it is a matter for national or local health systems to provide any resulting health benefits for the population. An opposing view argues that when wealthy countries or pharmaceutical companies sponsor research in resource-poor countries, they should not simply pack up and leave, with any resulting health benefits going to the sponsoring country and economic benefits to industry. This debate poses the question of what justice requires in the conduct of multinational research, the topic addressed in chapter 3.

An even more intense debate has arisen over research that could not – for ethical reasons – be conducted in an industrialized country, but is carried out in a developing country. In considering this possibility, the US National Bioethics Advisory Commission acknowledged the ethical dilemma but did not recommend prohibition of such research. The Commission's report on international research says that when the US or another industrialized country seeks to conduct research in another country, when that same research could not be conducted ethically in the sponsoring country, "the ethical concerns are more profound, and the research accordingly requires a more rigorous justification."[3]

Can there be a good justification for conducting research in a developing country when that same research could not ethically be conducted in the United States or Europe? One answer is a clear "no":

[O]ur ethical standards should not depend on where the research is performed . . . [T]he nature of investigators' responsibility for the welfare of their subjects should not be influenced by the political and economic conditions of the region . . . [A]ny other position could lead to the exploitation of people in developing countries, in order to conduct research that could not be performed in the sponsoring countries.[4]

The possibility that vulnerable people might be exploited is a cause for concern in developing countries that lack sufficient protections for human subjects of research. Yet the concept of exploitation remains fuzzy, and disagreements have arisen with regard to specific instances in which exploitation has been alleged. Chapter 4 examines the concept of exploitation, its different applications, and mechanisms to guard against it. One supposition underlying concerns about exploitation is that research subjects are exposed to risks, possibly unacceptable risks. This ethical worry focuses on the potential harms research subjects may experience.

However, a researcher from the Uganda Cancer Institute expressed an equally strong view defending research in his country that could not have been conducted in the United States or Western Europe:

Ugandan studies are responsive to the health needs and the priorities of the nation . . . [T]he appropriate authorities, including the national ethics review committee, have satisfied themselves that the research meets their own ethical requirements. With these requirements met, if Ugandans cannot carry out research on their people for the good of their nation, applying ethical standards in their local circumstances, then who will?[5]

This scenario puts a different twist on the matter. In the absence of research conducted in developing countries, the inhabitants are denied the potential benefits that may result. In many such places, the majority of people lack access to treatments available in industrialized countries or, for that matter, any treatments at all. If research is not conducted in developing countries, the public health benefits that could result may never be available to the population.

Still, the Ugandan researcher's comments pose another thorny question about the protection of human subjects of research in developing countries. Are the mechanisms for protecting the rights and welfare of human subjects adequate in those countries? According to one side in the debate, the ethical standards employed in the United States and Western European countries, and stipulated in international guidelines, should prevail wherever research is conducted, and review by an ethics committee should be required in both the sponsoring and the host countries. This is the position of the Public Citizen Health Research Group, as expressed in a letter criticizing a draft provision of the report of the US National Bioethics Advisory Commission:

We are dismayed and deeply disappointed that the National Bioethics Advisory Commission (NBAC) has seen fit to radically alter its draft report on the ethics of research in developing countries . . . to no longer require review by a US Institutional Review Board (IRB) of US government-funded research in developing countries. This ill-considered proposal would effectively remove the requirement for American ethical review of some American research and frequently leave participant protection solely to often inexperienced and unregulated foreign IRBs.[6]

Exactly the opposite position has been expressed by the Pharmaceutical Research and Manufacturers of America (PhRMA), the trade association for the US pharmaceutical manufacturers:

We understand that there is a strong movement to ensure that consistent ethical standards are applied to research globally. However, requiring ethics committee review in the sponsor's country as well as local ethics committee review would impose the standards of the sponsor's country on the host country. Moreover, we are not confident that ethics committees in sponsoring countries will have the resources to be involved routinely in such activity, given the demands already placed on such committees for review of protocols to be conducted in their own country.[7]

These opposing views call for an exploration of what ethical standards are in use or have been proposed in recent efforts to revise international guidelines, and whether it is a form of "ethical imperialism" for an industrialized country to impose its own standards on a developing country where it is sponsoring or conducting research. As discussed in chapter 2, a great deal of confusion surrounds the meaning of "ethical standards" in the review and conduct of research. One common shortcoming is a failure to distinguish between *ethical standards* and *procedural mechanisms*.

If it can be shown that the procedural mechanisms for protecting the rights and welfare of human subjects of research in developing countries are equivalent to the protections in place in the US and other industrialized countries, then it would surely be paternalistic to insist on ethical review of proposed research by a committee sitting in the US. On the other hand, someone from a developing country might argue that people there would balk at the requirement for obtaining informed consent in research because patients trust doctors to do what is in their best interest, and a local research ethics committee could accept that argument at face value. However, to abandon the requirement to obtain voluntary, informed consent from each prospective subject of research would amount to a significant departure from an internationally accepted ethical *standard* in the conduct of research. The question of what constitutes adequate safeguards for the protection of research subjects in developing countries is explored in chapter 5.

It is not uncommon to find references to ethical principles governing research as "American," "North American," or "Western," implying a contrast with "Asian," "African," or "Eastern" ethics. Such references misconceive the nature and scope of ethical principles. The author of an article about research in Africa on a preventive vaccine for AIDS, published in the *New Yorker*, makes this mistake when he asks: "Will scientific objectives drive the search for an AIDS vaccine, or will a series of ethical imperatives imposed by the West take precedence?"[8] This question actually embodies at least three mistakes; the same errors appear in a similar question under the article's title: "Has the race to save Africa from AIDS put Western science at odds with Western ethics?"[9]

The first mistake is in characterizing ethical imperatives for research as "imposed by the West." Three prominent documents containing guidelines for ethics in research were developed by international organizations and intended to apply to research that is multinational, as well as intranational. These are the Declaration of Helsinki, issued by the World Medical Association;[10] international ethical guidelines issued by the Council for International Organizations of Medical Sciences (CIOMS), a nongovernmental organization that works in collaboration with the World Health Organization (WHO);[11] and a guidance document for research on preventive HIV/AIDS vaccines, issued by the Joint United Nations Programme on HIV/AIDS (UNAIDS).[12]

The second error by the author of the *New Yorker* article is the presupposition that everyone in the "West" agrees on ethical imperatives. Researchers, ethicists, and health advocates from both industrialized and developing countries stand on both sides of debates that have occurred regarding key provisions in these international guidelines, especially the question of what is owed to research subjects during and after a trial. What the author of this misleading article identifies as "Western ethics" is the view that there exists an ethical obligation to provide antiretroviral treatment to research subjects who become infected while participating in a preventive HIV/AIDS vaccine trial in Africa. This is a question that assumes great importance as preventive HIV vaccine trials are going forward.

The vigorous and prolonged debate over what level of care should be provided to research subjects during a trial has, for the most part, occurred in a quite different context from that of HIV/AIDS preventive vaccine trials (see chapter 2). Contrary to the *New Yorker* author's statement, the strongest defenders of a "double standard" in research have been spokespersons from the West: officials at the US National Institutes of Health (NIH) and the Food and Drug Administration (FDA), and some of their counterparts from the UK. They have argued that it is ethically acceptable to provide a lower level of care and treatment to research subjects in less developed countries than research subjects receive in the US and in Europe (their views are discussed in detail in chapters 2 and 4).

The third error is setting scientific objectives in opposition to ethics in research. Guidelines for research that rest on universal ethical principles do not set science and ethics in opposition to one another. On the contrary, these documents proclaim the importance and necessity of conducting scientific research in striving for the goal of improving public health. The purpose of ethical guidelines is not to halt or slow scientific progress, but rather to ensure that the fruits of research are obtained with full attention to the rights and welfare of human beings.

In chapter 8 we return to the debate over whether researchers and sponsors of preventive HIV vaccine trials have an obligation to provide antiretroviral treatment to participants who become HIV-infected during the trial. We examine the merits of arguments on both sides of that debate, without the distracting assumptions that there exists a "Western" ethics, and that ethics and science are somehow incompatible elements in research.

Why do clinical research in developing countries?

A matter of growing concern is the increasing the number of studies that drug companies conduct in developing countries because the research can be done there more quickly and with less oversight, thereby enabling the companies to gain approval for marketing and realize a profit as soon as possible. Especially in countries that lack adequate mechanisms for the protection of human subjects, the dramatic rise in the testing of experimental drugs has become a matter of deep ethical concern. When the US National Bioethics Advisory Commission was holding meetings of its international project, one commissioner asked a fundamental question: "When is it ethically acceptable to conduct a trial in another country?" Another member responded that if all the ethical requirements are satisfied, the fact that it is cheaper to conduct the trial in another country is irrelevant.[13] Other commissioners disagreed.

When the Commission sought testimony from industry spokespersons at public hearings, that effort was thwarted by the refusal of industry to cooperate. However, a study commissioned by NBAC did succeed in getting a candid response from one pharmaceutical researcher regarding the reasons why industry conducts studies in developing countries:

The vast majority of the trials I have done in the third world possibly are dose response trials. Developing the profile of the knowledge on the drug to get profit and benefit elsewhere. That's extremely clear . . . I'm sure the simple fact that the pharmaceutical industry is a profitable business with all the drugs that we use just tells me that. It's not a charitable business. It's a Wall Street hardcore business. And doing clinical trials in the third world sometimes may be motivated by a variety of reasons. In general, the vast majority is access to the patient in large numbers and a faster rate. And sometimes the third argument, nevertheless, is also at a cheaper price.[14]

The pharmaceutical industry obtains unquestionable gains – scientific as well as financial – from testing new products in developing countries. One scientific reason for testing experimental medications on research subjects in developing countries is that they have been exposed to fewer other drugs than have patients in industrialized countries. As one industry spokesman is quoted as saying: "You want patients with no other disease states and no other treatments. Then you can say relatively clearly that whatever happens to those patients is from the drug."[15] Drug companies and researchers refer to such individuals as "naïve subjects," meaning that they have not been exposed to existing treatments for their condition and, therefore, are likely to yield more reliable results. A darker meaning of "naïve" may also be pertinent – a reference to people who are not well-educated, who are unacquainted with the precepts of modern science, or who submit themselves without questions to medical authority.

The financial advantages are several. It is unquestionably cheaper to carry out the research in countries that have lower costs for all of the ancillary goods and services necessary to set up and support the research, including labor costs for technical and scientific personnel in resource-poor countries. If the research can also be completed more rapidly, that is also a financial advantage because industrial sponsors can bring successful products to market more quickly and ensure an earlier profit. In the not-too-distant past, a factor that enabled research to be conducted more rapidly in developing countries was the virtual absence of prior ethical review by research ethics committees, a mechanism that has been required for decades in industrialized countries. Avoidance of the often time-consuming requirement for local or national ethical review is fast disappearing as an option, as an increasing number of developing countries have established such requirements and US agencies that oversee research also mandate such protections.

The US Department of Health and Human Services reported a significant increase in the number of foreign countries where US-supported clinical trials are carried out. In 1990, research involving human subjects was conducted in twenty-nine foreign countries; by 1999 that figure jumped to seventy-nine. The largest growth in these studies occurred in Russia, Eastern Europe, and Latin America.[16] By the middle of 2002, members of the US Congress had become concerned about reports of

unethical overseas research and a representative from California introduced a bill entitled "To promote safe and ethical clinical trials of drugs
and other test articles on people overseas." Among the findings in the
bill were that "Some researchers exploit the fragile regulatory systems,
high illiteracy rates, and public health failures of developing countries to
test their experimental drugs and devices on misinformed and unwilling human participants"; and that "existing law permits manufacturers
to profit from the misery and pain of uninformed, misinformed, and
unwilling patients in developing countries."[17] On the day the bill was
introduced, it was referred to the House Committee on International
Relations, where it has remained ever since.[18]

When asked whether India is increasingly becoming a favored destina-
tion for human trials, a distinguished Indian physician–researcher, who
established one of the first research ethics committees in that country,
made these observations.

The reasons for the popularity of the developing world are the following: (a) Large
population (b) Low cost (c) Legislative vacuum or infirmities (d) Ignorance about
the legal and ethical issues of human trials among the public and even health
care professionals and (e) Craze among the developing countries to link up with
Western institutions and at any cost.[19]

The Indian researcher added the important observation that adequate
readiness to conduct clinical trials should be assessed on an institution-
by-institution basis, and not for a developing country in general.

Still another factor that provides an advantage to the pharmaceutical
industry is the much greater opportunity in many developing countries
to conduct clinical research testing an experimental product against a
placebo, an inactive substance. Placebo-controlled studies can be completed with fewer research subjects and in a shorter period of time than
clinical studies that compare an experimental drug to an existing medication. In addition, the US Food and Drug Administration prefers a
placebo-controlled study whenever that design is ethically defensible[20]
(see chapter 2 for an extensive discussion of this issue). To industry's
advantage, the ability to compare a new drug with placebo shortens the
time of the study and makes the data more readily acceptable to the FDA,
both of which lead to quicker profits for experimental products that prove
to be efficacious.[21]

Of course, the single best reason to conduct clinical research in developing countries is that the diseases for which products are being tested
are prevalent in those countries and a public-health need exists to develop
effective prevention or treatment. But the investment in research on
tropical diseases has been paltry compared to the amount of money

and number of studies devoted to research on diseases prevalent in the United States, Europe, and Japan – the leading markets for pharmaceuticals. According to one estimate: "Just 0.3 percent of the drug industry's much-touted R&D [research and development] resulted in the handful of drugs approved for tropical diseases between 1975 and 1997, despite tens of thousands of industry-sponsored clinical trials conducted around the world every year."[22]

A leading example of this imbalance is the case of malaria. In 1993, the United Kingdom spent over $200 million on cancer research, whereas the total amount spent on malaria research throughout the world was only $84 million.[23] Yet in 2000, more than 1 million people died of malaria, most of them children in Africa. In contrast, only about 1,200 cases of malaria are diagnosed in the United States each year, most of them occurring in immigrants or travelers who have returned from areas where malaria is prevalent such as Africa, India, and Central America. There appears to be more basic research, such as studies of the mechanisms of action of drugs and disease transmission, and less research on ways of providing treatment against malaria to people in developing countries.[24] It is worth pondering what the expenditures on research would be if the toll malaria were to take in the United States even remotely approached the figures in developing countries.

Which countries are "developing"?

At a workshop on research ethics in which I participated in Buenos Aires in 2002, the need arose to distinguish between different countries typically referred to as "developing." I commented that Argentina is not in the same category as Rwanda: to which one participant, referring to the severe and worsening financial crisis the country was undergoing, replied: "We're getting there."

The terms "developed," "developing," and "underdeveloped" have typically been used to refer primarily, if not exclusively, to the comparative economic level of countries. In recent years, the requirement to use politically correct terminology led to a rejection of "underdeveloped" in favor of "developing." As late as 1993, however, the CIOMS international ethical guidelines included a guideline entitled "Research involving subjects in underdeveloped communities."[25] The revised version of the CIOMS guidelines, issued in 2002, abandons the term "underdeveloped," and the relevant guideline is entitled "Research in populations and communities with limited resources."[26] Other international documents now refer to "least developed countries" with the abbreviation LDCs.[27] An analogous move has resulted in a more frequent use of "industrialized" to replace "developed" when referring to wealthier countries. Another term used to refer to countries such as Brazil and Thailand is "newly industrialized," reflecting their status as somewhere between the richest countries in North America and Europe, and the poorest in Africa and Southeast Asia.

Nevertheless, a problem remains whenever a label is applied to countries, lumping them together as "industrialized' or "developing." For one thing, not all non-industrialized countries are moving in that direction at the same rate. Some may never become industrialized like European countries, the United States and Canada. Some are likely to remain poor indefinitely. Some countries characterized as "developing" have extremely low literacy rates, whereas others – such as Argentina, Costa Rica, and Chile – have a population whose literacy rate is as high as that of leading industrialized countries. In addition, it is not clear exactly how to characterize the countries that emerged from domination by the former Soviet Union at the end of the Cold War. Scientific and technological expertise has long been in the forefront in some of those countries, but awareness and implementation of ethical rules for the conduct of research has been rare, if present at all.

Is it a mistake to lump together as "developing" all countries except those in Western Europe, North America, Japan, Australia, and New Zealand? The answer is both "yes" and "no." It depends on the specific features of a country that bear on the research enterprise. It is appropriate to lump together countries that are resource-poor, since neither the government nor the majority of citizens can afford medical treatments that become largely available to residents of wealthier countries once research is concluded. It is appropriate to lump together countries that have few trained scientists and little experience of conducting biomedical research. And it is appropriate to lump together countries that lack ethical guidelines for research and have little or no capacity for conducting ethical review of research conducted there by industry or by scientists from industrialized countries.

Yet there is surely a continuum along which countries typically called "developing" fall with regard to the above characteristics. Most of the countries in sub-Saharan Africa are desperately poor, have little or no manufacturing capability, and have few highly trained and experienced biomedical researchers. South Africa is the key exception, with Uganda, Kenya, and Nigeria ranking somewhat above most other countries in these respects. A look at South America reveals that Brazil and Argentina boast many highly trained and experienced biomedical researchers. These countries have had an industrial infrastructure for many years. Yet Brazil is the country with the widest gap between the richest and poorest members of the population, and Argentina has slid from being a First World country (at the beginning of the twentieth century) to occupying the financial status of a Third World country (at the beginning of the twenty-first century).

Among Asian countries, Thailand, India, and China all have highly trained and experienced biomedical researchers and all also have the capability to manufacture drugs. In September 2000 the Indian Council for Medical Research (ICMR) issued a set of ethical guidelines governing research that is the equivalent of anything found in the industrialized West. Little is known about the existence and operation of research ethics committees in China. All three countries have a large population of poor people who lack access to modern medical treatment. Physicians from Myanmar, Laos, and Cambodia reported that awareness of ethical requirements in the conduct of research is entirely absent in their countries.[28]

A quite different meaning of "developed" and "underdeveloped" has been suggested, with considerable irony. Following a report in the *New York Times* that the newly elected president of Brazil had cancelled the purchase of military weapons in favor of buying food for the poorest segment of the country's population, a letter to the editor observed:

By choosing to buy food rather than weapons, [the Brazilian president] raises Brazil to the status of developed nation, well ahead of underdeveloped nations like the United States.

I speak in terms of moral development, of course, not economic.[29]

The letter-writer's remark contains more than wry humor. It reminds us that values other than economic development deserve to be recognized and promoted. Moral development is a concept conspicuously absent from international discourse, despite frequent allusions to the related, yet different, concept of human rights (see chapter 7).

In sum, then, there appear to be as many differences as there are similarities among so-called developing countries in respects relevant to the conduct of biomedical research. Recognizing that it is best to think of countries in the world as falling along an economic continuum from most-developed to least-developed, we may nevertheless, for the sake of convenience, continue to speak of the two groups as dichotomous: industrialized and developing. The chief distinction between the two groups is likely to lie in the opportunity for a majority of the population to have access to the successful products of research. This and subsequent chapters make distinctions between or among developing countries as appropriate to the context.

Health needs in developing countries

Despite longstanding and widespread knowledge of the devastating toll diseases continue to take on populations in the developing world, industrialized nations have largely avoided playing an active role in seeking to improve the health status of people in poor countries. Although it is true that the United States and European countries have for many years conducted or sponsored biomedical research in developing countries, once the research was concluded, the sponsors – wealthy countries as well as industry – considered their work done. A similar thing occurred with public health intervention programs. Decades ago, when the United States carried out programs of childhood immunization in Africa, it left no infrastructure in those places. Some hospital facilities there date from the 1940s and '50s. Today, there is wide agreement that the same mistakes should not happen again.

A new awakening in recent years began with a recognition that "safari research," as it has been critically termed, comes close to being a form of exploitation of poor countries and their populations from which research subjects are recruited. Some people argue that it is unacceptable to enter a developing country or community, set up facilities for carrying out biomedical research, and then simply depart with the healthcare personnel and equipment when the research is over. Others take a different view, maintaining that as long as the research is conducted carefully and with proper attention to the rights and welfare of the subjects, that is all that is ethically required. Today the conviction is growing among some researchers and sponsors that they have an obligation to "leave something behind" when the research is completed.

The chief means of fulfilling this obligation has been to help developing countries build their own capacity to conduct research independently. Elements of capacity-building include training scientists and other research personnel, contributing to the research and healthcare infrastructure in the community or country, and most recently, providing training for scientific and ethical review of research. Although establishing and strengthening scientific and technological capacity in developing countries was stated as an obligation in a United Nations Declaration more than a quarter of a century ago,[30] only recently has this obligation been affirmed and taken seriously by governmental and industrial sponsors of research in developing countries.

As beneficial as capacity-building is for poor countries, it is far from sufficient as a means of ameliorating the conditions created by historically prevalent diseases, such as malaria and tuberculosis, and in the past two decades, HIV/AIDS. Three million people died of AIDS in 2001;

tuberculosis accounted for 1.7 million deaths in 2000; and, as already noted, in the same year malaria killed more than 1 million people.

African nations have been hardest hit by HIV/AIDS, with an estimated number of more than 4 million HIV-infected individuals currently living in South Africa, 1 million infected in Malawi, and millions more in other sub-Saharan African countries. The next area predicted to experience an explosion of the epidemic is Asia, with the huge populations of China and India at risk of spread from relatively small numbers currently infected to the general population. It is abundantly clear that as important as education and behavioral interventions are in preventing the spread of HIV infection, they have not been successful in containing the disease.

Antiretroviral therapy (ART), now reasonably effective in prolonging the lives of HIV-infected people in most industrialized countries, has so far been available only to a tiny minority of wealthy individuals in all developing countries except Brazil. Since 1997, the Brazilian government has been providing free antiretrovirals to the general population. The following year, Brazil began to make copies of brand-name drugs to treat AIDS that are protected by patents in the US but not in Brazil. The domestic capacity to manufacture antiretroviral drugs does not exist in Rwanda, Malawi, and most other countries in Africa and Asia, and is unlikely to be developed in the foreseeable future. As a result of an agreement signed by member nations of the World Trade Organization, poor countries are not permitted to import cheaper generic drugs from countries that do manufacture them (a subject which is discussed in detail in chapters 6 and 7).

The conduct of clinical trials sponsored by industrialized countries and carried out in developing countries poses two chief questions: What is owed to research subjects during a clinical trial (often described in terms of the "standard of care")? and What is owed to research subjects, the larger community, and the developing country as a whole when the trial is over? A variety of answers have been proposed, some of which are in international ethical guidelines for research involving human beings and in recommendations in major reports that address these issues.

The controversy that launched debates

Since 1997, unprecedented worldwide attention has focused on ethical concerns in international research. These concerns pertain to biomedical research sponsored by industrialized countries or pharmaceutical companies and carried out in resource-poor countries. The specific questions that have prompted fierce debate and prolonged inquiry are as follows:

1 How can biomedical research be designed and conducted so as to contribute to the health needs of developing countries and at the same time contain adequate protections for the rights and welfare of the human subjects recruited for these studies?

2 If a particular study may not be conducted in the sponsoring country for ethical reasons, is it acceptable to carry out an identical study in a developing country, and, if so, with what justification?

3 When completed research yields successful products or other beneficial interventions, what obligations, if any, do the sponsors have to the community or country where the research was conducted?

4 Should the provisions of international ethical guidelines for research, such as the Declaration of Helsinki, be interpreted and applied in the same way in resource-poor countries as they are in wealthier countries?

These questions were prompted by an episode that arose and captured wide attention in 1997.

Although worries had long existed that exploitation can occur when industrialized countries and pharmaceutical companies conduct research in developing countries, a clinical trial that came to light in 1997 sparked new, worldwide attention to international research. That episode was the furious controversy that surrounded a set of studies of maternal-to-child HIV transmission carried out in several developing countries, in which some of the women were given a placebo even though a proven, effective treatment was available in industrialized countries. The reason for including a placebo group in a study like this is a methodological one. To determine whether the experimental treatment works (its efficacy), and just how well, it is necessary to compare it to something. In this case, the "something" was "nothing," an inactive substance that would have no efficacy in preventing transmission of HIV from mother to child.

The furor was initially prompted by an open letter addressed to US officials by a Washington, DC-based health advocacy group, the Public Citizen Health Research Group, which compared the trials (sponsored by the federal government research organizations) to the infamous Tuskegee experiments,[31] and newspaper stories that followed. The Public Citizen advocacy group argued that a proven treatment regimen can reduce the rate of mother-to-child transmission of the AIDS virus, so it is unethical to withhold that treatment from women in the trial. The proven regimen (known as "076" from the clinical trial in the United States that demonstrated its effectiveness) used a high dose of the drug AZT, begun midway through pregnancy and administered intravenously during childbirth to the woman. The international collaborative studies were carried out in developing countries that could not afford the expensive, high-dose AZT regimen routinely used in the US and European countries. These clinical trials were testing a lower dose of AZT, which was much cheaper and therefore presumed to be affordable to the poorer countries that would make it available to pregnant women. The developing country studies also began the cheaper AZT treatment much later in pregnancy, since women in those parts of the world do not routinely receive early prenatal care. And the AZT was administered by mouth rather than through a vein, which was more in line with the medical facilities used in these developing countries. These departures from the proven treatment available in industrialized countries were intended to adapt the treatment to the medical realities in the developing countries where it could be introduced.

For ethical reasons, clinical trials that included a placebo group (untreated women) to compare with the group receiving the experimental treatment could not be conducted in the United States. Once it had been shown to be effective in reducing the transmission of HIV from mother to child, the expensive AZT treatment became the standard therapy for HIV-positive pregnant women in the US and other industrialized countries. It would surely be unethical to withhold from women in a research study an effective treatment they could obtain as part of their routine medical care. But since women in the developing countries did not have access to any treatment whatsoever, they would not be made worse off by participating in the study than they would otherwise have been.

As a result of widespread publicity that followed the actions of the Public Citizen Research Group, an extended public debate ensued. Some of the discussions appeared in the pages of leading academic and professional journals and involved the sponsors of the research – the National Institutes of Health (NIH), the Centers for Disease Control and Prevention (CDC), and the Joint United Nations Program on HIV/AIDS (UNAIDS) – as well as opponents who criticized the studies. Other articles representing both sides of the controversy were published in bioethics journals.

Critics of this research conducted in developing countries argued that women in the trials should have been given the treatment proven to reduce the incidence of HIV infection in their infants, and many lives could have been saved. The rebuttal by defenders of the research included the following main points (not all defenders invoked all of these justifications). The first defense was that the "standard of care" for HIV-positive women in these developing countries is no treatment at all, so they are not being made worse off by being in the study. A second point was that a placebo-controlled trial can be carried out with many fewer subjects and completed in a much shorter time than could a study with a control arm containing an active treatment, so benefits to this population could be available much sooner.

A third justification was that the expensive AZT treatment that has become standard in the West is not, and will never be, available to this population, so its use in a research study cannot be justified. A final point was that the actual rate of transmission of HIV from mother to child was not precisely known. That meant there would be no way to tell if the new, experimental treatment would be better than no treatment, or sufficiently better to justify the expense of providing the new treatment. These points framed the debate that was to be carried on in numerous forums around the world.

At an early point in the controversy, a leading British medical journal took a position it claimed was absolutely self-evident. An editorial entitled "The Ethics Industry" appeared in the *Lancet*,[32] accusing "the ethics industry" of being "oddly parochial" and "rooted in armchair moral philosophy." And further: "Departments of ethics that are divorced from the medical profession, wallowing in theory and speculation, are quaintly redundant." This illustrates the cynicism with which philosophers and bioethicists continued to be viewed by some in prominent positions in mainstream medicine. Most interesting, however, is the *Lancet*'s quick and certain judgment of the most controversial piece of research of the past decade:

> Most of the dilemmas upon which ethicists thrive can be solved by appeal to principles fundamental to medical practice worldwide – that doctors do no harm to patients, that doctors do their best for patients . . . It does not require recourse to the opposing arguments of 18th century philosophers to work out that the placebo-controlled trials of antiretroviral drugs to prevent perinatal transmission of HIV infection . . . infringe the first principle. Women in the placebo-treated group were harmed by receiving no effective treatment to prevent transmission of HIV to their children.[33]

Without recourse to novel interpretations of "standard of care" or proposed new definitions, without appeal to debates about the proper role of efficiency and economics in international research, and surely without recourse to philosophical principles, the *Lancet* drew its conclusion about the ethics of the placebo-controlled trials. All it needed was an appeal to the "first principle" of medical practice worldwide – "that doctors do no harm to patients." Setting aside the editorial's attack on bioethicists, we may wonder how the *Lancet* arrived so quickly and easily at the opposite conclusion from that articulated by leading spokespersons for the Medical Research Council (MRC) in the UK[34] and the National Institutes of Health (NIH) in the US.[35]

I intend to spare readers of this book any further analysis of the placebo-controlled, mother-to-child HIV transmission studies conducted in Thailand, Uganda, and other developing countries in the late 1990s (although, of necessity, I will refer to that controversy at various points). Those clinical trials may well have surpassed the infamous Tuskegee study in the number of articles that have described, analyzed, and argued about them.[36] Most people who have given any thought to the matter have already formed an opinion, so there would be little point in my trying to convince them otherwise. Instead, it is worth examining a different placebo-controlled study, one that was proposed to be conducted in several Latin American countries.

The proposed Surfaxin study

Early in 2001, the Public Citizen Health Research Group – the same organization that brought attention to the placebo-controlled studies of maternal-to-child HIV transmission in developing countries – learned of a proposal to conduct a different placebo-controlled trial in several Latin American countries (Mexico, Ecuador, Bolivia, and Peru). This was to be a study of a treatment – a drug called Surfaxin – given to infants born prematurely with poorly functioning lungs common in prematurity, the condition known as respiratory distress syndrome. The company sponsoring the research was planning two different studies of its product: one in European countries, which was to compare the experimental product with four already approved treatments for respiratory distress syndrome in newborns, and one in Latin American countries that was to be placebo-controlled.

Public Citizen managed to obtain internal memos from the US Food and Drug Administration, which had planned to endorse the study. The internal FDA meeting at which the proposed trial was discussed was entitled "Use of placebo controls in life-threatening diseases: is the developing world the answer?"[37] The FDA had apparently made a determination in advance that a clinical trial comparing the experimental product with the existing products would not be approvable for methodological reasons. As a result, the company proposed a placebo-controlled trial, which could be conducted only in countries where the infants to be enrolled in the study would not otherwise have access to the existing medications (known as surfactants) already proven to be effective for respiratory distress syndrome.

In one of the internal memos Public Citizen obtained, the FDA acknowledged that "conduct of a placebo controlled surfactant trial for premature infants with RDS is considered unethical in the USA." The

FDA documents also said that surfactants are used in some hospitals in the countries where the study was proposed, but "surfactants are completely unavailable to infants at many other hospitals, secondary to rationing or economic limitations."

In a letter dated February 22, 2001 to Tommy Thompson, Secretary of the US Department of Health and Human Services, Public Citizen wrote the following:

> Particularly because the FDA approved another surfactant (Infasurf) in 1998 on the basis of studies performed between 1991 and 1993 in which all infants were treated with a presumably effective drug and none were given placebo, we call on you to immediately put a stop to plans for this unethical and exploitive study in its present design. The study is unethical because it violates the principle that placebos not be employed when there exists a standard treatment that may reduce or prevent harm, improve health or prolong life. If the study produces findings that are beneficial to patients in wealthier countries but the drug is not widely available in the countries in which it was tested, an additional dimension of unethical behavior will have been added. For the study to take place ethically, all infants must be provided with a treatment either known or expected to be effective; a comparison of the new surfactant to an already approved one would therefore be acceptable.

About six weeks later, Public Citizen announced that the company sponsoring the study planned to redesign the study with an active control instead of a placebo. No infants would receive a placebo in the newly designed study.[38] Yet the study with the original placebo control still had its defenders. At one meeting I attended, a participant said that infants who were to be enrolled in the trial as originally designed would have been made better off, and that "more babies would live if the trial had been done than if not. It is a shame that it was not."[39]

Dr. Peter Lurie, the deputy director of the Public Citizen Health Research Group, who was a leading critic of the placebo-controlled, mother-to-child HIV transmission studies conducted in developing countries, argued that those studies violated the Declaration of Helsinki. Lurie made the same charge for the placebo-controlled lung surfactant study, which was later modified to be consistent with the Declaration of Helsinki.

Revision of the Declaration of Helsinki

One question that emerged from the controversy over the use of placebos in research is whether widely respected international guidelines were sufficient to address the present and future conduct of international collaborative research, and what to do if provisions in these guidelines conflict with research practices that were being strongly defended. Specific items in the Declaration of Helsinki and the CIOMS international ethical guidelines were open to different interpretations, and the guidelines themselves could be questioned on grounds of internal consistency. These two documents are significant, as they are used for guidance and often as a definitive source of authority by the World Health Organization, by investigators in both developed and developing countries, and by national and local committees that review ethical aspects of research.

Guidelines and principles from the previous versions of these now-revised documents were cited both in support and in criticism of the trials in the controversy over the placebo-controlled AZT trials. The main focus of debate was the following provision in the Declaration of Helsinki: "In any medical study, every patient – including those of a control group, if any – should be assured of the best proven diagnostic and therapeutic method."[40] The Public Citizen group contended that the placebo-controlled studies violated this provision because the control group was denied the "best proven method" of reducing transmission of HIV from mother to child – a treatment that existed in the United States and Western Europe. One response to this charge claimed that this provision in the Declaration of Helsinki was never intended to refer to the best proven therapeutic method "anywhere in the world," but only in the country where the research was taking place.[41]

Regardless of what may have been the original intent of the framers of Helsinki, a much larger controversy arose over the substance of the rule governing the use of placebos in research conducted in resource-poor countries. Just because the "best proven" treatment was not available to most people in these countries outside the research context, did that mean it would be ethically acceptable to withhold such treatments from subjects in research when those treatments could be provided to them?

Interpretations of other clauses were debated. The Declaration of Helsinki contained the following statement: "Concern for the interests of the subject must always prevail over the interests of science and society."[42] Critics charged that in the placebo-controlled trials, the interests of society prevailed over the interests of the subjects enrolled in the study. However, supporters of the study could cite a different Helsinki principle: "Biomedical research involving human subjects cannot legitimately be carried out unless the importance of the objective is in proportion to the inherent risk to the subject."[43] According to this defense, although there did exist a risk to the subjects who received placebo, the importance of obtaining an affordable and practical regimen for reducing maternal-to-child HIV transmission for large numbers of people in poor countries is so overwhelming that it justifies the risk of not taking steps to prevent HIV transmission in the relatively small group of study participants.

As these ethical debates were mounted in the pages of medical journals, discussed in the bioethics literature, and reported in the news media, some groups suggested that the proper solution would be a revision of the ethical codes that were allegedly being violated. Those who sought the revisions argued that the provisions of the codes that were ostensibly violated were unreasonable, and therefore a thorough overhaul was needed. Others responded that this maneuver would be unconscionable. Should a longstanding code of research ethics – the Declaration of Helsinki – be revised just because some prominent governmental and international sponsors of research claimed that their studies were ethically sound despite a failure to adhere to provisions of this international code?

The World Medical Association (WMA), the organization that issued the Declaration of Helsinki, embarked on a process to revise the document, a process that became fraught with internal strife and external criticisms. After approximately a year and a half of work, a draft was widely circulated. That draft substantially revised the key paragraph mandating the "best proven therapeutic method," requiring instead that research subjects be provided only with whatever would otherwise be available to them if they were not enrolled in the study. Although that provision, as revised, had its defenders, opponents believed the revision unacceptably weakened the Declaration. After a long public comment period and several conferences devoted to the revised Declaration and its status as an international ethical guideline, that version was abandoned, and the process began anew. An entirely different drafting team was appointed, a new draft emerged, and in October 2000 – well over two years after the process of revision began – the World Medical Association adopted the revised Declaration.

Issuance of the revised Declaration of Helsinki did not quell the controversy, however. Debate continued to rage and finally led to the WMA issuing an alleged "clarification" a year after the revised Declaration had been approved. As we shall see in chapter 2, this "clarification" did little to clarify and left open to interpretation the key points under debate. It would be a mistake, therefore, to think that the newly revised Declaration laid to rest a spate of ongoing controversies and unresolved issues in international research, especially regarding studies that an industrialized country sponsors or conducts in a developing or resource-poor country.

One reason why the revised Declaration has not accomplished that task is that opponents in the fiercest controversies over key provisions remain locked in debate. The earlier principle that was most contentious ("the best proven method") was replaced with a paragraph that changed the wording but retained the substance: "The benefits, risks, burdens and effectiveness of a new method should be tested against those of the best current prophylactic, diagnostic, and therapeutic methods. This does not exclude the use of placebo, or no treatment, in studies where no proven prophylactic, diagnostic, or therapeutic method exists."[44] A close runner-up for contentiousness is the statement in Helsinki's paragraph 30: "At the conclusion of the study, every patient entered into the study should be assured of access to the best proven prophylactic, diagnostic and therapeutic methods identified by the study." Opponents on both of these controversial issues are not likely to reach a resolution because of their adherence to fundamentally different and incompatible viewpoints, despite apparent agreement on some underlying ethical premises.

Even those who endorse the intention that lies behind Helsinki's provisions may have reservations about the feasibility of providing the best current method worldwide in the context of research conducted in a developing country that has a poorly developed health infrastructure. For example, if providing the best current method to the control group would require construction of a cardiac intensive care unit solely in order to conduct the research, that clearly would not be feasible or even desirable, given that the unit could not likely be maintained after the research is concluded. How, precisely, to apply Helsinki's paragraph 29 to particular situations is a problem that has to be dealt with on a case-by-case basis. Nevertheless, those specific cases can be resolved after a thorough exploration of the options by those who are committed, in principle, to the high standard embodied in this provision of the Declaration of Helsinki.

Another reason why the Declaration, even in its current revision, cannot resolve ongoing controversies is that it simply does not address other important aspects of international research about which people disagree. Included in this category are these questions: What, precisely, is owed to the community or country where the research is conducted after the trial is over? and What specific mechanisms for prior review of research protocols and monitoring of studies already in progress can best protect the research participants? In seeking to identify the underpinnings of the debates surrounding these points, I contend that like the earlier items, these are unlikely to be easily resolved.

Procedural solutions

In addition to the substantive ethical concerns in these controversies, there is the crucial "who decides?" question. Who should have the ultimate authority to decide what is ethically acceptable in the design of clinical trials and in post-trial obligations: the developing country that hosts the trials? Should it be the industrialized country that sponsors or conducts the trials? If the relevant provisions of the Declaration of Helsinki or the CIOMS international guidelines should be the operative governing rules, who should make determinations of the key elements that require interpretation?

When agreement cannot be reached by an appeal to substantive ethical principles, one way to reach a resolution is to look for a fair method of resolving differences. This requires identifying and agreeing on a just procedure, a process that all parties agree is fair. An example outside the research context is that of "due process," ensuring that people who are accused of wrongdoing are given a fair hearing and a fair chance to defend themselves against the accusations. An example in the context of research is prospective review of protocols by a duly constituted body whose task is to protect the rights and welfare of human subjects of research.

In a letter to Dr. Harold Varmus, who was then director of the National Institutes of Health, Dr. Mbidde, the Ugandan researcher who defended trials in his country that could not have been conducted in the US, reiterated his position contending that criticism of the placebo-controlled trials by the Public Citizen group "reeked of ethical imperialism."[45] He argued that researchers from Uganda and representatives from the Ugandan Ministry of Health were full participants in the decision to initiate the trials. Other people from the developing countries in which the placebo-controlled AZT trials on maternal-to-child transmission were conducted have also been among the defenders. They argued along the same lines that the studies were ethically acceptable because they satisfied the relevant procedural requirements for approving and conducting research. They pointed out that the placebo-controlled studies were approved by ethical review committees in the developed countries that sponsored the trials and also in the developing countries where they were being conducted. Furthermore, they contended, researchers from the developing countries were carrying out the studies in their own countries and women enrolled in the studies granted their voluntary, informed consent to participate.

This defense of the studies rests on the premise that people from a given culture or country are in the best position to decide what is best for their country, and not some outsiders who are unrelated to the research and unfamiliar with the health needs of the region. Therefore, the argument goes, since the placebo-controlled trials adhered to ethically adequate *procedures* they must be considered ethically acceptable.

A reply to this procedural justification addressed its weakness: "Since the Tuskegee study was conducted by Americans on Americans, this argument obviously does not stand . . . Unethical research will not benefit developing countries in the long run, since it undermines human rights, which are the very foundation on which sustainable development needs to be built."[46] The question remains, then: when disagreement persists over a substantive ethical matter, can procedural solutions be an ethically acceptable means for providing a resolution? There is no easy answer.

Despite the value of seeking a fair procedure to resolve disagreements rooted in different substantive positions, a procedural solution can be flawed. For one thing, despite the search for a just procedure, when there is an imbalance in the power of individuals or groups engaged in the negotiation, it is more than likely that the more powerful will win out. In the case of research in a developing country sponsored by a large pharmaceutical company or a national research agency, such as the NIH or MRC, if the more powerful party sets conditions for the research different from those the Ministry of Health has proposed, the Ministry's desire for the research to be conducted is likely to lead it to accept the more powerful funding agency's conditions.

It is also entirely possible that a duly appointed authority can come to a "wrong" decision or a questionably right one. Only if one believes that whatever the designated authority says is right simply because that authority says so, can the authority's decision remain unquestioned. There can always be rational grounds for questioning a resolution stipulated by a duly appointed body. There is no better example than that of the judicial system in democratic countries. On the assumption that the judiciary is not corrupt, a decision by one court may legitimately be overruled by a higher court, or a court in a different jurisdiction may come to a different judgment. Since empirical evidence or good reasons can be marshaled to question an authority's ruling, this shows that even a fair process can yield misguided decisions or unethical judgments.

It cannot be correct, then, to claim that authorities in developing countries are always in the best position to determine what is best for their people when research is proposed or conducted. The Ministry of Health and other stakeholders are not disinterested parties. Although they may well have the interests of the people and the public's health as a priority, they also have competing interests. Local researchers stand to gain in experience and prestige when they collaborate with an international team sponsoring the research. Money flows into the pockets of those researchers, the hospitals or research institutions where the studies are conducted, and possibly into the coffers of the government itself. To say that the governmental decision-makers are not disinterested is not to imply that they are corrupt (although that can also sometimes be the case). It is only to say that a procedural solution aimed at reaching what is in the best public interest may not succeed in that aim when governmental authorities are the sole or ultimate decision-makers.

Wealthy and powerful sponsors of research can influence the behavior of local collaborators in developing countries. The less democratic the country, the fewer guarantees of freedom of speech, the greater is the opportunity for unethical practices in the conduct of research involving human beings. One example is a clinical trial in Nigeria, sponsored by Pfizer Inc., of antibiotics that had not yet been approved for use in the United States. In a six-part series of articles devoted to clinical drug testing in developing countries, the *Washington Post* reported that a Nigerian physician who said he was present during the trial "felt it was 'a bad thing,' but he did not object because Pfizer's test appeared to have backing from the government. 'I could not protest,' said the physician, Amir Imam Yola. 'The system you have in America and the system we have here, there is a wide gap. Freedom of speech is still not here.'"[47]

Agreement on underlying propositions

Soon after the revised version of the Declaration of Helsinki was issued, I wrote an article stating that underlying these controversies in international research ethics are several propositions on which opponents appear to agree. The propositions are:

1 research should be responsive to the health needs of the population in the country or region where the research is conducted;
2 research is needed in developing countries on common and serious diseases that rarely occur in industrialized countries (e.g., malaria), and on those that pose a huge risk to life and health even if the same diseases do exist in industrialized countries (e.g., HIV/AIDS, tuberculosis);
3 it is unacceptable to lower the ethical standards adopted in the industrialized world when carrying out research in developing or resource-poor countries;
4 it is unethical to exploit vulnerable populations or individual participants in the conduct of research.

Propositions 1 and 2 are discussed in this Chapter. Proposition 3 is addressed in chapter 2, and detailed interpretations of what is required by proposition 1 are addressed in chapter 3. The fourth proposition is examined in chapter 4.

Despite the apparent consensus on the above four fundamental propositions, once we peel off the layer of harmony we confront unanswered questions, as well as stark disagreements. Although I still maintain that widespread agreement exists on propositions 2, 3, and 4, I have come to be less certain about whether there is consensus on the first proposition. It has been questioned – and rejected soundly – by Dr. Robert Temple, a deputy director of medical policy at the Food and Drug Administration's Center for Drug Evaluation and Research (see chapter 3 for Dr. Temple's statement and a full discussion of this issue). Others have suggested that there are legitimate exceptions, and that this requirement should not be stated as an absolute prohibition.

Responsiveness to the health needs of the population

Although widespread agreement exists on the general principle, disagreement surrounds its interpretation. Is research responsive to the health needs of the population just so long as it addresses a health problem that is prominent in the country or region? Or must some steps be taken before the research is initiated to seek to ensure that successful products are made available to the population at the conclusion of the research? Opposing replies to these questions point to one of the gaps in the revised Declaration of Helsinki identified above: the question of what is owed to the community or country where the research is conducted after the trial is over. The 2000 revision of the Declaration contains a provision not included in the earlier versions. Paragraph 19 states: "Medical research is only justified if there is a reasonable likelihood that the populations in which the research is carried out stand to benefit from the results of the research." Although the provision as stated is laudable, it leaves wide open what are the criteria for determining "likelihood," and what degree of likelihood is necessary. This is precisely the point on which opponents disagree.

One prevailing view holds that as long as research projects investigate health problems of the population from which subjects are drawn, and if a study adheres to proper ethical rules for the conduct of research involving human subjects, then sponsors or researchers have no additional obligation to ensure availability of any resulting products. Others reply that failure to ensure in advance that products are made reasonably available in a timely manner to the participants and others in the community or country is a violation of distributive justice, and could constitute a reason not to embark on a trial at all.[48] Still others agree that something is owed to the community or country once a trial is concluded, but they say it need not be successful products of the research. Other benefits might equally well serve to fulfill the "responsiveness" proposition. It is evident, then, that these opponents agree on the underlying premise that research must be responsive to the health needs of the population; yet they disagree in their interpretation of what that proposition entails.

Opponents in the much discussed, placebo-controlled, HIV maternal-to-child transmission studies also agreed on the fundamental premise, yet disagreed over whether an alternative trial design would be responsive to the health needs of the population. Defenders of the placebo-controlled studies argued that to compare the shorter, cheaper experimental regimen with the treatment that is the "gold standard" in the United States and Western Europe would fail the "responsiveness" test, since the costly, more complex preventive regimen could never be implemented in resource-poor countries or those lacking the healthcare infrastructure to administer the treatment. Critics replied that the alternative research design was nonetheless responsive since it was not the expensive, complex treatment that was intended for this population but rather, the "short-course" regimen, which could be made available (this did occur in Thailand, but not in Uganda, where even the cheaper treatment remained too costly).

It is evident that the substantive views held by opponents in both debates – what is owed to research subjects during a trial, and what is owed to the country or community after a trial is completed – determine just how they interpret the proposition (accepted by most people) that research must be responsive to the health needs of the population in which the studies are conducted. But some problematic cases give rise to the question of whether legitimate exceptions to this general presumption should be allowed.

One such example is a paradoxical reverse of the situation for which this general presumption was established in the first place. Instead of an industrialized country or industry seeking to conduct an early phase of research in a developing country – research that is unrelated to that country's health needs – in this example the developing country requests that the study be carried out in the United States on a tropical disease. The US National Institutes of Health proposed to study a malaria vaccine in an African country where malaria is endemic. The African country insisted that the early phase of the study – to examine the safety of the vaccine – be conducted in the United States. Although a relatively small number of cases of malaria occur in the US every year (mostly acquired by travelers), it is surely not the case that malaria is a major health problem in the US. The African country's request conforms with a statement in the 1993 CIOMS ethical guidelines: "Phase I drug studies and Phase I and II vaccine studies should be conducted only in developed communities of the country of the sponsor."[49] That requirement was abandoned in the revised version of the CIOMS guidelines as being too paternalistic.

It is undeniable that research on malaria is not responsive to the health needs of the population in the US. Would it therefore be unethical to conduct this early phase study in the US, when any resulting benefits of the research would not be applicable to the industrialized country? On a strict interpretation of the ethical rule regarding "responsiveness" of the research, a study like this should not be permitted. Consistency would require a uniform application of the rule to all countries, industrialized as well as developing. What, then, could justify this exception to the rule? The most convincing justification would be that the developing country lacked the scientific or technical capacity to ensure a high degree of safety of the participants, but such protections are readily available for research conducted in the US. This justification relies on one of the cardinal principles of research, namely, that risks to research subjects be minimized insofar as possible.

Another possible justification is the insistence of the African country that is expected to be the ultimate beneficiary of the malaria vaccine if later phases of the research demonstrate its efficacy. If the consideration just discussed is the reason why the African country insists that the phase of the research to determine the vaccine's safety be conducted in the United States, then it could count as a legitimate exception to the "responsiveness" rule. However, if the African country offers no justification, or contends that residents of the sponsoring country should be exposed to the risks of early phases of research before residents of developing countries are exposed to those same risks, that would not constitute a sufficient reason to treat developing and developed countries differently in this context.

Beyond these debates lies a deeper question about the nature of ethical guidelines. Should they be "pragmatic" or "aspirational"? Adherents of the view that statements such as the Declaration of Helsinki and documents like the CIOMS international guidelines must be "pragmatic" are likely to rely on current and past practices as a guide to what is possible. The pragmatists dismiss "aspirational" guidelines as too lofty and, therefore, unrealistic.[50] For their part, the "aspirationists" tend to be reformers who judge past or current practices to be ethically insufficient to ensure that the highest standards for research apply everywhere, not just in wealthy, industrialized countries.[51]

Needed research in developing countries

Agreement is virtually universal that research is needed in developing countries on common and serious diseases that rarely occur in industrialized countries and on those that pose a huge risk to life and health even if the same diseases do exist in industrialized countries. Yet despite that consensus, sharp disagreement exists on a range of specific questions: Must the research design of a clinical trial demonstrate that a proposed treatment is better than nothing in resource-poor countries that lack a current, standard treatment available in wealthier countries? Or would a different design – known as an "equivalency" trial – be satisfactory, showing that an experimental treatment is as good, or almost as good, as the current treatment used in the wealthier country?[52] If studies with proven benefits have been conducted in one or more countries, when does it become ethically unacceptable to repeat those studies in still another country, rather than simply provide the proven treatment to the population in the country where no trials have taken place? Are observational studies of the "natural history" of diseases ethically permissible in resource-poor countries where effective treatments are not affordable to the majority of the people, but effective treatments for that same condition are available in the country sponsoring or conducting the research?

Answers to the above questions are ostensibly provided by paragraph 29 of the 2000 revision of the Declaration of Helsinki: "The benefits, risks, burdens and effectiveness of a new method should be tested against those of the best current prophylactic, diagnostic, and therapeutic methods. This does not exclude the use of placebo, or no treatment, in studies where no proven prophylactic, diagnostic, or therapeutic method exists." Although it may appear straightforward, this answer is not without ambiguity. Moreover, despite the apparent clarity with which the Helsinki proposition is stated, critics have concluded that it may warrant a rejection of the moral authority of the Declaration. Participants in a conference held at the NIH during the last week of November 2000 debated the Declaration's ban on the use of placebos in research except when no proven treatment exists. Robert J. Temple, who has been a longstanding defender of placebo-controlled trials, said that the revised Declaration of Helsinki takes an absolute position. "It would bar using placebos, for example, to evaluate a new drug for hay fever or migraine. But testing such a medicine against another drug approved to treat such conditions generally doesn't measure its effectiveness as well as testing it against a placebo."[53]

Robert J. Levine, a leading authority on research ethics who had earlier argued vehemently for abandonment of the "best proven treatment" provision in the previous version of the Declaration of Helsinki, was quoted as saying:

Forbidding the use of placebos rules out development of all new therapies for conditions for which there are proven therapies . . . If researchers had followed such rules in the past, he said, drugs currently used to treat high blood pressure or stomach ulcers never would have been developed because of the existence of older, less-effective treatments.[54]

Levine and Temple were countered by Kenneth J. Rothman, who defended Helsinki's position on placebos, saying the interests of the individual patient should always supersede the goals of science or society.

In a telling comment, Levine said that "The United States and most other countries have been ignoring the Declaration of Helsinki for years. I don't know why people think this revision . . . is going to bring about a great change in behavior." Levine's comment prompts two questions: first, why has the United States been "ignoring" the Declaration of Helsinki? and second, if that is the case, should we agree with Levine and Temple that there must be something wrong with the Declaration of Helsinki, or should we conclude that the United States and other countries have been unethical in ignoring it?

If it is true – and it probably is – that the United States has been ignoring the Declaration of Helsinki, it may well be because the US federal regulations governing research involving human beings are so detailed in their procedural aspects that researchers and Institutional Review Boards (IRBs) see no need for another, different set of ethical rules for research. Furthermore, the US regulations are just that – official regulations promulgated by a federal agency, with enforcement mechanisms and sanctions for noncompliance. The Declaration of Helsinki, on the other hand, is simply a "declaration," issued by an international association of medical professionals, which has no enforcement mechanisms and no sanctions for noncompliance. The United States has declined to become a signatory even to international instruments issued by the United Nations, such as the human rights treaty, the Covenant on Economic, Social, and Cultural Rights. So it is hardly surprising that researchers, ethical review bodies, and governmental agencies do not consider the Declaration of Helsinki to be a necessary adjunct to the official US research regulations, known as the Common Rule. While the US federal regulations are almost entirely procedural in their provisions, the Declaration of Helsinki tends toward a more substantive approach that incorporates ethical principles for research involving human subjects.

What, then, should we conclude about whether it is ethically sound or ethically misguided to ignore the Declaration of Helsinki? It is obvious that critics of the controversial paragraph 29 believe that the "best current" provision and its rejection of placebo controls for the vast majority of clinical trials are unreasonable, and therefore, it is not unethical to ignore that specific provision. Defenders would respond that US researchers and ethical review committees are remiss for not adhering to the Declaration of Helsinki in addition to complying with the US federal regulations. Here again, people's views on the substantive ethical issues at stake determine how they view the relevance of the Declaration of

Helsinki to research conducted in the United States or elsewhere in the world.

In sum, then, the broad consensus regarding the need for research in developing countries is a thin reed compared to the deep disagreement about acceptable research designs. Articles continue to appear in the scientific literature, not only about the ethics of placebo-controlled studies but also about their necessity and scientific merit.[55] Two epidemiologists who have opposed placebo-controlled trials contend that "most of these scientific arguments are either wrong or distorted."[56] Of course, their opponents disagree.

Ethical guidelines: pragmatic or aspirational?

These debates over the provisions and the status of the Declaration of Helsinki and the CIOMS ethical guidelines raise once again the fundamental question whether ethical guidelines should be "aspirational" or "pragmatic." I put these terms in quotation marks since those who debate questions surrounding the nature of ethical guidelines often use such terms to express a preferred value. Reference to guidelines as "aspirational" conveys the sense that they are impossibly ideal, not able to be realized in practice; whereas "pragmatic" suggests that the guidelines are truly usable in the practical world. The connotations of these terms imply the answer: pragmatic is better than aspirational.

But there is another way to describe the nature of guidelines. Are they prescriptive, stating what ought to be the case even if current practices fall quite short? Or are they merely descriptive of what is, in fact, done most of the time? Since ethics is about what *ought* to be, rather than simply what *is*, the answer to the prescriptive versus descriptive question is easy. The difficulty, however, is to craft guidelines that are usefully prescriptive without being hopelessly aspirational.

Perhaps a reminder is in order that moral progress has occurred in the past because forward-looking individuals or groups pointed out deficiencies in the current state of affairs and sought reforms. Whether it is establishing equal rights for minorities and women, the prohibition of cruel and unusual punishment of individuals convicted of crimes, or prohibition of female genital mutilation, those individuals or groups who sought reforms were often looked upon by others as "hopelessly aspirational," if not subversive of the established order and tradition. Although the protection of human subjects of research has been a prominent concern for more than three decades, new questions are being raised not only about what is owed to research subjects themselves, but also to others in the communities and countries where research is conducted. It is, therefore, not a legitimate defense against proposed changes to point to the status quo, arguing that the sought-after reforms are unrealistic.

Some of the difficulties in securing benefits for developing countries where research is conducted are a result of the pricing of drugs by the pharmaceutical industry. The justification of these high prices has always been that companies have to recoup their investment in research and development. Others have questioned whether that defense is adequate or even plausible to justify the high prices of drugs.[57] I will not attempt to tackle that debate in this book. One participant at a conference devoted to these issues said "You're not going to change the behavior of profit-making companies."[58] It is probably true that the behavior of profit-making companies will not be changed by issuing or revising ethical guidelines governing research. But other pressures, including international partnerships and collaborative efforts, have already begun to change the picture of research and its aftermath in developing countries.

NOTES

Portions of this chapter are excerpted from my book, *Against Relativism: Cultural Relativism and the Search for Ethical Universals in Medicine* (New York: Oxford University Press, 1999).

1. The meeting took place in February 2002 at the World Health Organization in Geneva, Switzerland. This was a conference of invited participants, convened to review a draft of *International Ethical Guidelines for Biomedical Research Involving Human Subjects*, issued by the Council for International Organizations of Medical Sciences (CIOMS). As a participant in the conference, I took notes on the meeting for my own scholarly use but did not request permission from any of the participants to quote their remarks with attribution. Therefore, I provide no identifying information for these or later quotations from this conference.

2. Peter Lurie, letter to Dr. Jack Bryant, President, Council for International Organizations of Medical Sciences, dated July 13, 2001, quoted with permission.

3. National Bioethics Advisory Commission (NBAC), *Ethical and Policy Issues in International Research: Clinical Trials in Developing Countries* (Bethesda, MD, 2001), 7.

4. Marcia Angell, "Investigators' Responsibilities for Human Subjects in Developing Countries," *New England Journal of Medicine* (hereinafter NEJM), 342 (2000), 967–969.

5. Edward K. Mbidde, Letter to the Editor, NEJM, 338 (1997), 836.

6. Public Citizen Health Research Group, letter to the NBAC criticizing their draft report on ethics of research in developing countries (HRG Publication #1550, December 6, 2000); http://www.citizen.org/publications/release.cfm?ID=6751, accessed June 2, 2002.

7. Bertram Spilker, comments on draft guidelines issued by CIOMS, July 23, 2001. Quoted with permission.
8. Michael Specter, "The Vaccine: Has the Race to Save Africa from AIDS Put Western Science at Odds with Western Ethics?" *The New Yorker* (February 3, 2003), 54–65 at 57.
9. Ibid., 54.
10. World Medical Association, 1964, as amended by the WMA 52nd General Assembly, Declaration of Helsinki (Edinburgh, 2000).
11. CIOMS, *International Ethical Guidelines for Biomedical Research Involving Human Subjects* (Geneva: CIOMS, 2002).
12. Joint United Nations Programme on HIV/AIDS (UNAIDS), *Ethical Considerations in HIV Preventive Vaccine Research* (2000).
13. This meeting of NBAC took place on July 11, 2000. I served as Senior Consultant to the project from July 2000 to July 2001 and was present at all but one of the Commission's meetings on the international project. My close collaboration with the Commission's staff during this period provided additional information presented here.
14. Nancy Kass and Adnan A. Hyder, "Attitudes and Experiences of US and Developing Country Investigators Regarding US Human Subjects Regulations," in NBAC, *Ethical and Policy Issues*, II (2001), B-1-220; 31–32.
15. Sonia Shah, "Globalizing Clinical Research," *The Nation* (July 1, 2002), 23.
16. The Deem Corporation, *Human Research Report*, 17:10 (2002), 9.
17. H. R. 5249, Sec. 2, 107th Congress, 2d session, House of Representatives, July 26, 2002.
18. http://thomas.loc.gov/cgi-bin/bdquery/, accessed February 13, 2003.
19. R. Krishnakumar, "Clinical Trials Should Promote Health Care," interview with Dr. M. S. Valiathan, *Frontline*, India's National Magazine 18:17 (August 18–31, 2001), no page numbers.
20. Karin B. Michels and Kenneth J. Rothman, "Update on Unethical Use of Placebos in Randomised Trials," *Bioethics*, 17:2 (2003), 188–204.
21. Ibid.
22. Shah, "Globalizing Clinical Research," 23.
23. Nuffield Council on Bioethics, *The Ethics of Research Related to Healthcare in Developing Countries* (London: Nuffield Council on Bioethics, 2002), 23.
24. Ibid., 23.
25. CIOMS, *International Ethical Guidelines for Biomedical Research Involving Human Subjects* (Geneva: CIOMS, 1993), 25.
26. CIOMS, *International Ethical Guidelines* (2002), 51.
27. See, for example, Carlos M. Correa, "Implications of the Doha Declaration on the TRIPS Agreement and Public Health," Essential Drugs and Medicines Policy, EDM Series No. 12, Annex 2 (Geneva: World Health Organization, 2002).
28. Physicians from these countries were participants in a training workshop on research ethics sponsored by the World Health Organization, conducted in New Delhi, India, in June 2000.
29. Glenn Cheney, Letter to the Editor, *New York Times* (January 8, 2003), A22.

30. UN Declaration on the Use of Scientific and Technological Progress, cited in George Andreopoulos, "Declarations and Covenants of Human Rights and International Codes of Research Ethics," in (eds.) Robert J. Levine and Samuel Gorovitz, with James Gallagher, *Biomedical Research Ethics: Updating International Guidelines: A Consultation* (Geneva: CIOMS, 2000), 193.

31. Public Citizen News Release, Media Advisory, April 22, 1997.

32. Editorial, "The Ethics Industry," *The Lancet*, 350 (1997), 897.

33. Ibid.

34. I am not aware of a published statement by the MRC regarding this particular placebo-controlled trial. However, on the more general question of whether it is necessary to provide the "best current" treatment to a control group in a clinical trial, the MRC had this to say: "It is . . . important to emphasise that administration of the 'best current therapy' available anywhere in the world may not only involve an expensive drug per se but also an accompanying level of administration/monitoring that is unachievable in a developing country." This comment was submitted on a draft guideline posted by CIOMS on its website (quoted here with permission).

35. The NIH position regarding the provision of "the best care anywhere in the world" to the control group in clinical trials in developing countries was stated in the NIH comment on a draft CIOMS guideline: "[This requirement] could easily result in a trial that yields information useless to the population involved in the study and render the study design unethical." NIH comments on CIOMS guidelines obtained by request through the Freedom of Information Act. See also Harold Varmus and David Satcher, "Ethical Complexities of Conducting Research in Developing Countries," NEJM, 337 (1997), 1003–1005, defending the placebo-controlled trials. Harold Varmus was Director of the NIH and David Satcher was Director of the CDC (Centers for Disease Control and Prevention) at the time they co-authored the article.

36. To cite only a few of these: Marcia Angell, "The Ethics of Clinical Research in the Third World," NEJM, 337 (1997), 847–849; George J. Annas and Michael A. Grodin, "Human Rights and Maternal-Fetal HIV Transmission Prevention Trials in Africa," *American Journal of Public Health*, 88:4 (1998), 560–563; Solomon R. Benatar and Peter A. Singer, "A New Look at International Research Ethics," *British Medical Journal*, 321 (2000), 824–826; Robert A. Crouch and John D. Arras, "AZT Trials and Tribulations," *Hastings Center Report*, 28:6 (1998), 26–34; Carlos Del Río, "Is Ethical Research Feasible in Developed and Developing Countries?" *Bioethics*, 12:4 (1998), 328–330; Christine Grady, "Science in the Service of Healing," *Hastings Center Report*, 28:6 (1998), 34–38; Leonard H. Glantz, George J. Annas, Michael A. Grodin, and Wendy K. Mariner, "Research in Developing Countries: Taking 'Benefit' Seriously," *Hastings Center Report*, 28:6 (1998), 38–42; Dirceu B. Greco, "Revising the Declaration of Helsinki: Ethics vs. Economics or the Fallacy of Urgency," *Canadian HIV/AIDS Policy and Law Newsletter*, 5:4 (2000), 94–97; Robert J. Levine, "The 'Best Proven Therapeutic Method' Standard in Clinical Trials in Technologically Developing Countries," *IRB: A Review of Human Subjects Research*, 20:1 (1998), 5–9; Reidar K. Lie, "Ethics of Placebo-controlled Trials in Developing Nations,"

Bioethics, 12:4 (1998), 307–311; Alex John London, "The Ambiguity and the Exigency: Clarifying 'Standard of Care' Arguments in International Research," *Journal of Medicine and Philosophy*, 25:4 (2000), 379–397; Peter Lurie and Sidney Wolfe, "Unethical Trials of Interventions to Reduce Perinatal Transmission of the Human Immunodeficiency Virus in Developing Countries," NEJM, 337 (1997), 853–856; David B. Resnik, "The Ethics of HIV Research in Developing Nations," *Bioethics*, 12:4 (1998), 286–306; Udo Schüklenk, "Unethical Perinatal HIV Transmission Trials Establish Bad Precedent," *Bioethics*, 12:4 (1998), 312–319; Udo Schüklenk and Richard Ashcroft, "International Research Ethics," *Bioethics*, 14:2 (2000), 158–172; Joe Thomas, "Ethical Challenges of HIV Clinical Trials in Developing Countries," *Bioethics*, 12:4 (1998), 320–327; Varmus and Satcher, "Ethical Complexities."

37. All information cited here was distributed by Public Citizen and is available on its website at http://www.citizen.org/hrg/PUBLICATIONS 1558.htm.

38. See http://www.citizen.org/hrg/PUBLICATIONS/1564.htm.

39. This was the same meeting referred to in note 1.

40. This is the wording used in the 1996 version of the Declaration of Helsinki. The revised wording is discussed further below.

41. Levine, "'Best Proven Therapeutic Method.'"

42. This wording is from the 1996 version of the Declaration. This provision now appears in the revised 2000 Declaration of Helsinki as follows: "In medical research on human subjects, considerations related to the well-being of the human subject should take precedence over the interests of science and society" (paragraph 5).

43. Declaration of Helsinki, 1996, Basic principle 4. In the 2000 revision, this has been revised to read: "Medical research involving human subjects should only be conducted if the importance of the objective outweighs the inherent risks and burdens to the subject" (paragraph 18).

44. Declaration of Helsinki, 2000, paragraph 29.

45. Dr. Mbidde's letter, dated May 8, 1997, was sent to Dr. Harold Varmus, then Director of the NIH, in response to the Public Citizen News Release of April 22, 1997. Public Citizen faxed copies of Dr. Mbidde's letter to individuals on their mailing list.

46. Carel B. IJsselmuiden, Letter to the Editor, NEJM, 338 (1998), 838.

47. Joe Stephens, "The Body Hunters: As Drug Testing Spreads, Profits and Lives Hang in Balance," *Washington Post* (December 17, 2000).

48. Crouch and Arras, "AZT Trials"; Glantz et al., "Research in Developing Countries"; Alice K. Page, "Prior Agreements in International Clinical Trials: Ensuring the Benefits of Research to Developing Countries," *Yale Journal of Health Policy, Law, and Ethics*, 3:1 (2002), 35–64.

49. CIOMS, *International Ethical Guidelines* (1993).

50. Grady, "Science in the Service of Healing"; Robert J. Levine, "The Need to Revise the Declaration of Helsinki," NEJM, 341 (1999), 531–534.

51. Glantz et al., "Research in Developing Countries"; Greco, "Revising the Declaration of Helsinki"; Schüklenk, "Unethical Perinatal HIV Transmission Trials"; Rothman, "The Shame."

52. Lurie and Wolfe, "Unethical Trials"; Lie, "Ethics of Placebo-controlled Trials"; Troyen A. Brennan, "Proposed Revisions to the Declaration of Helsinki – Will They Weaken the Ethical Principles Underlying Human Research?" NEJM, 341 (1999), 527–531.
53. Quoted in Susan Okie, "Health Officials Debate Ethics of Placebo Use," *Washington Post* (November 24, 2000), A3.
54. Ibid.
55. For an overview of the arguments and their proponents, see Michels and Rothman, "Update on Unethical Use of Placebos."
56. Ibid., 197.
57. Page, "Prior Agreements."
58. This was the same conference referred to in note 1.

2   Maintaining ethical standards in research

What substantive ethical standards ought to apply to research conducted in developing countries? Is it acceptable to permit a double standard, one for the industrialized world and a lower standard for developing countries, justified by the hope of providing future benefits to resource-poor countries? Some people maintain that exactly the same standards should be employed the world over, whereas others contend that different standards are required because different circumstances obtain. But does "different" necessarily mean "lower"? Controversies over what ethical standards are appropriate for the conduct of research in different parts of the world are complicated by confusion over what is meant by "ethical standards."

Debates about the justification for allowing different standards or requiring a single standard have arisen in two main contexts in international research. The first concerns what should be provided to a control group in clinical trials. Testing experimental medicines typically involves a comparison between the experimental product and an approved drug. In some situations, the experimental medicine is compared with a placebo, an inactive substance. One group of subjects receives the experimental product and the other – the control group – gets either the proven medicine or a placebo.

The ethical question focuses on what is provided to the control group. The phrase "standard of care" has been introduced in posing the question: Is it ethically acceptable to provide a control group in research with the standard of care in the developing country – whatever is routinely provided to people in that country with that medical condition? Or must a control group be provided with the best treatment available elsewhere – the "standard of care" in the sponsoring country?

The second context in which standards are debated is that of care and treatment provided to research participants if they become ill with a disease other than the one that is the focus of the study. A leading example exists in the context of preventive HIV/AIDS vaccine trials: What type or level of treatment should be provided to subjects who become HIV-infected in the course of the trial (not from the experimental vaccine but as a result of their health-risking behavior)? In the United States, those subjects would have access to triple therapy as the accepted, standard treatment for HIV-infected persons, subject to certain factors such as viral load. In resource-poor countries, access to triple therapy is available only to relatively few people and is not considered "standard" treatment for HIV infection. Arguments that rely on what is routinely available in resource-poor countries have been used to defend the care and treatment research participants receive during a trial when that care and treatment is substantially less than what would be provided in the industrialized country sponsoring the research.

A more sophisticated way of defending different levels of care and treatment in resource-rich and resource-poor countries is by appealing to the distinction between equitable treatment and equal treatment. In this connection, the *New Yorker* article on preventive vaccine trials (cited in chapter 1) quotes a comment by the chief of the bioethics branch at the NIH, who holds that it is not ethically required to provide the same care and treatment to subjects in vaccine trials in Africa that is available to subjects in similar trials in the US. The comment denies that "justice requires treating everyone, everywhere exactly the same way."[1]

This comment relies on a key distinction between justice as *equality* and justice as *equity*. How can we tell which conception of justice best applies to any particular situation?

To illustrate with examples of each conception in contexts outside of research ethics, consider first two possible systems of health insurance applied to individuals in society. One person lives alone, is young and healthy. Another person is old, has many illnesses and three children who are also sick. The first system of health insurance pays exactly the same sum of money to all individuals, whether or not they require money for medical care and treatment. The second system pays all individuals what they require for medical care but does not pay healthy people anything unless they become ill. The first system uses the principle of justice as equality: everyone receives exactly the same amount of money. The second system employs the principle of justice as equity: to each person according to his or her medical necessities. Without belaboring the analysis, it is intuitively obvious that the more appropriate principle in this context is justice as *equity*.

For a different example, consider two different systems of workplace earnings. Both companies employ men and women, and both groups do exactly the same work. In the first business, men are paid 50 percent more money than women. The boss reasons that it is likely that men have to support their families, and therefore they deserve more money than do women. In the second company, the boss pays women and men the same wages. In the first case, the boss uses the principle of *equity* (men deserve more money because they probably have greater expenditures in supporting their families). In the second case, the boss uses the principle of equality: equal pay for equal work.

What is clearly unjust in the first work place example is the division of the workers according to gender, without ascertaining whether some men are single and have no one else to support, some women are single parents and therefore, have children to support, and some couples both work and share in supporting their families. But suppose the boss made those distinctions and paid the single workers without families to support less money for the same work than the individuals with families to support. Using the principle of justice as equity in this situation bears some analogy with the system of health insurance, in which it seems obvious that the equity principle is the correct conception of justice. Yet using that same principle violates a cardinal principle of just compensation in the workplace: equal pay for equal work. The more appropriate principle in this situation is justice as *equality*. A just society should have other remedies for the needs of workers with families, such as tax breaks and medical insurance schemes that recognize such needs.

Since both principles of justice are legitimate and are potentially applicable to a variety of situations, it requires further argument and analysis to determine which is more applicable in a particular context. It is true but hardly sufficient to deny that justice requires treating everyone, everywhere, in exactly the same way. This chapter and the next explore various features of multinational research in which questions of justice arise.

Ethical standards and "standard of care"

The expression, *standard of care*, was introduced early on in debates over whether it is acceptable to use a placebo control when there exists a proven treatment for the condition under study. I first heard the term used in this context when a researcher who was involved in the maternal-to-child HIV transmission studies about to be launched in Thailand expressed concern about whether it would be ethical to withhold the proven treatment used in the US and, instead, give the pregnant Thai women in the control group a placebo. He consulted me on one brief occasion, and I was almost persuaded by the "standard of care" argument. However, I have since come to reject that basis for determining what is ethically acceptable to provide to members of a control group when research is conducted in developing countries.

The main reason why I reject the typical "standard of care" argument is that it is a lowest-common-denominator basis for determining ethical obligations. If the principle of beneficence has any relevance to the conduct of research, it requires researchers to *maximize benefits* as well as to minimize harms. Since the research subjects themselves are surely among those who should be counted in seeking to maximize benefits, it follows that providing a higher standard of care during the research, when that is feasible, is ethically preferable to providing the minimal standard dictated by background conditions in the country or region.

There is a second reason to reject the "standard of care" argument in debates over what should be provided to research subjects. It invites confusion because of its ambiguity and the many different interpretations placed upon it by commentators. Despite the widespread use of the phrase "standard of care" in discussions and debates, there has been little conceptual clarity. To illustrate the confused and confusing ways in which this term has entered the discussion, we begin with a brief survey from the literature.

That it is not even necessary to invoke the vague and ambiguous concept of standard of care is evident from the fact that it is nowhere to be found in any of the international declarations or guidelines that deal with the ethics of research involving human beings. It does not appear in the Declaration of Helsinki, issued by the World Medical Association; the *International Ethical Guidelines for Research Involving Human Beings*, issued by the Council for International Organizations of Medical Sciences (CIOMS); the *Guidance Document for Preventive HIV/AIDS Vaccines*, issued by the Joint United Nations Programme on HIV/AIDS (UNAIDS); the European Union Clinical Trials Directive; nor do other documents make use of the term "standard of care." The report on international research issued by the US National Bioethics Advisory Commission discusses the concept and explicitly rejects it. However, as discussed below, the report issued by the UK Nuffield Council on Ethics retains the term and defends its use.

Although the Declaration of Helsinki does not mention "standard" or "standard of care" anywhere (either in its earlier version or the substantially revised 2000 version), one commentator sought to interpret the Declaration's most controversial provision in those terms:

When Helsinki calls for the "best proven therapeutic method" does it mean the "best therapy available anywhere in the world"? Or does it mean the standard that prevails in the country in which the trial is conducted? . . . [T]he best proven therapy standard must necessarily mean the standard that prevails in the country in which the clinical trial is carried out.[2]

This interpretation is surprisingly dogmatic in light of the wide debate and conflicting interpretations of the problematic phrase that endured until the Declaration of Helsinki was revised in 2000. It is indeed puzzling that the author of this passage insists that "best proven therapy" *necessarily* means "the standard that prevails in the country in which the clinical trial is carried out." Why *necessarily*? (Necessary truths exist only in mathematics and deductive logic.) In any case, whereas this comment stipulates a single, unambiguous interpretation of the phrase used in the earlier version of the Declaration, other people have contended that the correct interpretation refers to the best current (proven) treatment anywhere in the world.[3]

The most problematic feature of the terms "standard" and "standard of care" is the different and often contradictory ways in which they have been used. Nevertheless, these terms continue to be widely employed, resulting in ongoing confusion and arguments at cross purposes. The National Bioethics Advisory Commission provides a brief analysis of the origin of the concept, questioning whether the concept can be uncritically imported into the research setting:

"Standard of care" is a concept borrowed from the medical–legal context, denoting the level of conduct against which a physician's or health provider's treatment of a patient will be judged in determining whether such conduct constitutes negligence. It generally means: "what a reasonably prudent physician (or specialist) would do in the same or similar circumstances". . . . Defined in this way, it can meaningfully describe the types or level of treatments provided to patients in the clinical setting, but it might not serve as a justification for what ought to be provided to participants in research.[4]

The key point to note here is the shift from a term used in a descriptive sense to one intended to play a justificatory role. NBAC goes on to identify the inherent ambiguity:

[A]n ambiguity lurks in the term "standard," which sometimes means "what is normally done," as in "standard practice." In this meaning, "standard practice" in some countries – such as reusing syringes or other disposable equipment – would not be acceptable to US researchers and would not constitute a justification to employ the local, unsafe practice. But "standard" can also refer to a level that must be attained, as in "a standard for admission to medical school," or "the standard for maintaining hygienic practice in treatment and research." In this latter sense, US researchers would be bound by the proper medical standard that prohibits the reuse of disposable equipment, even if reuse is standard practice in some countries.[5]

The distinction between these two senses of "standard" is critical. In the first sense, the meaning is purely descriptive, stating what *is* routinely done. The second sense is prescriptive, stating what *ought to be* done, a "standard that should be attained." The ability to slide imperceptibly between these two senses of "standard" lends credence to the view that the existing standard (the first meaning) is acceptable as a prescriptive standard (the second meaning). NBAC elected (wisely, in my view) to refrain from using the phrase "standard of care" after noting these ambiguities.

The Nuffield Council's report appeared one year after NBAC's, and in numerous places the Nuffield report cites or endorses NBAC's position. Not so on the use of the phrase "standard of care," however:

Rather than introduce a new term, we have chosen to adopt the term "standard of care" . . . and define it as: "the nature of the care and treatment that will be provided to participants in research". We use the term simply as a generic description of the range of preventive or curative treatments (or lack of them) and diagnostic interventions which are made available to participants.[6]

An opposing position directly contradicts Nuffield's statement that lack of preventive or curative treatments can properly count as a "standard of care," as shown by this observation:

Opponents [of placebo-controlled trials] contend that reference to the "standard of care" in developing countries to justify placebo-controlled trials is ethically suspect. When people receive no treatment at all, there can be no "standard" of care. Defenders say that women in the trial who receive placebo are not being made worse off than they would be if they were not in the trial at all. That is what is meant by "standard of care" in this context.[7]

The difference between these two positions is not "merely a matter of semantics," as some might put it. The second view clearly provides the correct analysis. What could possibly justify the claim that "no treatment" can be a "standard"? The only reasonable explanation is the desire for "standard" to play the role of justification. In providing no care or treatment to participants in research, the researchers are not making them worse off than they would be if they were not enrolled in research. In other words, sponsors and researchers attempt to justify providing less by way of care and treatment than they might be able to provide because they are not falling below the "standard."

The Nuffield Council's report acknowledges both the criticisms of the concept and its ambiguity. Nevertheless, Nuffield chose to retain the term rather than introduce a new one. The Nuffield report provides an additional clarification:

While the term "standard of care" is used in law to refer to the standard of treatment that a court would conclude that a reasonable physician would provide in the circumstances, the term is used here to describe what happens in practice, whether or not it could be considered to be reasonable or appropriate.[8]

This makes it clear that the Nuffield report is using the term in its purely descriptive sense.

Nuffield offers a further clarification, introducing a different phrase: "We use the term 'universal standard of care' to indicate the best current method of treatment available anywhere in the world for a particular disease or condition."[9] This move is intended to eliminate the doubts that have surrounded the interpretation of the Declaration of Helsinki's phrase, "best current treatment." Nevertheless, it is odd to use the term "universal" to mean anything other than what is universally applicable. It would be more appropriate to use the phrase "highest standard of care" to refer to the best current method of treatment available anywhere in the world for a particular disease or condition.

Other disagreements are more substantive than definitional. At one extreme is the position that there should be only one "standard of care," that which exists in the sponsoring (industrialized) country:

> Acceptance of a standard of care that does not conform to the standard in the sponsoring country results in a double standard in research. Such a double standard, which permits research designs that are unacceptable in the sponsoring country, creates an incentive to use as research subjects those with the least access to health care.[10]

And the same position, put somewhat differently:

> It is clear that the pressures to lower the ethical standards set by the DoH [Declaration of Helsinki] are primarily economic – it costs less to run a trial where you do not have to provide for medical care . . . So let us push to keep the highest ethical standards applied everywhere.[11]

A third, again in agreement:

> There are strong practical as well as principled reasons for Americans to follow American ethical standards when they do research abroad.[12]

A directly opposite view is stated in the following comments:

> [I]t has been incorrectly assumed that the standard set by developed countries can be considered the norm . . . It is arbitrary and not justifiable to select only one [requirement] . . . for example, which drugs are used – to compare the standard of care in developed and developing countries . . . The United States's standard of care should not be emulated throughout the world.[13]

And another statement expressing the same viewpoint, put somewhat differently:

> We can also see why we should not expect a single standard of research to govern all study designs. There are a variety of ethical principles that apply to research on human subjects, and they sometimes conflict . . . In order to achieve an optimal

balance of these different ethical standards, we need to take into account various social, cultural, economic, political, as well as scientific factors . . . One might even argue that it is unjust, unfair, and insensitive to demand that the exact same standards of research that govern study designs in developed nations should also be implemented in developing countries.[14]

These comments – the first three on one side, the second two in direct opposition – go to the heart of the debate. One side argues that different standards for research are acceptable, whereas the other maintains that a "double standard" is unethical.

The final comment to consider on "standard of care" is one that makes a careful attempt to untangle the ambiguities and lack of clarity in the term:

[T]his debate has been complicated by some unrecognized ambiguities in the notion of a standard of care . . . [T]his concept is ambiguous along two different axes, with the result that there are at least four possible standard of care arguments that must be clearly distinguished.[15]

The author identifies four different interpretations of "standard of care" culled from the literature. The first two interpretations arise as a result of two different relevant reference points, harking back to the question: "Does 'best proven therapy' mean the 'best therapy available anywhere in the world'? Or does it mean the standard that prevails in the country in which the trial is conducted?" These two reference points are termed "global" and "local", and give rise to two different judgments of what "standard of care" means. However, limiting the debate to these two reference points is simplistic and fails to capture a more subtle yet crucial distinction found in the second pair of interpretations. This latter pair is termed "de facto" and "de jure." The de facto interpretation uses "standard of care" to mean that the standard of medical practices in a community is determined by the actual medical practices in that community. In other words, the standard of care is no more than a description of what, in fact, occurs. The de jure concept, on the other hand, interprets the standard of care as determined by the judgment of experts in the medical community regarding which diagnostic and therapeutic practices have proven most effective in the illness in question.

The author concludes his careful analysis of these four interpretations by opting for the "local, de jure" interpretation of "standard of care" because it rejects the "bad, if not perfidious" local, de facto standard while still permitting research to go forward that may not meet the stringent requirements of the "global de jure" standard. However, the local, de jure standard would not permit researchers knowingly to deny subjects care that has proven effective for their illness in their population, and thus ensures that subjects of clinical research in developing countries are not exploited. At the same time, this standard requires attention to substantive differences in social, cultural, and economic contexts and their impact on the permissibility of international research.

Are opponents in this controversy over "standard of care" likely to resolve their differences? Alas, I fear not. My pessimism stems from several factors. First and foremost is the prevalence of "the method of tenacity" (borrowed from the philosopher, Charles Sanders Peirce) in maintaining a belief system. Defenders of the view that the local, *de facto* standard of care is ethically appropriate are not likely to alter their position when confronted with a *de jure* standard that may require more by way of care or treatment than research subjects would receive outside a trial. What counts for the *de facto* group is simply that research subjects are not made worse off as a result of their participation than they were before the research began. Those who interpret the Declaration of Helsinki in terms of the global, *de jure* standard – requiring the best current methods "anywhere in the world" – are not likely to be persuaded by the subtlety of arguments that would permit the local *de jure* standard in some circumstances. As long as the sponsor of the research is able to provide the best current methods to a control group in a clinical trial, it matters not where the research is conducted. Geography is irrelevant.

A second factor that makes resolution of disagreements unlikely is the limited power of "stipulative definitions," ones that intend to persuade people to adopt a new meaning for a familiar word or phrase. Those who understand "standard of care" in its narrowest meaning – referring only to which drugs are used for a control group in a clinical trial – are not likely to abandon that meaning in favor of an expanded or alternative concept proposed by even the most thoughtful commentators who argue both for the need to attend to morally relevant considerations of context and for the equally important need to reduce the huge inequities in global health.[18]

Treat like cases alike

A different way of approaching this debate is to try to determine whether it is unjust to have one standard for the design and conduct of research in resource-poor countries and another for wealthier countries. One familiar formulation of what justice requires is expressed as a formal principle: "Treat like cases alike, and different cases differently." This formal principle differs from the conception of distributive justice (discussed in detail in chapter 3), which refers to "fairness in distribution" of benefits and burdens. The formal principle, "treat like cases alike," lacks content and is difficult to apply in specific contexts. The key to applying this principle is to ascertain the relevant respects in which cases are alike or different. Difficulties arise when there is disagreement about which similarities or differences are relevant and which are not. How can this formal principle of justice be used to determine what should be provided to research subjects in clinical trials conducted in developing countries?

One interpretation of the formal principle provides a justification for the following proposition: If it is unethical to carry out a particular type of research in a developed country, it is unethical to conduct that same research in a developing country. If the research has the same hypothesis, basically the same design, the same methodology, it is similar in relevant respects. Yet a different interpretation is possible, and therefore a dispute arises regarding the "sameness" or "difference" in the two contexts. One consideration lies in the background conditions. If the vast majority of the population in a developing country lack access to the best current treatment routinely available in the industrialized country, are the two situations sufficiently different to warrant a different research design – one in which some people are assigned to a placebo group that receives no treatment?

According to the first interpretation, the ethically relevant consideration is the research design. If a placebo-controlled trial would not be ethically acceptable in an industrialized country, it should not be ethically acceptable in a developing country that lacks the resources to purchase the best current treatment. However, according to a quite different interpretation, the two situations are unlike in the following respect. In the rich country, the best current treatment would be available to research subjects outside the research context, but in the poor country the best current treatment is available only to a very small minority of wealthy individuals. Rich country and poor country are not like cases, on this interpretation, so it would be permissible to do a placebo-controlled trial in the poor country even though it would be ethically prohibited in the rich country. How can we determine which interpretation of this formal principle of justice should apply to international research?

One approach is to look at the harm–benefit ratios in the different settings. It is sometimes argued that different harm–benefit ratios between industrialized and developing countries provide a basis for determining whether the two settings are relevantly similar or different. In the wealthier country, people who need treatment can normally get the best current treatment outside of a clinical trial, therefore they would suffer greater harm by participating in the trial than by not participating. In the resource-poor country, on the other hand, the research subjects would not have access to the best current treatment or to the experimental intervention. Not only would they *not* suffer harm, but they would potentially benefit from participation. Therefore, the benefit–harm ratio is different in the two situations.

The question remains, however, whether this specific difference in the two situations is relevant to warrant treating the cases differently, with the result that the best current treatment may ethically be withheld from participants in the clinical trial in the developing country. What the two situations have in common is that participants in the control group would be denied an effective treatment that could be made available within the research context – regardless of what is available outside the trial – and would thereby suffer harmful consequences of leaving their condition untreated or treated with an inferior therapy. In this respect – harm to the untreated subjects – the two cases are alike.

Another leading argument contends that the economic conditions in industrialized and resource-poor countries constitute the relevant difference that makes the two cases unlike. The great disparity in both the wealth of the nation as a whole and the majority of the population in these different settings compels the conclusion that they are unlike in relevant respects, thereby justifying a double standard of care and treatment for research subjects. Others maintain that economic conditions are irrelevant to ethics regarding this particular question[17] (it does not follow, however, that economic circumstances are irrelevant for all purposes).

The Nuffield Council's report is a leading example of the view that the economic conditions in a developing country are the governing factor in determining what standard of care is ethically appropriate in research. Chapter 2 is entitled "Healthcare: the economic context," setting the stage for the account that follows. The report reminds readers that "the best current method of treatment is frequently not available in developing countries, since the majority of people are economically and medically disadvantaged."[18] According to this view, economic and medical disadvantages in the society as a whole become the benchmark for determining what level of care and treatment is ethically acceptable in the conduct of research. But it is reasonable to ask why, if a higher level of care and treatment *could* be provided to research subjects living in a disadvantaged country, would it not be desirable or even obligatory to provide that higher level, even if it were limited to people enrolled in the trial?

A critique of the assumptions regarding background economic conditions in developing countries rejects the argument of the Nuffield report: "In developing countries, the standard of care . . . is not based on a consideration of alternative treatments or previous clinical data, but is instead an economically determined policy of governments that cannot afford the prices set by drug companies."[19] The implication is that if drug companies charged lower prices, or if developing countries were to obtain generic copies of expensive drugs for which pharmaceutical companies hold patents, then poor countries would be able to afford a better standard of care for their populations than is possible under current pricing constraints.

In light of these various interpretations, how should the economic conditions of a country bear on the meaning and application of the principle, "treat like cases alike, different cases differently"? If the relevant difference between rich and poor countries is their ability to afford drugs at the prices determined by industry, then it is clear that the countries are relevantly different in this respect. But it does not automatically follow that the standard of care for research participants should be based on this difference. What is relevant to the economic condition of resource-poor countries is the need for the population to have access to affordable drugs.

There is a huge gap, however, between the acknowledgment of that need and the conclusion that the only way of making affordable drugs available is to provide the locally available "standard of care" (which can be no treatment) to a control group in a clinical trial in order to test low-cost experimental medications. Many intermediate steps are needed to move from the premise that it is ethically desirable to provide for the needs of resource-poor countries and the conclusion that to achieve that end, it is scientifically necessary and ethically acceptable to design clinical trials that provide no treatment or inferior treatment to subjects in a control group. What is and is not affordable is a shifting picture, and several alternative paths to making drugs accessible in poor countries have also been opening up. These developments are discussed further in chapter 5.

What do the guidelines say?

Largely because of the controversy spawned by the placebo-controlled, maternal-to-child HIV transmission studies, revisions in existing international guidelines and newly commissioned reports all grappled with the question of what should be provided to a control group in randomized, controlled clinical trials. The Declaration of Helsinki was a point of departure for these other guidelines and recommendations from the two main reports, NBAC and Nuffield.

Declaration of Helsinki

Here again is the controversial paragraph 29:

The benefits, risks, burdens and effectiveness of a new method should be tested against those of the best current prophylactic, diagnostic, and therapeutic methods. This does not exclude the use of placebo, or no treatment, in studies where no proven prophylactic, diagnostic or therapeutic method exists.

This paragraph in the 2000 revision of the Declaration prompted both serious opposition and strong support. After protracted debate and at least two conferences devoted to the now-revised Declaration, in November 2001 the World Medical Association published the following "clarification" of paragraph 29.

NOTE OF CLARIFICATION ON PARAGRAPH 29 of the WMA DECLARATION OF HELSINKI

The WMA is concerned that paragraph 29 of the revised Declaration of Helsinki (October 2000) has led to diverse interpretations and possible confusion. It hereby reaffirms its position that extreme care must be taken in making use of a placebo-controlled trial and that in general this methodology should only be used in the absence of existing proven therapy. However, a placebo-controlled trial may be ethically acceptable, even if proven therapy is available, under the following circumstances:

– Where for compelling and scientifically sound methodological reasons its use is necessary to determine the efficacy or safety of a prophylactic, diagnostic or therapeutic method; or
– Where a prophylactic, diagnostic or therapeutic method is being investigated for a minor condition and the patients who receive placebo will not be subject to any additional risk of serious or irreversible harm.

All other provisions of the Declaration of Helsinki must be adhered to, especially the need for appropriate ethical and scientific review.

The World Medical Assembly approved this clarification as a footnote to the Declaration at its annual meeting in 2002 in Washington, DC. However, a major problem is that the clarification fails to clarify. The second of the two circumstances that can permit departure from the placebo rule is relatively uncontroversial, and very few people who have objected to placebo-controlled studies are likely to reject this condition. But the first of the two conditions simply reopens the door to the very controversy that led to the revision of the Declaration in the first place.

Just what should count as "compelling and scientifically sound methodological reasons . . . necessary to determine the efficacy or safety" of a new method? In the case that created the furor, it was precisely the controversy over whether a placebo-controlled trial was necessary or whether a different research design – one that compared the experimental, short course AZT against the 076 treatment – could serve as a scientifically sound methodology. The alleged clarification is flawed on three separate counts: first, it provides no criteria for the "compelling reasons" that could justify departure from the principle; second, the requirement for scientifically sound methodology is redundant, as it is required in every study and stated elsewhere in the Declaration of Helsinki; and third, it would allow participants in research to be subject to predictable serious or irreversible harm.

Granted, the sort of detailed analysis that would have to be provided for elucidating the "compelling reasons" is beyond the scope of a document like Helsinki. The Declaration consists of thirty-two numbered paragraphs, with only one paragraph providing anything in the way of detail – the paragraph that stipulates the elements to be disclosed in the informed consent process. Nevertheless, something called a "clarification" should succeed in clarifying rather than do the opposite. The addition of this "note" leaves those who seek to conform to the Declaration of Helsinki in a distinct quandary.

The CIOMS International Guidelines

The task of elucidating the provisions of the Declaration of Helsinki was taken on by the Council for International Organizations of Medical Sciences (CIOMS) in the late 1970s when it prepared a document entitled *Proposed International Guidelines for Biomedical Research Involving Human Subjects*, which it issued in 1982:

The purpose of the *Proposed Guidelines* was to indicate how the ethical principles that should guide the conduct of biomedical research involving human subjects, as set forth in the Declaration of Helsinki, could be effectively applied, particularly in developing countries, given their socioeconomic circumstances, laws and regulations, and executive and administrative arrangements.[20]

The 1993 version of the CIOMS guidelines, prepared in collaboration with the World Health Organization, superseded the earlier version. Most people have thought of the CIOMS guidelines as having adopted and endorsed the provisions of Helsinki, elucidating them in greater detail and applying them in the context of international research. It is of interest that the 1993 CIOMS document did not include a guideline that specifically addressed what should be provided to control groups in clinical trials. CIOMS did, however, use the term "standards" in elucidating the guidelines. Under the heading "Externally sponsored research," Guideline 15 was entitled "Obligations of sponsoring and host countries." The first of two provisions was as follows:

An external sponsoring agency should submit the research protocol to ethical and scientific review according to the standards of the country of the sponsoring agency, and the ethical standards applied should be no less exacting than they would be in the case of research carried out in that country.

Although this appears to be a procedural requirement, the substantive aspect is the clause that mentions "ethical standards" – that they should be no less exacting than they would be in the case of research carried out in the sponsoring country. The commentary under the guideline makes no attempt to explicate the meaning of "ethical standards."

The use of placebos was mentioned in a lengthy commentary under Guideline 14 of the 1993 CIOMS guidelines, entitled "Constitution and responsibilities of ethical review committees." Although the guideline itself stated procedural requirements for the proper scientific and ethical review of research proposals, a substantive ethical requirement was embedded in the commentary, where it could easily have escaped notice. This requirement endorsed the Helsinki provision in the then current 1989 version of the Declaration:

[A]s required by the Declaration of Helsinki, Article II.3, "every patient – including those of a control group, if any – should be assured of the best proven diagnostic and therapeutic method." Therefore, if there is already an approved and accepted drug for the condition that a candidate drug is designed to treat, placebo for controls usually cannot be justified.[21]

When the furor erupted over the placebo-controlled, maternal-to-child HIV transmission studies in developing countries, prompting the decision to revise the Declaration of Helsinki, the CIOMS secretariat decided that it should revisit its own 1993 guidelines. The process that commenced was fraught with no less controversy than that which accompanied the revision of the Declaration of Helsinki. A steering committee was appointed to convene and discuss the substance of a draft prepared by the CIOMS consultant assigned for the project. The steering committee consisted of about thirty people, including representation from the World Health Organization, the Joint United Nations Programme on HIV/AIDS (UNAIDS), and the World Medical Association. When the committee met for the first time in May 1999, participants discussed the draft and suggested a list of topics for new or amended guidelines. The committee also recommended papers to be commissioned on those topics.

The next step was a consultation convened by CIOMS in March 2000, at which members of the steering committee were joined by the authors of the commissioned papers and designated commentators, who were invited in order to add specific areas of expertise to the group.[22] At this consultation, several people who had been at the initial meeting of the steering committee expressed disapproval of the progress report that the CIOMS consultant who had written the original draft provided in his introductory remarks. The disapproving participants contended that the consultant had not heeded their recommendations for substantive changes in the draft.

Further disagreement erupted in discussions following some of the subsequent presentations. Not surprisingly, this disagreement focused on the contentious issue of the use of placebos in clinical trials in developing countries – the very issue that had prompted the decision to revise the Declaration of Helsinki. The draft guideline submitted for review at the CIOMS consultation in 2000 allowed exceptions to Helsinki's strict requirement that the control group receive "the best proven" method (the wording in the 1996 version of Helsinki, still in force at the time), as well as a departure from Helsinki's stipulation regarding when placebos may be used. The CIOMS consultant-drafter substituted the phrase "highest attainable and sustainable" for Helsinki's wording, "best proven treatment". Since these departures from Helsinki were specifically intended to apply to developing countries, dissenters claimed that the guideline introduced an unacceptable double standard into the CIOMS document.

Participants in the March 2000 consultation decided on the procedural step of broadening the process of drafting the guidelines by forming subcommittees of members with expertise or interest in the contents of specific guidelines. Naturally this lengthened the process. The next step was the appointment of a small, unofficial writing group, which met for one week in New York in January 2001, and subsequently engaged in electronic communications over a period of several months.[23] Some months after this informal group was appointed, the CIOMS secretariat added two more individuals.[24] Members of this small writing group were in substantial agreement on almost all of the proposed draft guidelines, but a split occurred, once again, over the placebo guideline.

The CIOMS consultant initially appointed to prepare the revised guidelines remained as the chief drafter and continued to insist on departures from Helsinki's paragraph 29, with its strict requirement regarding placebo controls. Two members of the informal group, who represented developing countries, argued that this loophole could be used to justify research in which established, effective treatments could be withheld from research subjects in their own resource-poor countries, resulting in serious harm or death to the subjects. Since such treatments would be available in industrialized countries, the research could not be done in those places. The consequence, once again, would be a double standard in research. Members of the writing group continued to be sharply divided on this issue.

The CIOMS secretariat posted the draft guidelines on its website, calling for comments by all stakeholders and interested parties. The comments received were collated and organized by the secretariat, and sent, once again, to the informal writing group for their responses.[25]

Predictably, the comments on the contentious placebo guideline that was posted on the CIOMS website ran the gamut from strong approval to strong disapproval, with several people observing that the guideline was self-contradictory or that it should entirely omit reference to the Declaration of Helsinki. This is the version that was posted for comment:

In biomedical research, "the benefits, risks, burdens and effectiveness of a new method should be tested against those of the best current prophylactic, diagnostic, and therapeutic methods. This does not exclude the use of placebo, or no treatment, in studies where no proven prophylactic, diagnostic or therapeutic method exists." (Declaration of Helsinki, Paragraph 29). Any departure from this principle requires a sound scientific and ethical reason to use a control other than the best current method.

Some who objected maintained that the final sentence was a loophole that opened the door to research that could be ethically unacceptable because of the risks to subjects who received placebo rather than the best current therapeutic method. Those who agreed with the guideline held that such departures were acceptable. A few comments that gave unqualified support to the guideline as written were the following:

This is an excellent guideline on the ethical position regarding the use of placebos in research.[26]

Basically agree.[27]

Support acceptable "departures" from DoH requirements.[28]

As a whole, the commentary is quite reasonable, giving examples for the needed use of placebos. It is a useful complement to the unclear provisions of the Declaration of Helsinki by describing situations where placebo-controlled studies are scientifically justified and necessary. Indeed, some regulatory authorities (e.g., US FDA and EMEA) require placebo-controlled studies in certain circumstances.[29]

The next set of comments came from people who were opposed to the Declaration of Helsinki's restriction on the use of placebos and were critical of the CIOMS guideline for not unequivocally rejecting the Helsinki provision.

The Guideline is an almost verbatim quote of Article 29 of the Declaration of Helsinki, stating that all participants in a clinical trial should receive state-of-the-art care and that control arms should be equivalent to the best care available anywhere in the world. This suggests that CIOMS agrees with the DOH, which is misleading. Only the last sentence of this guideline begins to clarify the difference in positions, which is further described in the commentary. Such a requirement could easily result in a trial that yields information useless to the population involved in the study and render the study design unethical.[30]

We find it surprising and unfortunate that CIOMS has adopted Article 29 almost in its entirety, then provided for the waiving of the expressed principle as an afterthought (*"[A]ny departure from this principle . . . best current method"*). CIOMS is clearly aware of the problems implicit in the phrasing of Article 29; we suggest that CIOMS should propose new language for [this guideline] that avoids these problems. As it is, the Guideline compounds the WMA's unrealistic position on placebo-controlled trials.[31]

The Commentary is well done but the Guideline is wrong and contradictory. It should be changed . . . Moreover, the use of placebos is *not* controversial, except in the eyes of a tiny cadre of absolutists.[32]

Next is a sample of commentators who disagreed because of the departure from Helsinki's strict requirement for the use of placebos:

The Guideline needs to emphasise more strongly that it is not acceptable to use only a placebo in the control group where significant harm may come to those participants.[33]

The DOH requires that "The benefits, risks, burdens and effectiveness of a new method should be tested against those of the best current prophylactic, diagnostic, and therapeutic methods," (Article 29). Linking the use of placebo with the "standard of care" available in a study location is like snatching a life jacket from the clutches of a drowning man. Sometimes, I think it would be helpful if privileged researchers and scientists who take such important decisions on ethics, experienced the pains of poverty. Sometime they should ask themselves this question: Given what I know about research and ethics, what would I do if I was in the position of the vulnerable and the poor?[34]

When a proven effective treatment for a serious condition is available, a placebo control can rarely if ever be justified. From the perspective of the public good, the important question is whether a new treatment is better than the established one – not whether it is merely as good (i.e., "equivalent"), or whether it is better than a placebo. For this reason, the case for placebo controls based on the assertion that it is difficult and expensive to prove equivalent is largely irrelevant. It is important to recognize that new treatments that are no better than established ones over the broad range of a condition may still deserve approval because they are superior in subsets of that condition – e.g., for patients who do poorly with the established treatment or suffer unusually severe side-effects. Evidence for such superiority is best obtained by controlled side-by-side trials in such patients – a process that is discouraged if treatments can be approved simply based on their superiority to a placebo.[35]

I think the best available protection against exploitation is watchful and independent scrutiny by local ethics committee, rather than any guideline text. I'd rather we stuck to Helsinki 2000 and let people fight it out; at least they will do it in the open air, and recognise that a defence is required.[36]

Given this sample of contrasting and opposing views, the problem loomed of how CIOMS should proceed. One possibility was not to have a guideline dealing with this topic at all. The writing group and CIOMS secretariat rejected that prospect on the grounds that the issue was so important, and so widely discussed, that to omit it would threaten the credibility of the CIOMS guidelines altogether. Another possibility was to include a discussion of the controversy in the commentary to the guideline. Indeed, one person who submitted a comment argued in favor of this:

> I think it is appropriate that you mention that there is no agreement on this. What is disturbing obviously is that only the views of those who think differential standards are ethically acceptable feature prominently here. The least you should do is to report the views of the other side (incidentally the side whose views are reflected in the October 2000 version of the Declaration of Helsinki!) too, and to stress the point that that is the view taken by the WMA. Omitting this seems much like another exercise in campaigning to me.[37]

In the end, the following is the solution the CIOMS secretariat elected to adopt.

In February 2002, CIOMS convened a conference to discuss the latest draft of the guidelines. This meeting included many members of the steering committee and participants in the 2000 consultation, some individuals who had commented on the website posting, and other significant stakeholders from the pharmaceutical industry. In what was by now a predictable development, sharp disagreements arose over the placebo guideline, with relatively minor controversies or none at all accompanying most other guidelines.

What had remained unclear up to this point was where the final authority lay for approval of the guidelines once the drafting stage was completed. According to one view, the previously appointed steering committee should have the final say, as that appeared to be the understanding when the process first began. However, this seemed unwise in light of the fact that CIOMS convened two later meetings that included additional participants who made significant contributions to the discussion. Moreover, as it emerged, it was not entirely clear just who were the members of the original steering committee. Most important, however, was the question why any of these groups should be granted the authority to determine final approval of a document intended for international consumption and issued under the auspices of a nongovernmental, international organization.

The Executive Committee of CIOMS met just prior to the opening of the February 2002 conference and resolved that the final authority should rest with it, the executive body of the organization, since the guidelines are a product of the organization as a whole, not the individuals who happened to be invited to the several meetings, nor the informal writing group appointed to work on the draft. A final version of the guidelines was sent to members of the executive committee in August 2002, and following their approval, was posted on the CIOMS website on August 29. Here is the final form of the controversial Guideline 11:

Guideline 11: Choice of control in clinical trials

As a general rule, research subjects in the control group of a trial of a diagnostic, therapeutic, or preventive intervention should receive an established effective intervention. In some circumstances it may be ethically acceptable to use an alternative comparator, such as placebo or "no treatment".

Placebo may be used:
– when there is no established effective intervention;
– when withholding an established effective intervention would expose subjects to, at most, temporary discomfort or delay in relief of symptoms;
– when use of an established effective intervention as comparator would not yield scientifically reliable results and use of placebo would not add any risk of serious or irreversible harm to the subjects.

The commentary under this guideline describes the possible exception that previously stood as part of the guideline itself, under the heading "Exceptional use of a comparator other than an established effective intervention." The exception is stated as follows:

An exception to the general rule is applicable in some studies designed to develop a therapeutic, preventive or diagnostic intervention for use in a country or community in which an established effective intervention is not available and unlikely in the foreseeable future to become available, usually for economic or logistic reasons. The purpose of such a study is to make available to the population of the country or community an effective alternative to an established effective intervention that is locally unavailable. Accordingly, the proposed investigational intervention must be responsive to the health needs of the population from which the research subjects are recruited and there must be assurance that, if it proves to be safe and effective, it will be made reasonably available to that population. Also, the scientific and ethical review committees must be satisfied that the established effective intervention cannot be used as comparator because its use would not yield scientifically reliable results that would be relevant to the health needs of the study population. In these circumstances an ethical review committee can approve a clinical trial in which the comparator is other than an established effective intervention, such as placebo or no treatment or a local remedy.[38]

This passage is followed by the objections to the above-described exception raised by those who reject a double standard – one for use of placebo in industrialized countries, and another in developing countries.

- Placebo control could expose research subjects to risk of serious or irreversible harm when the use of an established effective intervention as comparator could avoid the risk.
- Not all scientific experts agree about conditions under which an established effective intervention used as a comparator would not yield scientifically reliable results.
- An economic reason for the unavailability of an established effective intervention cannot justify a placebo-controlled study in a country of limited resources when it would be unethical to conduct a study with the same design in a population with general access to the effective intervention outside the study.[39]

Thus the compromise eventually reached in this lengthy process was to incorporate the positions of both sides of the controversy in the commentary under the guideline itself. What could not be accomplished in the brief paragraphs of the Declaration of Helsinki became possible in the CIOMS guidelines in the elucidation section that follows the statement of the guideline itself.

The UNAIDS Guidance Document

Another set of international guidelines that weighed in on the placebo question was the Guidance Document issued by UNAIDS for preventive HIV/AIDS vaccine trials. Guidance Point 11 allows for the use of placebo in a control arm under the same conditions as stipulated by Helsinki: "As long as there is no known effective HIV preventive vaccine, a placebo control arm should be considered ethically acceptable in a phase III HIV preventive vaccine trial."[40] It was easy for the drafters of the document to issue this guideline without qualifications, since up to the present time an effective, preventive HIV vaccine does not exist. However, with regard to a future time when at least one preventive vaccine will have been proven effective but other, possibly more effective candidates still need to be tested, a dilemma could arise. The commentary under Guidance Point 11 addresses this future scenario and allows for the possibility of an exception to the requirement based on a scientific rationale for use of placebo in the control arm even when a safe and effective HIV vaccine exists. "Participants in the control arm of a future phase III HIV preventive vaccine trial should receive an HIV vaccine known to be safe and effective when such is available, unless there are compelling scientific reasons which justify the use of a placebo."[41] What are the "compelling scientific reasons"? Unlike the Helsinki "clarification," which offers no clue, the UNAIDS Guidance Document mentions the following: "[t]he effective HIV vaccine is not believed to be effective against the virus that is prevalent in the research population"; and "[t]here are convincing reasons to believe that the biological conditions that prevailed during the initial trial demonstrating efficacy were so different from the conditions in the proposed research population that the results of the initial trial cannot be directly applied to the research population under consideration." These potential exceptions do not actually weaken the provision, since a flawed scientific design is ethically unacceptable in any case. The rationale specifies substantive criteria for permitting the exception, and it limits any departures from the placebo guideline to situations where there is a scientific justification. In contrast, both the NBAC and Nuffield reports permit justifications of the use of placebo on economic grounds as well as for compelling scientific reasons.

The NBAC Report

As already noted, the US National Bioethics Advisory Commission chose not to use the term "standard of care." NBAC also elected to use the phrase "established, effective treatment" instead of "best proven therapeutic method." (The revised CIOMS Guideline 11 also uses the phrase "established, effective treatment," adopting the NBAC language.) Aside from this difference in terminology, NBAC's position on the design of randomized, controlled trials is decidedly weaker than that of the Declaration of Helsinki, CIOMS guideline 11, and the UNAIDS Guidance Document. Recommendation 2.2 of NBAC says:

Researchers and sponsors should design clinical trials that provide members of any control group with an established effective treatment, whether or not such treatment is available in the host country. Any study that would not provide the control group with an established effective treatment should include a justification for using an alternative design. Ethics review committees must assess the justification provided, including the risks to participants, and the overall ethical acceptability of the research design.

Unlike the UNAIDS exception, which offers substantive criteria that an ethics review committee could use if it intends to depart from the strict requirement in the Declaration of Helsinki, the NBAC report simply leaves the matter up to the committee without providing criteria that would make the departure acceptable. This results in undue reliance on the judgment of ethics review committees. It may be the case that committees in developing countries, whether they are experienced or newly established, will pay more attention to matters that have largely been ignored by review committees in industrialized countries. On the other hand, evidence suggests that many committees in developing countries are inexperienced, and others do a less than adequate job protecting the rights and welfare of research subjects (see chapter 5, below). Moreover, if a study to be carried out in a developing country is approved by the ethics review committee in the sponsoring country, there is likely to be great pressure on the committee in the developing country to accept whatever justification the researchers provide for departures from the Helsinki requirement.

The Nuffield Council Report

Stated explicitly or implicitly throughout the Nuffield report is the premise that research is needed in developing countries on serious diseases that never or rarely occur in industrialized countries. The Nuffield report's discussion of standards of care endorses two of the other general premises on which there is widespread agreement: "Research conducted in developing countries should be relevant to the healthcare needs of that country;"[42] and "the need to avoid exploitation is imperative."[43] Like the others who reject Helsinki's "best proven treatment" requirement, Nuffield begins with the premise that research should be responsive to the healthcare needs of the country. This is followed by a detailed factual accounting of economic disadvantages in most developing countries. Nuffield concludes from the economic facts that research in developing countries need not adhere to the "universal standard" defined as "the best treatment available anywhere in the world, wherever the research is conducted."

Firmly endorsing the need to avoid exploitation, the report contends that "insisting upon a universal standard of care may not always be the best way to respect this principle." In defense of this position, Nuffield refers to the putative requirement of justice "that we treat people identically, regardless of context, because justice demands equal respect," and proceeds to reject the idea that people must be treated identically. Rather, "parity of respect requires us to address the specific needs and circumstances of individuals in determining how to behave toward them."[44] This is another way of stating the formal principle of justice discussed earlier in this chapter – "treat like cases alike, different cases differently." But here we are confronted, once again, with the need to determine which similarities and which differences are relevant to determining when identical treatment is warranted and when it may justifiably be forgone.

Nuffield provides a list of factors that should be used by researchers, sponsors, and research ethics committees in determining the appropriate standard of care to be provided to participants in a clinical trial. These factors include two of those discussed above in connection with the pro-placebo argument: "The appropriate research design(s) to answer the research question"; and "the standard(s) of care which can be afforded by the host and sponsoring country(ies) for the disease being studied." Although it is surely the case that the research design must be appropriate for answering the research question, the formulation of the research question itself is a value-laden matter. What is selected as *the* research question can and should be determined, at least in part, by the ethically optimal research design. The alternative to formulating the research question and then selecting the appropriate design is first to identify the research design that minimizes harms and maximizes benefits to the research subjects, and then to frame the research question accordingly.

Nuffield's second factor to be used in determining the standard of care for a research study is "the standard of care which can be afforded by the host and sponsoring countries." It is obvious that whatever is provided to the control group must be affordable by the sponsoring country or industrial sponsor, but this is only very rarely likely to be an economic barrier to industry, which supplies the drugs for virtually every clinical trial. What remains entirely unexplained is why the preventive or therapeutic method given to the control group must be afforded by the *host country*. It is only the *experimental* method that has to be affordable by the host country, since if the trial is successful, that is the method that presumably will be introduced into the country.

Among the other factors Nuffield mentions are two that we have not yet discussed: "the standard(s) of care which can effectively be delivered in the host country(ies) during research"; and "the standard(s) of care which can be provided in the host country(ies) on a sustainable basis." The first of these is a feasibility criterion, which obviously must be fulfilled. It is a basic prerequisite of any ethical imperative, an instance of the maxim known as "ought implies can." A precondition for any ethical injunction that something ought to be done is the possibility or feasibility of doing it. So, to use the example Nuffield offers:

if a treatment was sought for a condition such as liver cancer . . . the universal standard of care includes surgery to remove the tumour or a liver transplant. While the sophisticated infrastructure required to provide such treatments is available in developed countries (including intensive care units, trained surgeons and health-care staff) it is very limited or absent in the majority of developing countries.[45]

No reasonable defender of the Helsinki "best current treatment" provision would require the establishment of this highly skilled and technologically advanced infrastructure in order to be able to test a feasible treatment for liver cancer in a developing country. But this leaves open the question of where to draw the line between what is judged to be technically unfeasible and what is simply very costly to provide for the control group. Why not spend money to build the intensive care unit, train the local surgeons or import some from the sponsoring country in order to provide the control group with the best current treatment? The answer, albeit somewhat unsatisfactory, is that the difficulty of drawing a line does not mean that the line should not be drawn somewhere. What is ethically required in any circumstances may be constrained by practical realities. "The sky's the limit" is not a reality-based place to draw the line.

The other heretofore unmentioned item on Nuffield's list of considerations is "the standard(s) of care which can be provided in the host country(ies) on a sustainable basis." This item, like the affordability of the method provided to the control group, is irrelevant. It is the experimental intervention that has to be able to be sustainable, not what is provided to the control group. Unlike the preceding item – the feasibility of providing the best current method during the research – the sustainability of the best current method after the research is not a matter of concern for the host country or the sponsoring country.

Nuffield's recommendation regarding the standard of care for the control group is as follows:

A suitable standard of care can only be defined in consultation with those who work within the country and must be justified to the relevant research ethics committees. Wherever appropriate, participants in the control group should be offered a universal standard of care for the disease being studied. Where it is not appropriate to offer a universal standard of care, the minimum standard of care that should be offered to the control group is the best intervention available for that disease as part of the national public health system.[46]

The minimum standard of care stipulated in this recommendation can be implausibly low. It can be nothing at all.

In a subsequent recommendation that addresses care and treatment of subjects who develop a disease being studied in research into preventive measures, Nuffield claims to endorse Guidance Point 16 of the UNAIDS Guidance Document for preventive vaccine research. In this recommendation, as in the preceding one, Nuffield recommends the universal standard of care "whenever appropriate." But "where it is not appropriate to offer a universal standard of care, the minimum standard of care that should be offered is the best available intervention as part of the national public health system for that disease."[47]

This is not, however, what Guidance Point 16 of the UNAIDS document actually says about the minimum that should be offered. Guidance Point 16 says that the "ideal" is to provide "the best proven therapy," and "the minimum to provide the highest level of care attainable in the host country" in light of a set of circumstances that are listed. Those circumstances include "level of care and treatment available in the sponsor country," "highest level of care available in the host country," and "highest level of treatment available in the host country, including the availability of antiretroviral therapy outside the research context in the host country."[48] Nowhere does the UNAIDS document mention "the best available intervention as part of the national public health system." The "minimum" required by Nuffield, then, is likely to be considerably lower than the minimum prescribed in the UNAIDS document. It can be nothing at all for the disease in question.

US Regulations and the FDA

The federal regulations governing research in the United States make no mention of placebos. The Common Rule (the federal human research subject protection policy) does not say anything about the design of clinical trials beyond the following criteria for IRB approval:

a) In order to approve research covered by this policy the IRB shall determine that all of the following requirements are satisfied:
(1) Risks to subjects are minimized: (i) by using procedures which are consistent with sound research design and which do not unnecessarily expose subjects to risk, and (ii) whenever appropriate, by using procedures already being performed on the subjects for diagnostic or treatment purposes.
(2) Risks to subjects are reasonable in relation to anticipated benefits, if any, to subjects, and the importance of the knowledge that may reasonably be expected to result.[49]

In March 2001 the FDA issued a document entitled "Guidance for Industry: Acceptance of Foreign Clinical Studies."[50]

This document is not an official regulation, and contains the following disclaimer: This guidance represents the Food and Drug Administration's (FDA's) current thinking on this topic. It does not create or confer any rights for or on any person and does not operate to bind FDA or the public. An alternative approach may be used if such approach satisfies the requirements of the applicable statutes and regulations.[51]

What is interesting about this document is its reference to the Declaration of Helsinki – not the version approved by the World Medical Association in October 2000, nor even the immediately previous version in 1996, but an earlier version dated 1989.

The reference to the Declaration of Helsinki appears in connection with a rather technical point of FDA review and approval of new drug applications submitted to the agency. Specifically, the point is as follows: "FDA will accept a foreign clinical study not conducted under an IND [an Investigational New Drug application] only if the study conforms to the ethical principles contained in the Declaration of Helsinki . . . incorporating the 1989 version of the Declaration." The FDA Guidance mentions that the WMA revised the Declaration in October 2000, and goes on to say that "FDA has not taken action to incorporate those revisions into its regulations. FDA is making available this guidance document to clarify that the action of the World Medical Association did not change FDA regulations."

Why does this FDA document hark back to the 1989 version of the Declaration of Helsinki rather than refer to the subsequent version in 1996? The "Guidance for Industry" does not say. The difference between the 1989 and 1996 versions of Helsinki is the addition to the later version of a provision specifying when it is acceptable to use placebos in research. The 1989 version contains only the following clause relating to the design of research: "In any medical study, every patient – including those of a control group, if any – should be assured of the best proven diagnostic and therapeutic method." This statement was retained in the 1996 version, and as described earlier in chapter 1, was at the heart of the controversy that led to calls for revising the Declaration.

The allegation cited earlier – that "The United States and most other countries have been ignoring the Declaration of Helsinki for years" – was directed at this paragraph mandating the "best proven diagnostic and therapeutic method." The 1996 version of Helsinki added the following statement to the "best proven" clause in the 1989 version: "This does not exclude the use of placebo, or no treatment, in studies where no proven . . . method exists." If this means that the "best proven method" must be used for the control group whenever such a method exists, the FDA would object even more strongly to the addition of the placebo clause. The placebo-controlled, double-blind, randomized clinical trial remains the gold standard in the FDA's reviews and approval process. As a result, it is altogether less controversial for the FDA to cite the 1989 version of the Declaration of Helsinki in preference to the 1996 version.

The section of the FDA regulations that mentions adherence to the Declaration of Helsinki and includes the entire Declaration[52] was revised on April 1, 2001. However, the published regulation does not state which version of the Declaration of Helsinki is the one quoted, does not acknowledge that it is not the most recent and official version adopted by the World Medical Association in 2000, and does not indicate that it is the 1989 version instead of the version subsequently revised in 1996. One can only wonder at the motives of those responsible for this elliptical and misleading account provided by the nation's drug regulatory agency.

ICH Guidelines for Good Clinical Practice

PhRMA, the trade association representing the research-based pharmaceutical industry in the US, understandably has a great stake in the debates over placebo-controlled trials. For one thing, industry sponsors a majority of the trials conducted in developing countries. For another, US pharmaceutical companies are eager to receive FDA approval for their products, since otherwise they could not market those products in the US. Since FDA's preference for placebo-controlled studies is abundantly evident, US industry and its trade group would like to have the broadest possible latitude to conduct placebo-controlled studies. The Declaration of Helsinki looms as an obstacle to that goal.

PhRMA issued a "Discussion Paper on the Declaration of Helsinki as Revised in October 2000." The paper is a wonderful example of selective quotations and incomplete references. One section of the discussion paper is devoted to placebo-controlled trials. The paper says:

A placebo-controlled trial design is often the only design that permits the unambiguous assessment of efficacy, safety, and tolerability. Alternative designs such as active-controlled equivalence/non-inferiority trials often cannot rule out the possibility that two therapies were equally ineffective, rather than equally effective, no matter how large the trial (as explained in ICH Guideline E-10 Clinical Trial Design: Choice of Control Group).[53]

This requires a look at the referenced document: ICH, which stands for International Conference on Harmonisation, Tripartite Guideline.[54] These ICH guidelines make recommendations on how to interpret and apply technical requirements for product registration in these regions of the world. The aim is to harmonize the different countries' individual requirements and thereby reduce the need to duplicate the testing of new drugs during research and development. The ICH Tripartite Guideline contains a section entitled "Detailed consideration of types of control," a subsection under that entitled "Placebo control," and a subsection under that entitled "Ethical issues."

In the "Ethical issues" subsection, the ICH document says:

When a new treatment is tested for a condition for which no effective treatment is known, there is usually no ethical problem with a study comparing the new treatment to placebo. Use of a placebo control may raise problems of ethics, acceptability, and feasibility, however, when an effective treatment is available for the condition under study in a proposed trial. In cases where an available treatment is known to prevent serious harm, such as death or irreversible morbidity in the study population, it is generally inappropriate to use a placebo control. There are occasional exceptions, however, such as cases in which standard therapy has toxicity so severe that many patients have refused to receive it.[55]

So, although it is true that the ICH document elsewhere makes the point that the PhRMA discussion paper cites, and it is also true that the ICH guidelines say that placebo-controlled trials are as free of assumptions as it is possible to be in seeking to show the efficacy of an experimental product, these guidelines clearly state the conditions under which placebo-controlled trials are ethically unacceptable.

But, one might object, the guideline has an escape clause in the inclusion of the term "generally": "it is generally inappropriate to use a placebo control." Few guidelines are couched in absolute terms like "never" and "always," so this is not surprising. It does, however, open the door for the PhRMA discussion paper to say: "In our opinion, the overall clinical assessment of any new medicine, including the use of placebo or active therapies as controls, should be considered in the context of the overall knowledge about existing therapies."[56] And even more to the point: "There is also a need to provide an explanation of the applicability of Article 29 [of the Declaration of Helsinki] to clinical research under the different circumstances found around the world."[57]

PhRMA is well aware that the 2000 version of the Declaration of Helsinki was subjected to great scrutiny around the world, and that a much weaker clause than the one in paragraph 29 was rejected by the World Medical Association after receiving many comments on the double standard that would result. Paragraph 29 (before the 2001 "Clarification" was added) was intended to stipulate a single standard for the use of placebos in research, including in those parts of the world where the "best current treatment" is not routinely available to the majority of the population.

Conclusions

Most defenders of the view that it is unreasonable to require the same "standard of care" in developing countries as that provided to research subjects in the industrialized world are motivated by the same laudable intentions as those who argue for the same standards. Among the former group are researchers from industrialized countries who have devoted years of their working lives in countries in Africa and Asia in the hopes of improving public health in those regions. Opponents in this controversy both seek to improve the health conditions of populations in poor countries and are eager to provide these populations with access to essential drugs.

The flaws in the position of the defenders of the double standard are threefold. First is their belief that the only relevant research question responsive to the health needs of these countries is "Is the experimental product being studied better than the 'nothing' now available to the population?" Second is the insistence on the gold standard, placebo-controlled trial in circumstances where using that methodology requires a compromise in ethical standards. And third is the assumption that the only way – or the best way – of obtaining affordable products is to design trials to test cheap interventions to replace the expensive ones used in industrialized countries. This last assumption is discussed in detail in chapter 5.

Some people question whether this entire discussion of what should be provided to a control group in research is somewhat beside the point, as it fails to confront a much larger issue: the disease burden suffered by populations in developing countries and the extraordinary need that millions of people have for affordable, effective treatments. Concern for the larger issue is without doubt paramount. Nevertheless, attention to the narrow question that arises in the conduct of research in developing countries is not intended to detract from the much larger problem. Nor is it a step toward beginning to solve the larger problem. It is, rather, a sharp focus on the question of what is owed to the human subjects of research, and whether that should differ depending on whether they live in a wealthy or a poor country. What is a first step in approaching the larger question is the subject of the next chapter: what is owed to research subjects, the wider community, and the developing country as a whole when research is concluded.

NOTES

Portions of this chapter are excerpted from my previously published article, "After Helsinki," *Kennedy Institute of Ethics Journal*, 11:1 (2001), 17–36.

1. Michael Specter, "The Vaccine: Has the Race to Save Africa from AIDS Put Western Science at Odds with Western Ethics?" *The New Yorker* (February 3, 2003), 54–65 at 65.
2. Robert J. Levine, "The 'Best Proven Therapeutic Method' Standard in Clinical Trials in Technologically Developing Countries," *IRB: A Review of Human Subjects Research*, 20:1 (1998), 5–9 at 6.
3. Peter Lurie and Sidney Wolfe, "Unethical Trials of Interventions to Reduce Perinatal Transmission of the Human Immunodeficiency Virus in Developing Countries," NEJM, 337 (1997), 853–856.
4. National Bioethics Advisory Commission, *Ethical and Policy Issues in International Research: Clinical Trials in Developing Countries* (Bethesda, MD, 2001), 13.
5. Ibid.
6. Nuffield Council on Bioethics, *The Ethics of Research Related to Healthcare in Developing Countries* (London: Nuffield Council on Bioethics, 2002), Box 7.1, 87.
7. Carol Levine, "Placebos and HIV: Lessons Learned," *Hastings Center Report*, 28:6 (1998), 43–48 at 47.

8. Nuffield, *Ethics of Research*, Box 7.1, note 2, 87.
9. Ibid., Box 7.1, 87.
10. Lurie and Wolfe, "Unethical Trials," 855.
11. Dirceu B. Greco, "Revising the Declaration of Helsinki: Ethics vs. Economics or the Fallacy of Urgency," *Canadian HIV/AIDS Policy and Law Newsletter*, 5:4 (2000), 94–97 at 97.
12. David J. Rothman, "The Shame of Medical Research," *New York Review of Books*, http://www.nybooks.com/nyrev/WWWfeatdisplay.cgi?20001130060, accessed November 15, 2000.
13. Solomon R. Benatar and Peter A. Singer, "A New Look at International Research Ethics," *British Medical Journal*, 321 (2000), 824–825.
14. David B. Resnik, "The Ethics of HIV Research in Developing Nations," *Bioethics*, 12:4 (1998), 286–306 at 304–305.
15. Alex John London, "The Ambiguity and the Exigency: Clarifying 'Standard of Care' Arguments in International Research," *Journal of Medicine and Philosophy*, 25:4 (2000), 379–397 at 381.
16. This is the view of Benatar and Singer, "A New Look."
17. This is the view of Lurie and Wolfe, "Unethical Trials," and Greco, "Revising the Declaration of Helsinki."
18. Nuffield, *Ethics of Research*, 87.
19. Lurie and Wolfe, "Unethical Trials," 855.
20. CIOMS, *International Ethical Guidelines for Biomedical Research Involving Human Subjects* (Geneva: CIOMS, 1993), 5–6.
21. Ibid., 39.
22. I was the author of one of the commissioned papers, and was therefore a participant in the March 2000 consultation. I attended all subsequent meetings of the CIOMS steering committee.
23. The members of this group and their nationalities were: Robert J. Levine, United States; Fernando Lolas, Chile; Leonardo de Castro, Philippines; Godfrey Tangwa, Cameroon; myself, United States, and Jack Bryant, President of CIOMS, *ex officio*, United States.
24. Florencia Luna, Argentina, and Rodolfo Saracci, France. This process was coordinated and helped by the very able assistance of Dr. James Gallagher of the CIOMS secretariat, who worked behind the scenes from beginning to end, along with Dr. Juhana Idänpään-Heikkilä, the Secretary General of CIOMS.
25. As a member of the writing group, I had access to all of the comments, along with the identity of the authors or organizations that submitted them. In preparation for writing this book, I contacted the individuals or representatives of the organizations and sought permission to quote their remarks, with or without attribution. All who were contacted granted permission, with one organization requesting that it not be identified. All responses to the CIOMS draft guidelines quoted in this and other chapters are, therefore, with the permission of their authors. The identifying information for each author or organization is what was provided to me.
26. Permission granted to quote without attribution.
27. Swiss Academy of Medical Sciences.

28. Norway Ethics Council.
29. International Federation of Pharmaceutical Manufacturers Associations.
30. National Institutes of Health.
31. PhRMA, comment submitted by Dr. Bertram H. Spilker representing PhRMA.
32. Dr. Robert Temple.
33. Australia HEC.
34. Dr. Oyewale Tomori.
35. Frederick Moolten.
36. Richard Ashcroft.
37. Udo Schüklenk.
38. CIOMS, *International Ethical Guidelines for Biomedical Research Involving Human Subjects* (Geneva: CIOMS, 2002), 56–57 at 57.
39. Ibid.
40. Joint United Nations Programme on HIV/AIDS (UNAIDS), *Ethical Considerations in HIV Preventive Vaccine Research* (2000), 31.
41. Ibid.
42. Nuffield, *Ethics of Research*, 87.
43. Ibid., 90.
44. Ibid.
45. Ibid., 93.
46. Ibid., 94–95.
47. Ibid., 96.
48. UNAIDS, *Vaccine Research*, 41.
49. Department of Health and Human Services, Code of Federal Regulations (1991), 45 CFR 46.111 Criteria for IRB approval of research.
50. Available at http://www.fda.gov/cber/gdlns/clinical031301.pdf, accessed May 6, 2003.
51. FDA Guidance for Industry, 1.
52. Code of Federal Regulations, Title 21, Volume 5 (21 CFR 312.120).
53. PhRMA Discussion Paper on the Declaration of Helsinki as Revised in October 2000, issued by the Pharmaceutical Research and Manufacturers of America (June 2001), 1; http://www.phrma.org/, accessed May 22, 2002.
54. The full name of the ICH is "International Conference on Harmonisation of Technical Requirements for Registration of Pharmaceuticals for Human Use." This project brings together the regulatory authorities of Europe, the United States and Japan to discuss scientific and technical aspects of product registration; http://www.ifpma.org/ich1.html.
55. ICH, 2.1.3, 13.
56. PhRMA Discussion Paper, 1.
57. Ibid., 2.

3   Striving for justice in research

What does justice require when industrialized countries sponsor or conduct research in developing countries? Diverse interpretations of the concept of justice are one source of controversy regarding what – if anything – industrialized country sponsors owe to research subjects, to the community, or country as a whole when research yields successful products or contributions to knowledge.

An even more problematic question asks why biomedical research should be the place to seek to redress the gross inequalities that characterize access to all sorts of goods and services in the world. This was a recurrent theme in meetings of the National Bioethics Advisory Commission in its international project. Some commissioners readily acknowledged the existence of pervasive global injustices, yet they rejected the idea that providing beneficial products resulting from clinical trials was an appropriate way to begin to address unequal distribution of resources – medical or otherwise. According to that viewpoint, pharmaceutical products are just one more commodity that is distributed inequitably in a global system in which market forces govern. A sharply contrasting view is that drugs and other items necessary for maintaining or improving the health of people in all societies should be removed entirely from the market system.[1] This "radical" view could find support in a human rights analysis of obligations regarding public health (see chapter 7).

Concerns about justice in international research have focused mostly on worries about exploitation of research subjects or entire populations in developing countries in the process of recruiting subjects and conducting the study. The chief concerns have been flawed or cursory procedures in gaining informed consent, inadequate or nonexistent local or national ethical review of proposed research, or lack of proper skills on the part of local researchers in developing countries. These shortcomings have not disappeared, and charges continue to surface, alleging that one or another research project is guilty of exploiting subjects or the population from which they are drawn. In chapter 4 we return to these concerns in examining the concept of exploitation in research and assessing which charges are justified, and on what grounds.

As one author notes: "The focus on protecting the vulnerable from the imposition of greater health-related risks is precisely the animating concern of the dominant norm of justice in research as protection."[2] That dominant norm was rarely cast in the language of justice, but this has changed considerably at the turn of the twenty-first century. One early exception was the *Belmont Report* of the US National Commission for the Protection of Human Subjects of Biomedical and Behavioral Research. In explaining what justice requires in the research context, the *Belmont Report* stated that "research should not unduly involve persons from groups unlikely to be among the beneficiaries of subsequent applications of the research."[3]

Distributive justice in global research

The relevant conception of justice in this context is *distributive justice*, which mandates a fair distribution of the benefits and burdens of research. The twin ethical concerns in any research are an imposition of undue burdens and the absence of expected benefits. Although risks to subjects are an enduring concern, the failure to share in the benefits of research when successful products or contributions to knowledge result has only recently been acknowledged as a major shortcoming in research sponsored by industrialized countries and conducted in resource-poor countries.

Despite the intuitive plausibility of viewing unfair distributions of benefits and burdens as a relevant concern for justice on a global scale, a skeptical view questions the very application of distributive justice in this context. The reviewer of a manuscript submitted for publication made the following comments:

There are two problems with this use of the term "distributive justice": First, it is controversial to think of the interaction between *countries* as being governed by distributive justice. The parties are simply too distant in their relationship. The concept covers *social* benefits and burdens, which means those benefits and burdens that result and arise from a group of people living together in a society.[4]

In reply to this objection, it is notable that the literature in research ethics does not support the reviewer's contention that the scope of distributive justice lies within a single country. To cite one prominent example from a report published by the Institute of Medicine of the National Academy of Sciences: "Beneficiaries of the research outcomes must include people in the developing countries where the research is conducted, as well as" in the developed country that sponsors the research.[5]

Moreover, in the conduct of multinational research, the interaction is not between countries. The research may be sponsored by a governmental agency such as the US NIH or, in the UK, the Medical Research Council (MRC), by private industry, by a private foundation (Ford Foundation, Gates Foundation, Rockefeller Foundation), by an international organization such as WHO, or some combination thereof. The collaboration takes place among the researchers from the industrialized country, the sponsors, the researchers in the developing country and the local host institution, and sometimes also the host country Ministry of Health (which usually must grant approval for the research).

Thus a close relationship exists among the group of collaborators in international research, regardless of any geographical distance that may separate the countries involved. It is surely the case that the industrialized country researchers form a relationship both with their developing country collaborators and with the research subjects in the country where the research is conducted. US researchers who testified at meetings of the National Bioethics Advisory Commission in its international project spoke at length of the collaborative relationships forged during their research carried out in developing countries.

The skeptical manuscript reviewer noted that the concept of distributive justice covers *social* benefits and burdens. While that is true, it is also the case that the concept covers health benefits, financial benefits, and others – all of which may be construed as social benefits. But there is nothing inherent in the concept of distributive justice that requires those benefits and burdens to "result and arise from a group of people living together in a society," as the reviewer claimed.

A precise general definition of what constitutes a fair distribution is hard to arrive at. This is because the criteria for fairness may differ from one context to another.[6] In the context of research involving human subjects, equity is the core concept of fair distribution. Equity requires that no one group – gender, racial, ethnic, geographic, or socioeconomic – receive disproportionate benefits or bear disproportionate burdens.[7] A striking illustration of inequity on a global scale is the disparity between the magnitude of disease burden in the world and the allocation of research funding. According to the Global Forum for Health Research: "Every year more than US $70 billion is spent on health research and development by the public and private sectors. An estimated 10% of this is used for research into 90% of the world's health problems. This is what is called 'the 10/90 gap.'"[8] The central objective of the Global Forum for Health Research is to help correct the 10/90 gap by focusing research efforts on diseases representing the heaviest burden on the world's health and facilitating collaboration between partners in both the public and private sectors.

It is a well-documented fact that disadvantaged people in developing countries suffer a disproportionate burden of bearing the risks of research without the opportunity to enjoy any lasting benefits that may accrue. Residents of developing countries lack access to the products of research carried out in their countries if the medications are too expensive for individuals or the ministries of health to afford. One report specifies two conditions that must be fulfilled in order to meet the requirements of distributive justice in international research:

1. The design and determination of acceptable risk–benefit ratios must be evaluated with the same standards as when such research is carried out in the sponsoring country;
2. Beneficiaries of the research outcomes must include people in the developing countries where the research is conducted, as well as in the United States.[9]

These conditions make it clear that it is not only the benefits and burdens accruing to the research participants, but also the potentially beneficial outcomes to the larger community that count in determining equity.

This issue became prominent early on when AIDS vaccine trials were first contemplated in Africa.[10] One writer puts the matter as follows: "Although there may be scientific interest in studying groups of Africans with different transmission risks in order to evaluate the efficacy of a vaccine, it would be unethical to subject Africans to a disproportionate share of the research risks without an equal share of the benefits."[11] A proposed solution is for developed countries to make a commitment to provide an affordable or subsidized vaccine to African countries following international collaborative vaccine trials conducted there, a move that would satisfy this requirement of justice.

To provide a general theory of global justice is beyond the scope of this book, although some people argue that without such a theory, there can be no sound justification for the claim that an obligation exists to provide benefits to research subjects or to the larger community following clinical trials conducted in a developing country. In this chapter I examine one of two related, yet different global developments that demonstrate a new-found recognition of the need to help the world's poorest, both in providing access to beneficial medical therapies and in bettering the social conditions that have been shown to contribute largely to health inequities. The first of these two efforts relates to obligations on the part of sponsors of research when the research is concluded. The second effort, described in detail in chapter 6, is that of newly forged public–private partnerships, such as the Global Fund to Fight AIDS, Tuberculosis, and Malaria, a joint initiative launched in 2001 by several United Nations agencies.

Global disparities and health equity

A wealth of empirical data exists demonstrating an array of inequalities throughout the world related to specific diseases. Statistics regarding HIV/AIDS in Africa are the most striking. AIDS killed 2.4 million African people in 2002. The estimated 3.5 million new HIV infections in sub-Saharan Africa in that year means that 29.4 million Africans are living with HIV/AIDS. Botswana has an HIV prevalence rate among the adult population of 38.8 percent, and other countries in Southern Africa have a prevalence rate of higher than 30 percent. In the 15–24 age range, 10 million people are HIV-infected and almost 3 million children under the age of 15 are living with HIV.[12] Nearly 70 percent of all new HIV infections the world over occur in sub-Saharan Africa. In those countries, HIV is spread primarily through heterosexual activity.

According to UNAIDS, the vast majority of the 42 million adults and children living with HIV/AIDS are in developing countries, an additional 45 million may be infected by HIV by 2010, and up to 70 million people could die of AIDS by 2020. At the end of 2001, in low- and middle-income countries fewer than 4 percent of those infected had access to antiretroviral therapy. However, this marks an improvement over the previous year, when fewer than 1 percent of people needing antiretroviral treatment had access. UNAIDS reports that in countries like India, the national prevalence rate is not a good indicator of the growth of the epidemic. At the end of 2001, the national adult HIV prevalence rate was under 1 percent, yet this meant that the actual number of Indians living with HIV/AIDS was estimated at 3.97 million – more than in any country other than South Africa.[13] The fastest growing rate of HIV/AIDS in 2002 was in Eastern Europe and Central Asia. In that year there were about 250,000 new infections in those regions.[14]

High-income countries generally have a much lower rate of incidence and prevalence of the disease than do other parts of the world. Despite the staggering figures of HIV infection in Africa and India, the only effective treatment for the disease – highly active antiretroviral therapy – is available only to a tiny minority in those countries and most other developing countries (with the exception of Brazil), whereas in the United States and other industrialized countries, most infected individuals are treated.

The worldwide focus on the AIDS pandemic and its devastating consequences in Africa partially obscures the equally burdensome consequences of two other diseases prevalent in developing countries in the South: tuberculosis and malaria. Like HIV/AIDS, tuberculosis is a disease occurring in both North and South, prevalent in developed as well as developing countries. The Global Alliance for TB Drug Development, one of several newly formed international partnerships, has as its mission to accelerate the discovery and/or development of cost-effective new drugs that would shorten or simplify treatment of TB and provide more effective treatments of new TB strains.

According to the Global Alliance for TB Drug Development, it is imperative to develop new drugs to fight TB. The Alliance notes that "No new drug to treat TB has been developed in more than 30 years, mostly because it appeared to be defeated. But the number of new cases of TB clearly indicate that TB is still a significant public health threat worldwide." Not only is the number of people estimated to have latent TB infection around 1.86 billion; also, multidrug-resistant strains have developed as a result of poor adherence to treatment, instances of misdiagnosis, misprescribing treatment, and poor drug supply.[15] The Global Alliance contends that contrary to popular belief, there is a sufficient market for anti-TB drugs, larger than what has been estimated. The Alliance also maintains that private industry could recoup its investment in new anti-TB drugs.

The third major disease – malaria – is found predominantly in the South. Malaria is a public health problem in over 100 countries worldwide, comprising about 40 percent of the world population. Countries in sub-Saharan Africa account for more than 90 percent of the 300 million cases diagnosed each year. Mortality from malaria is estimated at almost 1 million deaths worldwide per year, mostly among young children in Africa and especially in remote rural areas with poor access to health services. As with TB at the present time, there is increasing resistance to medicines that are currently in use. The result is likely to be an increasing demand for effective medications in the near future.[16]

Today malaria is almost exclusively confined to developing countries. In the past, however, malaria was found in the United States and was epidemic as far north as Finland. According to one expert, "at present many epidemic prone situations will, by their nature, stretch across national boundaries."[17] We have only to think about another mosquito-borne disease – West Nile virus in the United States – to recognize the possibility that malaria may return to countries in the North at some point in the future. Some international measures are in place in an attempt to keep malaria from spreading to places where the disease does not now exist. Anyone who has been on an airplane departing from countries where malaria and other insect-borne diseases are prevalent has no doubt experienced spraying of the cabin, with the flight attendants warning passengers to cover their faces. Aircrafts, ships, and other vehicles may be sprayed with insecticide upon arrival if there is reason to suspect importation of malaria mosquitoes. Another step is for countries where the disease is prevalent to enforce and maintain rigid antimosquito sanitation within the mosquito flight range of all ports and airports. Also, in special circumstances antimalarial drugs may be administered to potentially infected migrants, refugees, seasonal workers, or other persons moving into areas or countries where malaria has been eliminated. As diligent as airlines and health authorities may be in this regard, the effort was either nonexistent or ineffective in keeping the West Nile virus from traveling from Africa to the New York metropolitan area, and following that, spreading throughout the United States.

The examples cited above of global disparities in access to effective treatments and inequities in the global burden of disease all pertain to diseases that are epidemic in many developing countries. Another broad area where social inequalities are prominent is that of women's reproductive health. Maternal mortality remains unacceptably high in many developing countries, a consequence of limited health infrastructure, poorly trained birth attendants, and women's inevitable recourse to illegal and unsafe abortions. From 1990 to 2000, the rate of maternal mortality remained highest in Africa, with 9.4 deaths per 1,000 live births. The death rate for Southeast Asian women was 6.1. In contrast, the rate was 1.4 for North and South America taken together, 0.6 for Europe, and 0.1 for the United States.[18]

The World Health Organization (WHO) reports the following problems regarding sexually transmitted infections specific to women, making women more vulnerable than men with such infections:

Women are much more vulnerable biologically, culturally, and socioeconomically than men;

The majority of sexually transmitted infections (STIs) are asymptomatic in women (60–70 percent of gonococcal and chlamydial infections);

The consequences of sexually transmitted infections are very serious in women, sometimes even fatal (eg cervical cancer, ectopic pregnancy, sepsis) and in their babies (stillbirth, blindness);

Women tend not to seek treatment because, in addition to the absence of obvious symptoms, more stigma is attached to STIs in women and they often have neither time nor money for health care.[19]

Although much of the attention and most of the data on health disparities have focused on girls and women of reproductive age in developing countries, information is now emerging on the health status of older women. WHO has reported the following facts:

There are powerful economic, social, political and cultural determinants which influence how women age, with far-reaching consequences for health and quality of life, as well as costs to the health care systems. For example, poverty at older ages often reflects poor economic status earlier in life and is a determinant of health at all stages of life. Countries that have data on poverty by age and sex (mostly the developed countries) show that older women are more likely to be poor than older men . . .

Poverty is also linked to inadequate access to food and nutrition and the health of older women often reflects the cumulative impact of poor diets. For example, years of child bearing and sacrificing her own nutrition to that of the family can leave the older woman with chronic anaemia . . .

Older women everywhere are far more likely to be widowed than older men and most women can expect widowhood to be a normal part of their adult daily lives. While most women adjust both emotionally and financially to their changed situation, traditional widowhood practices in some countries result in situations of violence and abuse and pose a serious threat to older women's health and well-being.[20]

In every country in the world, the rich live longer than the poor and the poor are sicker than the rich.[21] And the gap in income between rich and poor has been increasing in every country.[22] Stark disparities in health status exist between rich and poor classes around the globe, both within nations and between nations. There are vast inequalities between and among nations regarding access to health care among large sectors of the population. Among the poor in countries in which women are disvalued, girl children suffer from malnutrition, which leads to growth retardation, and from medical neglect; both conditions result in increased morbidity and mortality.

The South African physician–ethicist, Solomon Benatar, has traced many of the existing inequities in health status and access to health care to poverty brought about by the huge world expenditures on military goods and services, including military aid provided by industrialized countries to developing countries. In addition, modern international economic policies and market-driven health care have contributed to poverty, thereby threatening physical and mental health as the prerequisites for a decent human life and global survival.[23]

Justice, health care, and research

Leading scholars in health policy have argued that health care is a special form of social good, one not strictly commensurate with or replaceable by commodities in the marketplace. Following the concept introduced by John Rawls in *A Theory of Justice* and elaborated by the philosopher, Norman Daniels, this line of reasoning adopts the premise that health is a "primary good."[24] "Primary goods" are things that every rational person would want because they are needed to carry out a personal life plan.[25] Although health care and medications are not sufficient to guarantee good health, they are surely among the necessary conditions for attaining or restoring health in the case of treatable diseases. Daniels makes a compelling argument that access to basic health care is a requirement of justice, as it is necessary in order for human beings to function in a way that is normal or typical for the species.[26]

The relationship between justice and health pertains not only to the health of individuals in society, but to a country's public health status as well. Daniels and colleagues argue that a goal of public health and medicine is to keep people as close as possible to the ideal of normal functioning, under reasonable resource constraints. In an article that focuses on the social determinants of public health, Daniels and colleagues contend that concentration on medical care, on the part of both bioethicists and the public, is a misplaced emphasis.[27]

Another bioethicist, Dan W. Brock, has also made a compelling case for shifting attention away from the provision of medical services toward the direction of social determinants such as socioeconomic inequality and class.[28] Brock notes that "[M]ost general theories of justice appear to assume that it is possible to determine which socioeconomic inequalities are unjust independent of their effects on health"; he maintains that "it is a mistake to assume that the justice of socioeconomic inequalities can be assessed independent of their substantial effects on health."[29] The leading global public health agency, the World Health Organization (WHO), has devoted increasing attention to inequalities in health status and the policies and causes that create or mitigate them.

The application of theories of justice to health policy has focused primarily on access to health care, both preventive services and therapeutic care. According to one account, different norms of justice have been dominant in different spheres of health policy.[30] Bioethicists and political theorists who have studied inequalities in health care in the United States have tended to follow the lines of an egalitarian conception of justice in health policy. As noted earlier, a rather different focus initially marked concerns about justice in the context of research. The conception of justice most frequently invoked was that of protecting the vulnerable from exploitation – either by ensuring that their consent to participate was informed, understanding, and fully voluntary, or by establishing protective mechanisms such as prior ethical review of research protocols by an independent committee. (These safeguards are discussed in detail in chapter 5.) A third, somewhat distinct norm of justice has been dominant in occupational and environmental health policy:

[T]raditional approaches to environmental and occupational health issues reject the almost exclusive focus on either benefits or risks which both egalitarian and protective conceptions of justice employ. They adopt instead an approach which involves a simultaneous reflection on benefits and burdens. The assumption is that every option involves both benefits and burdens, necessitating some trade-offs, and often the trade-offs occur in cases where the burdens are not borne by the beneficiaries.[31]

It is true, of course, that the application of the classic conception of distributive justice to research requires a balancing of benefits and burdens. But the problem is more acute and takes on different dimensions when research is conducted in developing countries because access to health benefits outside the context of research is so limited. Although it is still the case that millions of people in the US are uninsured, and thus lack access to adequate or any health care, they constitute a minority of the population. In contrast, the majority in most developing countries are without access to adequate or effective healthcare services. Poor access to medical care in the US could be remedied with considerable ease, but for a lack of political will on the part of elected officials: socially conservative legislators and Presidents. No comparable solution exists within countries that rank among the poorest in the world.

A related, yet different concern of justice in research is the setting of research priorities. Only a small fraction of research dollars spent by the pharmaceutical industry and major national research agencies has been devoted to the diseases that are prevalent in developing countries (the 10/90 gap described above). This is not surprising where industry is concerned, since the goal of pharmaceutical and biotechnology companies is to make a profit. Major profits are not forthcoming from sales of drugs in countries where neither the government nor the majority of the people have money to pay for expensive medications and there is little in the way of private insurance. As a result, if research that is most relevant to the health needs of developing countries is given a low priority, the likelihood of research benefits flowing to the populations in those countries is slim. Nevertheless, industrialized country sponsors are increasing the research they conduct in developing countries, so we have to ask what, if anything, justice requires for the populations in those countries.

Post-trial benefits of research: obligation or charity?

According to a main tenet of distributive justice, it is not fair that populations in resource-poor countries suffer the potential burdens of research without the prospect of deriving benefits when research demonstrates the safety and effectiveness of an experimental drug. It is unjust when the products of research conducted in developing countries are available only to individuals who can afford them, both in the resource-poor countries and in industrialized countries where private or public insurance or governments assume the burden of healthcare costs.

However, there is far from universal agreement on what justice requires in this sphere. One commentator finds two different interpretations of the distributive justice principle, with roots in the opposing theories of capitalism and Marxism. Cooley writes:

Distributive justice requires that each social member receives a just distribution of the benefits and burdens of society, i.e., what he or she deserves from being a member of the society. The question here is why do the members of the community who did not participate in the experiment deserve to receive the benefits of the experiment? They did not have to bear burdens as the test subjects do – or those the sponsoring agencies or pharmaceutical companies are required to shoulder – but receive an enormous benefit at no real cost to themselves . . . [C]apitalist justice requires that only those who have contributed to achieving their group's goals may receive benefits.[32]

Cooley argues that a conception of distributive justice that would require that successful products be made available to the entire community or developing country is "more closely aligned with Marxism, which requires that people work according to their abilities, while they receive according to their needs."[33] He argues further that such a requirement is actually more extreme than Marxism, since the principle of distributive justice "requires no contribution from those receiving benefits."[34]

Cooley's analysis is both tendentious and circular. It is tendentious because it relies on an appeal to the "victory" capitalism achieved over Marxism by the end of the twentieth century. If capitalism has become the dominant economic system in today's globalized world and Marxism is a discredited vestige of the past, then the reader is led to reject an interpretation of distributive justice that seems to derive from Marxism, and even more readily, one that is "more extreme than Marxism." Cooley supports the conduct of research in developing countries but his approach does not rely on the principle of justice, which he finds vague and ambiguous. Rather, Cooley defends research conducted in developing countries on utilitarian grounds and the autonomous choice of the subjects to participate in such research. Solomon Benatar criticizes Cooley's approach as serving "only to entrench further a neo-liberal economic mind-set deeply inimical to the progress required to rectify some of the widening disparities in wealth and health that characterize an increasingly unstable world."[35]

Cooley's analysis is circular because it begs the central question under examination. It simply assumes, without argument, that those who have not contributed to the research do not deserve to share in the benefits:

[T]he non-participating population loses nothing if the experiment is performed in its community and can not be made useful to it. Those who do not contribute have no reasonable expectation of benefit in the first place, especially if the experiment is not done. In order to have a reasonable expectation of a benefit, there must be something that justifies such a desert.[36]

What *could* justify such a desert? Cooley dismisses need alone as a justifying factor, claiming that to justify desert individuals must have made some contribution to the effort. In contrast, a brief statement in the UNAIDS Guidance Document for preventive HIV/AIDS vaccine research suggests that dire human need *can* justify this interpretation of what distributive justice requires:

Given the severity of the epidemic, it is imperative that sufficient incentives exist, both through financial rewards in the marketplace and through public subsidies, to foster development of effective vaccines while also ensuring that vaccines are produced and distributed in a fashion that actually makes them available to the populations at greatest risk.[37]

More needs to be said about this attempted justification. A worrisome feature is that the principle may apply only in the case of devastating diseases such as AIDS. Arguably, however, it could also apply to tuberculosis and malaria, the two other killer diseases targeted for collaborative international assistance in the Global Fund to Fight AIDS, Tuberculosis, and Malaria.

A basis for a response to Cooley's position is the idea that justice or equity lies in maximizing health benefits for a population ("equity as maximization"). According to one account, some people consider it self-evident that health policy should aim to produce as much health as possible for a given population.[38] The article in question contends that maximizing principles can serve as candidates for principles of justice or equity:

The fundamental moral assumption of maximizing principles is that we express equal respect for each person by giving her interests the very same weight as others. Behind a maximizing principle is a principle of equality: each person's interests, in this case their health, counts just as much and no more than anyone else's.[39]

Unlike Cooley's interpretation of distributive justice, this line of reasoning does not require a contribution on the part of individuals to make them deserving of measures to improve their health status. On this account, justice requires that the entire population in need – not only the research subjects who have contributed to development of a successful product – deserves the benefits of research.

Another candidate for a principle of justice or equity as applied to health is "equity as priority to the sickest."[40] This position relies on the urgency of people's needs: those who have the shortest life expectancy and most serious diseases and injuries have the greatest urgency. On this view, the sickest people should have priority. But there is a problem with this if the individuals who have served as research subjects received the benefits during the research of a product that has proven to be successful; then they are no longer the sickest. The sickest are those who were not involved in the research and did not have access to any treatments because none were available outside the research. Since the entire population of non-subjects is worse off than those who served as subjects and received the beneficial product, on this principle they deserve priority for receiving the product.

But what about the research subjects who still need the product when the research is over? Does the principle of priority to the sickest mean that they should no longer receive the product when the research is over because they have already been helped by it? The answer is "no," but this shows only that no single principle of justice is appropriate for all situations. The situation in which research subjects still require a successful product that they received during their participation in research requires a different ethical principle: individuals who serve as research subjects should not be made worse off after a clinical trial is over than they were while the research was being carried out.

The international report of the US National Bioethics Advisory Commission describes the above situation as an "existential loss" that the research subjects would experience. Although I cannot see what describing the loss as "existential" contributes to the analysis, I concur in the conclusion that leaving subjects worse off after a trial is over than they were during the research is ethically unacceptable. The NBAC report locates post-trial obligations to research subjects in the principle of "justice as reciprocity," a justification similar to Cooley's reasoning discussed earlier.

> Justice as reciprocity . . . is concerned with what people deserve as a function of what they have contributed to an enterprise or to society. In the context of clinical trials, justice as reciprocity could mean that something is owed to research participants even after their participation in a trial has ended, because it is only through their acceptance of risk and inconvenience that researchers are able to generate findings necessary to advance knowledge and develop new medical interventions.[41]

The NBAC report goes on to note that the principle of reciprocity applies not only to research subjects who have participated in a clinical trial that has had successful results, but also to subjects in research that did not yield any successful products or knowledge. This is because in both cases, the subjects accepted risks and inconvenience in agreeing to participate.

A final conception of justice that may be applicable in this context is that of "compensatory justice." This concept is usually applied to the research context in two circumstances. First, in cases in which people have been injured in the course of research, they deserve money or other benefits to compensate them for the injury. Although monetary compensation is rarely offered by sponsors of research, it is nevertheless reasonable to hold that such compensation is owed to injured subjects on the model of compensation for injuries sustained in the workplace. The second situation is one in which research subjects have lost time from work in order to participate in the research, or have paid out of pocket for expenses related to the research. These include expenses such as travel to the site of the research or child care. In both situations, compensation is owed or provided to research subjects for something they did or that happened to them.

Compensatory justice has been applied in a broader context to cover situations that have occurred in the past:

The notion of *compensatory justice* goes beyond that of fairness in distribution in an attempt to remedy or redress past wrongs. An example from the history of human subjects research is that of monetary payments made to survivors of the Tuskegee syphilis study or to their relatives, to compensate them for the harm or wrong done by the study.[42]

Payment to the survivors of the Tuskegee syphilis study is an extension of the usual type of compensation since it is based on something that was done to the research subjects themselves, even though the actual events took place many years earlier. Payment to the relatives of the men who were subjects in the Tuskegee study is a departure from the usual form of compensation. An analogy from a different context is compensation provided to family members of victims of the Holocaust in Nazi Germany.

Although some would argue that it stretches the notion of compensatory justice too far, a case could be made for benefiting developing countries or the communities where research is conducted today as compensation for past research from which no benefits flowed to those communities or countries. When past research conducted in developing countries yielded successful products, those products were available in industrialized countries but only much later, if at all, in developing countries. A broad concept of compensatory justice could justify providing benefits from current research because of past injustices.

What the guidelines say

What do the leading international ethical guidelines and the two comprehensive reports on international research say about what is owed to research subjects and to others at the conclusion of a trial? All of the guidelines and reports express the general idea that research must be responsive to the health needs of the population where the research is conducted and should potentially benefit that population. As noted in chapter 1, the latter statement is by now so widely accepted that few commentators see the need to argue for it explicitly (but see the position of Dr. Robert Temple of the FDA quoted below, p. 88).

The documents compared in what follows have already been discussed in a different context in earlier chapters: the Declaration of Helsinki, as revised in 2000; the report of the US National Bioethics Advisory Commission (NBAC), issued in 2001; the 2002 revised version of the CIOMS *International Ethical Guidelines for Biomedical Research Involving Human Subjects* (CIOMS); the UNAIDS Guidance Document, *Ethical Considerations in HIV Preventive Vaccine Research* issued in 2000; and the 2002 report of the Nuffield Council on Bioethics (Nuffield). The UNAIDS Guidance Document makes a stronger statement and provides for a wider range of benefits than do these other documents.[43] Because of that, the UNAIDS provisions are subject to the criticism that they are too "aspirational" and not sufficiently "pragmatic."

Earlier versions of the Declaration of Helsinki did not include any statement expressing a general requirement for making successful products available to research subjects or to others. The 2000 revision of Helsinki, however, addresses the point in two separate paragraphs: 9 and 30. Paragraph 19 says:

Medical research is only justified if there is a reasonable likelihood that the populations in which the research is carried out stand to benefit from the results of the research.

The brevity of the items in the Declaration of Helsinki and the absence of any commentary or explication leaves crucial questions wide open. For example, what are the criteria by which "likelihood of benefit" is to be determined? And what degree of likelihood is necessary?

Helsinki also addresses the question of benefits to the subject population in a strong requirement in paragraph 30:

At the conclusion of the study, every patient entered into the study should be assured of access to the best proven prophylactic, diagnostic and therapeutic methods identified by the study.

In this paragraph, Helsinki contains the same strong requirement found in Guidance Point 2 of the UNAIDS Guidance Document for preventive vaccine research, regarding what should be made available to research participants: "Any HIV preventive vaccine demonstrated to be safe and effective . . . should be made available as soon as possible to all participants in the trials in which it was tested." However, Helsinki is silent on the question of what, if anything, must be made available to others in the country or community at the conclusion of successful trials.

In contrast, UNAIDS Guidance Point 2 continues with an even stronger requirement not found in other guidelines or documents: "Any HIV preventive vaccine demonstrated to be safe and effective . . . should be made available as soon as possible . . . *to other populations at high risk of HIV infection*" (emphasis added). It may well be that this requirement is easier to fulfill in the case of HIV/AIDS preventive vaccines than for other potential products, since vaccines are generally less expensive than many therapeutic agents and what would be required is a one-time administration followed by boosters rather than, say, a lifetime of frequent administration of a pharmaceutical product. The commentary following Guidance Point 2 states that the discussion about making a successful vaccine available should begin before the trial commences, mentions the elements that should be included in the discussion, and indicates who should be the parties to the discussion. Unlike NBAC (see below), the UNAIDS document does not retreat from its bold requirement by adding that it is permissible to depart from the provision as long as an acceptable justification is provided.

Like UNAIDS, the NBAC report and the Nuffield Council report address two separate points regarding availability of successful products after a trial is completed: availability to the research participants themselves (the only point addressed in the Declaration of Helsinki), and availability of successful products to others in the country or community. The first point is stated in NBAC's Recommendation 4.1:

Researchers and sponsors in clinical trials should make reasonable, good faith efforts before the initiation of a trial to secure, at its conclusion, continued access for all participants to needed experimental interventions that have been proven effective for the participants. Although the details of the arrangements will depend on a number of factors (including but not limited to the results of a trial), research protocols should typically describe the duration, extent, and financing of such continued access. When no arrangements have been negotiated, the researcher should justify to the ethics review committee why this is the case.[44]

Whereas the Declaration of Helsinki stipulates that "every patient entered into the study should be assured of access," NBAC requires only "reasonable, good faith efforts" on the part of researchers and sponsors, and permits the researcher to justify to the ethics review committee any failure to negotiate advance arrangements to make successful products available to participants who still need them at the end of the trial. NBAC Recommendation 4.1 provides no criteria for what would constitute a sound or acceptable justification for such failures. NBAC states only the procedural requirement that researchers submitting a protocol to an ethics review committee provide the justification to the committee.

How many research ethics committees are accustomed to deliberating on this issue? Research ethics committees (IRBs) in the United States virtually never raise this question, even when they review research conducted in domestic resource-poor communities, such as uninsured or under-insured populations. Nothing in the US Code of Federal Regulations governing research with human subjects deals with this point, and most US IRBs see themselves as bound only by those regulations, along with any other US guidance or state regulations. Therefore, NBAC's call for a justification to the research ethics committee will more than likely result in committees accepting whatever justification a researcher provides. Moreover, the justification need be provided only to the US IRB. An ethical review committee in the host country would, of course, also have to approve the protocol, and could withhold approval unless the strong requirement in Helsinki's paragraph 30 is fulfilled. If the successful product is an HIV/AIDS preventive vaccine, then the similarly strong provision in UNAIDS Guidance Point 2 would apply.

The report issued by the Nuffield Council on Bioethics is even more circumspect than the NBAC report on providing post-trial benefits to research participants and to others in the community or country. Nuffield begins the section entitled "What happens once research is over?" with the observation that if sponsors of research – including large pharmaceutical companies – were required to provide post-trial benefits in the form of successful products, many would simply cease to sponsor and conduct research in developing countries. The reason is that they would be unable to afford the cost without curtailing other research.[45] On a more hopeful note, the Nuffield report observes that although products of research may initially be too costly to be made widely available, the cost may fall later on. But the fact that such products are initially too expensive to provide should not be a reason to consider it unethical, Nuffield argues, as that may lead to the loss of opportunity to improve health care.[46]

Nuffield's wording in its recommendations on post-trial benefits is tentative:

[W]e recommend that the following issues are clearly considered by researchers, sponsors, national healthcare authorities, international agencies and research ethics committees as part of any research protocol before research relating to healthcare involving the testing of new interventions is undertaken.[47]

My own view, albeit somewhat cynical, is that recommending that individuals, committees, or agencies "clearly consider" something leaves the door wide open for the response: "We clearly considered it and found it not feasible to make such a commitment at this time."

With respect to providing successful products of research to the trial participants once the research is concluded, the Nuffield report essentially agrees with the NBAC recommendation:

We . . . endorse the US National Bioethics Advisory Commission (NBAC) recommendation that researchers should endeavor before the initiation of a trial to secure post-trial access for effective intervention for participants in the trial and that lack of such arrangements should have to be justified to a research ethics committee.[48]

On the second, more problematic, issue – availability to others at the conclusion of a study – the NBAC report once again states a presumption (in Recommendation 4.2) in favor of making successful interventions available, in this case to the wider community or country:

Research proposals submitted to ethics review committees should include an explanation of how new interventions that are proven to be effective from the research will become available to some or all of the host country population beyond the research participants themselves. Where applicable, the investigator should describe any pre-research negotiations among sponsors, host country officials, and other appropriate parties aimed at making such interventions available. In cases in which investigators do not believe that successful interventions will become available to the host country population, they should explain to the relevant ethics review committee(s) why the research is nonetheless responsive to the health needs of the country and presents a reasonable risk/benefit ratio.[49]

On this same point – providing post-trial benefits to the wider community – the Nuffield report once again closely follows the NBAC recommendation:

We endorse the NBAC recommendation that research proposals submitted to those committees should include an explanation of how new proven interventions could be made available to some or all of the host country population and that investigators should justify to the relevant research ethics committee why the research should be carried out if this is not thought possible.[50]

Here again, as in the case of providing post-trial benefits to research subjects, researchers are called upon to provide explanations and justifications to the ethics review committee. It is hardly conceivable that an ethics review committee will disapprove a research protocol on these grounds alone, however feeble may be the explanation or justification the researcher offers.

One criticism that has been repeatedly leveled against a requirement that prior agreements be negotiated in advance of a study to make any resulting safe and effective products reasonably available is: This has never been done (or required) before.[51] That observation may well be true, but what is being called for now is a reform – not a continuation – of past practices in international research. To object meaningfully to efforts to introduce this social reform rooted in considerations of justice, a persuasive argument would have to be mounted showing that such prior agreements could not reasonably be expected to be forthcoming, but if required, the result would be the abandonment of all research in developing countries. Emerging evidence is beginning to show that supposition to be false (as described below in chapter 6).

Unlike Helsinki, which contains rather brief statements of its principles, the CIOMS guidelines include a rather detailed commentary under each guideline. The 2002 revised CIOMS document contains both the more general statement of responsiveness to the health needs of the population found in UNAIDS, and also the more explicit requirement that successful products be made "reasonably available" to the population. Both points are included in Guideline 10:

Before undertaking research in a population or community with limited resources, the sponsor and the researcher must make every effort to ensure that:
– the research is responsive to the health needs and the priorities of the population or community in which it is to be carried out; and
– any product developed will be made reasonably available to that population or community.[52]

It is instructive to note the way in which this guideline in the 2002 CIOMS international guidelines differs from the earlier version that appeared in the 1993 CIOMS guidelines. Old CIOMS Guideline 8 was the previous version of the now-revised CIOMS Guideline 10. Old Guideline 8 was entitled: "Research involving subjects in underdeveloped communities." (As noted in chapter 1, even way back in 1993 the term "underdeveloped" had been abandoned as politically incorrect.) The old guideline read as follows:

Before undertaking research involving subjects in underdeveloped communities, whether in developed or developing countries, the investigator must ensure that:
• persons in underdeveloped communities will not ordinarily be involved in research that could be carried out reasonably well in developed communities;

- the research is responsive to the health needs and the priorities of the community in which it is to be carried out;
- every effort will be made to secure the ethical imperative that the consent of individual subjects be informed; and
- the proposals for the research have been reviewed and approved by an ethical review committee that has among its members or consultants persons who are thoroughly familiar with the customs and traditions of the community.[53]

In addition to abandoning the term 'underdeveloped', the revised CIOMS guideline made the following changes.

First, the revised guideline abandons the presumption stated in the first bullet point. A sufficient number of researchers, policy-makers, and health advocates from developing countries have objected to the protectionist stance of this item. They point out that to require that research be conducted first in developed countries will result in delay in bringing successful products to the developing country. In addition, many developing countries have been building capacity for the conduct of research, as well as scientific and ethical review of research protocols. So there is no longer a need for such protection from industrialized countries as once there may have been.

Second, the item pertaining to informed consent is not retained in the new CIOMS Guideline 10. This is because the revised CIOMS document contains several new guidelines outlining the requirements for informed consent, much expanded from the 1993 version.

Third, the bullet point on ethical review committees has been taken out of this guideline and, here again, more extensive guidelines pertaining to ethical review committees are included in the new CIOMS document.

Finally, the following item is retained in the 2002 Guideline 10:

- the research is responsive to the health needs and the priorities of the community in which it is to be carried out;

and is supplemented with the additional item:

- any product developed will be made reasonably available to that population or community.

This latter point did appear in the commentary under Guideline 8 in the 1993 CIOMS document, and could also be found embedded in the commentary on the old Guideline 15: "As a general rule, the sponsoring agency should agree in advance of the research that any product developed through such research will be made reasonably available to the inhabitants of the host community or country at the completion of successful testing."[54] In the newly revised guideline, this item appears in bold, elevated from the commentary section to the guideline itself. But as shown below, it has given rise to major objections, including an urging by an FDA official to delete the guideline altogether.

Responses to the CIOMS guideline

As described in chapter 2, the CIOMS secretariat solicited comments after posting on its website the new draft guidelines prepared by the small, informal editorial group that met in January 2001. The comments CIOMS received in response to its website posting included some sharp disagreements. The strength as well as the polarity of the opposing views expressed by commentators once again poses the question of whether there ought to be a guideline on an issue about which such major disagreements exist. Among the comments most critical of the guideline were the following.

The first comment quoted below was submitted by Dr. Robert Temple of the FDA, whose comments on Guideline 11 were quoted in chapter 2. Dr. Temple's remarks are the most critical of all those submitted on this guideline, calling for its deletion from the CIOMS document. Other commentators who expressed various degrees of skepticism about the ability to fulfill the main provision of the guideline did not call for its abandonment. It is somewhat of a mystery why a spokesperson for the FDA – a drug regulatory agency – would be so highly critical of a guideline that seeks to provide post-trial benefits to populations in developing countries. One can only surmise that the close relationship between the FDA and industrial sponsors of research has cemented a strong pro-industry bias on the part of the regulatory agency, with the result that the best interest of the sponsor is the FDA's main concern in international collaborative research. What is curious, however, is that Dr. Temple's remarks are much more critical than those submitted by respondents from the trade associations that represent pharmaceutical manufacturing companies.

Dr. Temple commented that:

This guideline is wrong in principle and is at odds with others, namely to build local infrastructure. It should be deleted. If a new anti-depressant is studied in Eastern Europe (limited resources), the study *brings* resources and trains people; i.e., it provides a tangible benefit to the community. Individual patients may also be given access to treatments otherwise unavailable to them (how can they possibly be "exploited" by this?). It is not likely that the country's resources will go to purchasing the new agent anytime soon; they will (sensibly) rely mostly on generics until they're a lot richer.

The next comment, submitted by the US National Institutes of Health, is critical of the entire burden being placed on sponsors and researchers.

But it does not deny that such a responsibility might exist and should be fulfilled by a broader partnership.

> [T]his Guideline could be seen as unrealistic and paternalistic in placing the obligation to *ensure* "reasonable availability" totally on the sponsor and researchers. Such an obligation could seriously curtail research needed to address the health concerns of developing nations. The responsibility should rest, instead, on a *partnership* of sponsor, host country government, NGOs, and others.

Among the comments that endorsed the guideline or found it generally acceptable, but expressed some reservations, were these:
The Medical Research Council of the UK stated:

> Medical research often proceeds ahead of certainty that treatments will be made available; this is not unique to developing countries. We welcome discussion of these issues in the Commentary, which might also emphasise that availability may depend not only on cost but also on cultural factors and professional/political inertia.

Dr. David Wendler, a bioethicist who works at the NIH, submitted these comments in his own name, not officially on behalf of the NIH. Dr. Wendler did not express opposition to the guideline in principle, but called for a less forceful way of phrasing it.

> On other important issues, the draft stipulates a presumption, but not a strict requirement. Couldn't the same approach be used here: there should be a STRONG presumption that research must be community relevant, but exceptions can be made in specific cases if there are compelling reasons to do so, and this is approved by the funding and local IRB.

The next comment was submitted jointly by two groups comprising a consortium of representatives of pharmaceutical manufacturers. The first is PhRMA, the trade association representing the research-based pharmaceutical industry in the United States,[55] and the second is its international counterpart, the International Federation of Pharmaceutical Manufacturers Associations (IFPMA). It is worth noting that these industry groups do not call for a deletion of the guideline, but simply point out an array of difficulties in implementing its provisions.

> The statement "the sponsor and the researcher must make every effort to ensure that . . . any product developed will be made reasonably available to that population or community" is not clear to us. The availability of a product in any given locality will depend upon factors beyond the control of the sponsor of a clinical trial, such as the decision by local authorities as to whether to permit the marketing and use of the product . . . It is frequently the case that the evidence from a single study is an insufficient basis upon which to use the product safely in larger numbers of patients, and that other studies are necessary.

Other comments expressed unqualified support for the guideline. A bioethicist from the United Kingdom, Professor Richard Ashcroft, said:

This guideline is very good.

The Australia Health Ethics Council stated that it

strongly supports this guideline and its valuable commentary.

The Swedish Society of Medicine commented:

We fully approve the wording of the guideline and appreciate the importance for future research in developing countries.

The Swedish Research Council said that they

Fully agree with guideline and commentary.

Tadahiro Mitsuishi, from Japan, submitted a comment aimed at making the wording in the guideline even stronger:

The phrases "make every effort" and "reasonably" should be deleted because they will create another loophole.

The range of disagreements in these comments is representative of views expressed by individuals at conferences and meetings devoted to these same issues. It is remarkable that the most negative criticisms of the CIOMS guideline, which calls for strong obligations on the part of sponsors and researchers, are from the two most relevant US government agencies: the NIH, which sponsors and conducts research in developing countries, and the FDA, which regulates US-sponsored research and data submitted by foreign researchers seeking FDA approval of their research products. Also worth noting are the positive comments from two Swedish groups, as Sweden is a relatively small country and yet is one of the largest financial contributors to programs of the World Health Organization.

The FDA and PhRMA

In chapter 2 we examined the document issued by the FDA in March 2001, "Guidance for Industry: Acceptance of Foreign Clinical Studies." We noted that the FDA document refers to the 1989 version of the Declaration of Helsinki, not the version approved by the World Medical Association in October 2000 or even the immediately previous version in 1996. The discussion of this point in chapter 2 focused on the absence of any mention of placebos in the 1989 Declaration, and offered a guess that the reason for the FDA's reference to that earlier version might be related to the agency's wish to finesse the current controversy over the use of placebos.

Another guess, pertinent to the discussion in this chapter, suggests an additional reason for the FDA's reluctance to cite the latest revision of the Declaration of Helsinki. Two paragraphs in the 2000 version of the Declaration likely to be questioned, if not rejected by the FDA, are the ones quoted earlier in this chapter (neither of these two paragraphs appears in the 1996 version of the Declaration).

Paragraph 19 says:

Medical research is only justified if there is a reasonable likelihood that the populations in which the research is carried out stand to benefit from the results of the research.

And paragraph 30 states:

At the conclusion of the study, every patient entered into the study should be assured of access to the best proven prophylactic, diagnostic and therapeutic methods identified by the study.

In light of the comments the FDA's Dr. Robert Temple submitted on the CIOMS guideline on this same issue, it is not surprising to find the FDA avoiding mention of the 2000 revision of the Declaration of Helsinki.

In fact, paragraph 30 is criticized in the PhRMA discussion paper on the Declaration of Helsinki, the document that is also highly critical of paragraph 29 on placebo-controlled trials. The PhRMA discussion paper offers a strong interpretation of paragraph 30, saying that it

appears to require research sponsors to supply research participants, at the conclusion of a clinical trial, with whatever treatments were found to be best in that particular clinical trial. This raises important ethical and practical concerns, as well as the spectre of an unintended consequence – the establishment of unnecessary barriers to research and treatments for the developing world.[56]

As it is written in the passive voice – an evasive form of language that avoids identifying an agent responsible for actions – paragraph 30 of the Declaration of Helsinki does not specify who must "assure" that every patient has access to the best methods identified by the study. It could be the researchers who have to give the "assurance" at the time of enrollment. It could be the government or agency such as the Ministry of Health that makes the assurance to the researchers or to the pharmaceutical company seeking permission to carry out the trial. In any case, the requirement to "assure every patient of access" is not at all the same as to require research sponsors to supply participants with treatments found to be best in the trial. PhRMA has over-interpreted this paragraph in Helsinki.

National regulations and guidelines

Examination of a sample of national regulations and guidelines governing research involving human subjects reveals a range of viewpoints on post-trial obligations of sponsors and researchers. At one end of this continuum are the US federal regulations that govern research involving human subjects. These regulations say absolutely nothing about what is owed to research subjects or to others at the conclusion of clinical trials.

Although most national regulations and guidelines do not contain as bold a requirement as stated in UNAIDS Guidance Point 2, some countries have directly addressed post-trial benefits to research subjects and have begun to establish a presumption in favor of wider benefits to the community or country. Especially interesting are several developing countries' guidelines, which reflect the realities of their respective economic and political situations. A few illustrative examples from industrialized countries and developing countries follow.[57]

The UK Medical Research Council (the British counterpart to the US NIH) has this paragraph in its 1998 "Guidelines for Good Clinical Practice in Clinical Trials": "The [Trial Steering Committee] should ensure that appropriate efforts are made to ensure that the results of the trial are adequately disseminated and due consideration is given to the implementation of the results into clinical practice."[58] The number and types of qualification in this guideline are truly remarkable. First, the burden falls to the steering committee of each clinical trial. It is not clear what authority such committees have in making policy once the trial they are steering is concluded. Secondly, the guideline does not specify or even suggest who should be making the efforts to ensure what is supposed to be ensured (first the steering committee should "ensure"; but who is to make the "appropriate efforts" to ensure that the results are disseminated?). Thirdly, what must be ensured? Dissemination of the results of the trial is a rather straightforward matter and should, of course, be done. But the only thing this second agent (whoever it may be) should ensure is that "due consideration is given to the implementation of the results into clinical practice." Once again, there is a recommendation to "consider" something. As a guideline for effective action, this MRC paragraph could hardly be more vague or indirect.

A South African Department of Health committee issued a document in 2000 that contained the following provision: "Where a patient has a therapeutic response to a study drug, that patient should be offered ongoing treatment. In designing studies, consideration should be given to the costs of long term provision of study drugs and of clinical monitoring, including the costs of medical staff."[59] It is apparent that numerous guidelines include the form of words used here: "consideration should be given . . ." Although the spirit of this type of urging is understandable, as a guideline it is vague and ineffectual. Its vagueness lies in failure to specify *who* should be taking such considerations into account and *what criteria* they should use in accepting or rejecting the item under consideration. As I have already suggested, it opens the door to whoever does the considering to say "We considered and rejected it."

In 2002 the Medical Research Council of South Africa issued updates of its 1993 ethical guidelines for research involving human subjects. A statement by Professor Peter Cleaton-Jones, head of the South Africa MRC's Research Ethics Committee, refers to benefits to the community in which research is conducted, in addition to the research subjects themselves: "The revised guidelines have tried to ensure that the concept of the 'best interest of the research participant' is clear and to emphasise that developing communities must not be exploited. Participating communities must also benefit from the research done in or with them."[60]

Going back as far as 1996, a resolution by the National Health Council of Brazil contained strong presumptions in favor of post-trial benefits:

Research involving human subjects must whenever possible guarantee that:
- research in communities is translated into benefits whose effects continue to be felt after the research is concluded;
- . . . the individuals and communities where the research was undertaken [receive] a return on the benefits obtained in the research;
- to ensure the research subjects the benefits resulting from the research project, in terms of social return, access to procedures, products, or research agents.[61]

The Indian Council of Medical Research included a statement in its ethical guidelines issued in 2000 that requires a restricted set of post-trial benefits to research participants: "After the clinical trial is over, if need be, it should be made mandatory that the sponsoring agency should provide the drug to the patient till it is marketed in the country."[62] The phrase "if need be" presumably refers to the situation in which the patient who was a subject in the research still needs the study medication after the research is over. However, the length of time during which the drug is provided free of charge may be insufficient for people of little means who have chronic conditions for which the drug has proven to be helpful.

The Indian guidelines do not explicitly mandate post-trial benefits to the community or country, yet the guidelines include a section that specifically addresses international collaboration and assistance from international sponsors of health research. One item in this section addresses the concerns of distributive justice in very general terms: "The research protocol should outline the benefits that persons/communities/countries participating in such research should experience as a result of their participation . . . The burden and the benefit should be equally borne by the collaborating countries."[63]

Uganda's ethical guidelines for research, issued in 1997, contain the following paragraph:

The investigator must provide assurances that, if the investigational product is found to be beneficial, the investigator will make every effort to ensure its provision, without charge, to participants in the trial following the conclusion of the trial. In addition, the investigator shall make a reasonable effort to secure the product's availability to the local community in which the research occurred.[64]

This statement makes it clear that the product is to be made available free of charge, and sets up a presumption of availability to the local community – but not the country as a whole. It also places a burden on the investigator both to provide the assurances and to make efforts to ensure the provision of the product.

Conclusions

The different interpretations of the requirements of distributive justice discussed in this chapter range from minimalist conceptions of justice to robust conceptions. These differences raise the question posed in chapter 1 of whether ethical guidelines should be pragmatic or "aspirational." In the matter of providing post-trial benefits to developing countries, as required by CIOMS Guideline 10, Solomon Benatar comes down squarely in rejecting the pragmatic approach in favor of one that stresses the ideals of justice. Benatar criticizes the more pragmatic position, faulting one advocate on the following grounds:

- a particular perspective on the legitimacy of reaching agreements about post-trial drug availability, and on whose interests should predominate, which may not be shared by many in deprived countries;
- an emphasis on so-called realistic considerations, rather than on ethical ideals;
- complacency with the reality of what 'is' and acceptance that this determines what we 'ought' to do;
- a pandering to the pervasive market forces and business ethics, which are eclipsing professional ethics;
- viewing daunting obstacles and logistic difficulties as barriers to expressing ideals;
- being more concerned about intellectual property rights than about distributive justice.[65]

A dramatic shift has already begun to be evident, away from viewing as hopelessly aspirational the provision of needed drugs and public health interventions to resource-poor countries, toward seeing such efforts as a moral obligation of wealthy nations. In chapter 6 we explore several of these efforts, returning to the objection that requiring pre-trial agreements to make drugs available when research is concluded is doomed to failure.

A growing consensus is emerging that something is owed to a developing country after the completion of research conducted by an industrialized country or pharmaceutical company. But there is much less agreement on whether what is owed to the country is a successful product that results from the research. We return to these issues in the next chapter, which explores the charge that CIOMS Guideline 10 is "overly paternalistic," and again in chapter 8, which examines the related view that other benefits besides a specific product may fulfill the prohibition against exploitation of the population in resource-poor countries.

NOTES

This chapter includes portions of my previously published papers: "International Ethics and Equity," *Notizie di Politeia*, 18:67 (2002), 9–14; "After Helsinki," *Kennedy Institute of Ethics Journal*, 11:1 (2001), 17–36; "Bioethics and Public Policy in the Next Millennium," *Bioethics*, 15 (2001), 373–381; "Four Forward-looking Guidance Points," *Developing World Bioethics*, 1 (2001), 121–134. Permission granted by Blackwell Publishing to reprint excerpts from the latter two articles.

1. This view was expressed by a few participants at the Rockefeller Foundation's Study and Conference Center in Bellagio, Italy, when I made an informal presentation there during my residency in May 2002.
2. Madison Powers, "Justice Theories in a Research Context," in (eds.) Jeffrey P. Kahn, Anna C. Mastroianni, and Jeremy Sugarman, *Beyond Consent* (New York: Oxford University Press, 1998), 151.
3. National Commission for the Protection of Human Subjects of Biomedical and Behavioral Research, *The Belmont Report: Ethical Principles and Guidelines for the Protection of Human Subjects of Research* (April 18, 1979), 5.
4. Personal communication. The manuscript was submitted to a journal by a colleague, who sought my response to the reviewer's comments. I do not know the identity of the reviewer.
5. Anna C. Mastroianni, Ruth Faden, and Daniel Federman (eds.), *Women and Health Research: Ethical and Legal Issues of Including Women in Clinical Studies*, vol. I (Washington, DC: National Academy Press, 1994), 78.
6. Mastroianni et al., *Women and Health Research*, 76.
7. Ibid.
8. Global Forum for Health Research, available at http://www.globalforum health.org/pages/page1_0002_1.htm?center/page=page1_0002_1.htm.
9. These two conditions are stipulated in Mastroianni et al., *Women and Health Research*, 78.
10. Nicholas A. Christakis, "The Ethical Design of an AIDS Vaccine Trial in Africa," *Hastings Center Report*, 18:3 (1988), 31–37.

11. Michele Barry, "Ethical Considerations of Human Investigation in Developing Countries: The AIDS Dilemma," NEJM, 319 (1988), 1083–1086 at 1085.
12. Joint United Nations Programme on HIV/AIDS (UNAIDS) and World Health Organization (WHO), *AIDS Epidemic Update* (UNAIDS/WHO, December 2002), 16.
13. Ibid., 7.
14. Ibid., 12.
15. http://www.tballiance.org/, accessed August 28, 2002.
16. Roll Back Malaria, http://mosquito.who.int, primary contributions and scientific review by Aafje Rietveld.
17. Ibid.
18. William H. Helfand, Jan Lazarus, and Paul Theerman, "Safe Motherhood Means: Social Equity for Women," *American Journal of Public Health*, 90:9 (2000), 1382.
19. WHO Fact Sheet No. 249, *Women and Sexually Transmitted Infections* (June 2000).
20. WHO Fact Sheet No. 252, *Women, Ageing, and Health* (June 2000).
21. Sarah Marchand, Daniel Wikler, and Bruce Landesman, "Class, Health, and Justice," *The Milbank Quarterly*, 76 (1998), 449–467.
22. Solomon R. Benatar, "Global Disparities in Health and Human Rights: A Critical Commentary," *American Journal of Public Health*, 88:2 (1998), 295–300.
23. Ibid.
24. Norman Daniels, *Just Health Care* (New York: Cambridge University Press, 1985).
25. John Rawls, *A Theory of Justice* (Cambridge, MA: Belknap Press, 1971).
26. Daniels, *Just Health Care*.
27. Norman Daniels, Bruce P. Kennedy, and Ichiro Kawachi, "Why Justice is Good for Our Health: The Social Determinants of Health Inequalities," *Daedalus*, 128 (1998), 215–251.
28. Dan W. Brock, "Broadening the Bioethics Agenda," *Kennedy Institute of Ethics Journal*, 10:1 (2000), 21–38.
29. Ibid., 35.
30. Powers, "Justice Theories."
31. Ibid., 152.
32. D. R. Cooley, "Distributive Justice and Clinical Trials in the Third World," *Theoretical Medicine*, 22 (2001), 151–167 at 157.
33. Ibid., 157–158.
34. Ibid., 158.
35. Solomon R. Benatar, "Distributive Justice and Clinical Trials in the Third World," *Theoretical Medicine*, 22 (2001), 169–176 at 169.
36. Cooley, "Distributive Justice," 158.
37. Joint United Nations Programme on HIV/AIDS (UNAIDS), *Ethical Considerations in HIV Preventive Vaccine Research* (2000), 13.
38. Marchand et al., "Class, Health and Justice," 456.
39. Ibid.

40. Ibid., 461.

41. National Bioethics Advisory Commission (NBAC), *Ethical and Policy Issues in International Research: Clinical Trials in Developing Countries* (Bethesda, MD, 2001), 59.

42. Mastroianni et al., *Women and Health Research*, 76.

43. An acknowledgment is in order. I was one of a small group of individuals who worked on the UNAIDS Guidance Document from the outset. My views in this chapter can, therefore, hardly be considered "objective," as I contributed to the process of developing the Guidance Document and ended up agreeing with virtually all of the Guidance Points. Nevertheless, my lack of objectivity does not distinguish the arguments in this chapter from those of any authors who seek to defend substantive positions in ethics that they embrace.

44. NBAC, *Ethical and Policy Issues*, 74.

45. Nuffield Council on Bioethics, *The Ethics of Research Related to Healthcare in Developing Countries* (London: Nuffield Council on Bioethics, 2002), 123.

46. Ibid., 124.

47. Ibid., 125.

48. Ibid., 121.

49. NBAC, *Ethical and Policy Issues*, 74.

50. Nuffield, *Ethics of Research*, 125.

51. NBAC, *Ethical and Policy Issues*, chapter 4; Alice K. Page, "Prior Agreements in International Clinical Trials: Ensuring the Benefits of Research to Developing Countries," *Yale Journal of Health Policy, Law, and Ethics*, 3:1 (2002), 35–64.

52. CIOMS, *International Ethical Guidelines for Biomedical Research Involving Human Subjects* (Geneva: CIOMS, 2002), 51.

53. CIOMS, *International Ethical Guidelines for Biomedical Research Involving Human Subjects* (Geneva: CIOMS, 1993), 25.

54. Ibid., 45.

55. Comments submitted by Dr. Bertram H. Spilker representing PhRMA.

56. Pharmaceutical Research and Manufacturers of America, "PhRMA Discussion Paper on the Declaration of Helsinki as Revised in October 2000" (June 2001), 2; http://www.phrma.org/, accessed May 22, 2002.

57. For additional examples, see Nuffield, *Ethics of Research*, Appendix 1, Table 5, 156–157, and NBAC, *Ethical and Policy Issues*, vol. II, D48–D57.

58. Nuffield, *Ethics of Research*, Appendix 1, Table 5, 157.

59. Clinical Trials Working Group of the South African Department of Health, "Guidelines for Good Practice in the Conduct of Clinical Trials in Human Participants in South Africa" (2000), Paragraph 9.7.3.

60. http://www.mrc.ac.za/pressreleases/2002/7pres2002.htm, accessed May 14, 2002.

61. National Health Council of Brazil, "Resolution No. 196/96 on Research Involving Human Subjects (1996), Paragraph III.3m"; cited in Nuffield, *Ethics of Research*, Appendix I, Table 5, 156.

62. India Council of Medical Research (ICMR) New Delhi, "Ethical Guidelines for Biomedical Research on Human Subjects" (2000), 23. Available at http://icmr.nic.in/ethical.pdf.

63. Ibid.
64. National Consensus Conference on Bioethics and Health Research in Uganda, "Guidelines for the Conduct of Health Research Involving Human Subjects in Uganda," (1997). V. D.(4).
65. Solomon R. Benatar, "Justice and International Research: A Response to Reidar K. Lie," in (eds.) Robert J. Levine and Samuel Gorovitz, with James Gallagher, *Biomedical Research Ethics: Updating International Guidelines: A Consultation* (Geneva: CIOMS, 2000), 41–50 at 42.

It may be easier to recognize exploitation when we see it than it is to define the concept. A case in point is a clinical trial sponsored by Pfizer in 1996 in Nigeria during an epidemic of meningitis in children. The company was testing trovafloxacin (under the trade name, Trovan), a drug that had not yet been approved by the FDA for use in the United States. Critics charged that it was unethical to use the circumstances of an epidemic to test a new drug. A meningitis specialist from the US who co-authored industry guidelines for conducting meningitis experiments expressed surprise that Pfizer embarked on this experiment since the guidelines did not envision tests conducted under such conditions – "testing an antibiotic amid a terrible epidemic in a squalid, short-staffed medical camp lacking basic diagnostic equipment."[1] The meningitis specialist was reported as saying: "I just wouldn't do a study that way myself. I know they wanted to get the data. They wanted to go fast. They wanted to move ahead. I'm not sure they made a smart decision."[2]

Unlike some other examples of international research that have been criticized as unethical, the Nigerian meningitis experiments actually resulted in significant harm to participants. Eleven children who received the experimental drug died, and 200 others became deaf, blind, or lame. A frequent allegation in studies conducted in countries that have few or no mechanisms for proper review of research proposals, or in which the population is illiterate or otherwise vulnerable, is the partial or complete absence of informed consent to participate in research. Often such cases have not involved physical harm to the subjects, although participants were nevertheless wronged by being enrolled without their properly informed, voluntary consent.

When news of the Nigerian experiment and its serious consequences was made public, the company defended the study. Pfizer claimed that the aim was to study the safety and effectiveness of the product, and at the same time, to pioneer "a breakthrough treatment for the Third World." Pfizer cited the number of children who showed improvement and reported a rate of death of about 6 percent, a rate comparable to patients with the same condition who are treated at US hospitals.[3] Despite these claims, investigation revealed that most of the Nigerian children were given Trovan orally – by mouth – whereas children treated for meningitis in the US are normally given medicine intravenously, a faster-acting route of administration. Pfizer acknowledged that the oral form of its product had never been tested before in children.

The Nigerian experiment had all the earmarks of exploitation, as that concept is typically employed. There was an epidemic raging in a very poor part of a developing country. Children were desperately ill and no other treatment was readily available for them. The trial was conducted by a rich and powerful pharmaceutical company. The trial was in apparent violation of established industry guidelines for studies of meningitis, not only because it was carried out during an epidemic, but also because the guidelines say that a follow-up spinal tap should be done a day or so after the drug is administered to see if it is working. Those follow-up tests were optional in the study in Nigeria. In addition, the children were supposed to have blood tests on two separate occasions, but the requirement for the second blood test was abandoned because of a shortage of staff, according to the company's report.[4]

These features of the experiment are only part of the story. In addition, questions were raised about whether the research subjects – the children – or their parents were fully aware that they were part of a clinical trial. One laboratory technician was reported as saying that participants did not know they were involved in research, they knew only that they were sick. The company claimed that local nurses had explained the research to the families, a procedure that could have been valid if it met the well-established requirements of informed consent. It is impossible to know what the nurses told the families, whether they made it clear that the children were participants in research rather than patients receiving a "new treatment" for the terrible disease they were suffering. In any case, the company produced no signed consent forms to document the consent process. An undisputed criterion for determining that research is, in fact, exploitative is failure to provide the information necessary for properly obtained consent: telling potential subjects that they are being invited to participate in research, lack of an adequate explanation of the risks, potential benefits, procedures to be performed and alternative treatments, and failure to ensure that the potential subjects understand what they have been told and agree voluntarily to participate. To the extent that these elements were lacking in the Nigerian study, it counts as a case of exploitation.

Reports of this clinical trial included several procedural flaws, as well as these substantive ethical concerns. Although flaws in procedural aspects – such as failure to keep proper records and absence of prior review of the research plans by an independent ethics review committee – may not rise to the level of exploitation, they are nevertheless unethical features of research involving human subjects. One item that emerged from the inquiry into the Nigerian study was the disappearance of the medical records of more than 300 children from the hospital where the trial took place.[5] The maintenance of proper records of each research subject is an important procedural requirement both for documenting any benefits the study may show and for recording serious adverse effects subjects may experience from the experimental drug.

It also emerged that there were shortcomings in the process of ethical review by a properly constituted, independent committee – if such review took place at all. Once an investigation into the study began, the Nigerian physician who was in charge of local aspects of the study admitted that his office had created a backdated document containing ethical approval of the study by an ethics review board. The medical director of the hospital confirmed that the hospital did not have an ethics review committee at the time the research was initiated. When the sponsoring company, Pfizer, requested evidence that the study had been approved by a properly constituted ethics committee – a procedure required by the FDA in its review of the data and conduct of clinical trials – that was apparently when a false document was created and backdated to include a date six days before the experiment began. An FDA official was reported as saying that knowing submission of false documents to a US government agency is a violation of federal law.[6]

When reports of a study like the Nigerian experiment are publicized, they obviously require careful investigation of the allegations made against the company and the local physicians in charge of the trial. It would be unfair to render a final judgment in the absence of full documentation. We can, nevertheless, ask the hypothetical question whether the Nigerian study would count as a case of exploitation if the charges turned out to be true. The answer requires an examination of what we mean by "exploitation" in the research context.

Definitional debates

I offer a tentative, general definition of "exploitation" before applying it to the specific context of research involving human beings: "Exploitation occurs when wealthy or powerful individuals or agencies take advantage of the poverty, powerlessness, or dependency of others by using the latter to serve their own ends (those of the wealthy or powerful) without adequate compensating benefits for the less powerful or disadvantaged individuals or groups."[7] The central feature of this definition is that exploitation involves harm or wrong to persons or groups. It also contains an element of moral condemnation, and seeks to distinguish exploitation from other wrongful actions, since only a subset of wrongful actions can properly be considered acts of exploitation. Some situations may be unjust without being exploitative, and some unethical behavior may be a function of harm inflicted on people without their having been exploited.

There are also cases in which researchers can be said to exploit a very unfortunate situation without thereby exploiting the individuals they have chosen to study. An example might be an epidemiological study of the aftermath of a natural disaster such as an earthquake, tornado, or volcanic eruption. Finally, it may be the case that individuals or groups can *be* exploited without *feeling* exploited, or without believing they are exploited. This last situation is controversial, but a telling example might be individuals who are enslaved but treated humanely by their masters. These individuals may not feel exploited, especially if their circumstances are better than they would be if they were not slaves. Nevertheless, since slavery is an intrinsically degrading condition for human beings as it involves an absolute denial of individual liberty, it is reasonable to assume that people in that condition are, in fact, exploited even if they do not consider themselves so.

Some analyses of the concept maintain that people can be exploited even when they are not harmed or wronged. One author distinguishes between fair and unfair exploitation, thereby rejecting the view that exploitation includes only unfair practices.[8] On this analysis, exploitation is unfair "if the other person does not give truly voluntary consent; the other person is harmed; the exploiter is profiting off the desperation of other persons; or the exploiter's gain is disproportionate when compared with the exploited person's gain."[9]

The most extensive analysis and discussion of the concept of exploitation has occurred in the Marxist tradition of political and moral philosophy.[10] However, since that tradition ties exploitation to the labor theory of value, it is both too narrow and fraught with too many questionable ideological presuppositions to be applied to the context of research. In contrast, a "lowest common denominator definition" that has been proposed is arguably too broad: "A exploits B when A takes unfair advantage of B."[11] This definition embraces acts of injustice and cheating that could count as exploitation only by making the concept overly broad. For example, if a worker intentionally misstates the time she has worked on a job, taking advantage of an honor system in order to receive more compensation, she is taking unfair advantage of her employer's use of the honor system. However, it would be hard to argue that she is exploiting her employer. She is simply cheating him. A feature of my proposed definition is that the exploited individual has less wealth or power than the exploiter, or is dependent in some way on the exploiter. This is a feature that distinguishes acts of exploitation from simple cheating and other unfair acts.

Or, suppose two students are vying for top honors that can be awarded to only one of them. Student A knows that B is highly sensitive about being overweight and gets rattled whenever anyone refers to his obesity. Just before they sit down to take the test that will determine who gets the honors, A says to B: "How're you doing, fatso?" B gets predictably upset and has trouble concentrating on the test. A has taken unfair advantage of B, but here again, A has not exploited B. The two students are equally matched in the contest, A has no advantage of power or wealth over B, and B is not dependent in any way on A.

Several other definitions have been proposed,[12] not specifically in the context of research but intended to apply generally to a range of possible situations.

1 "To exploit a person involves the *harmful, merely instrumental utilization* of him or his capacities, for one's own advantage or for the sake of one's own ends."[13]

This differs from my proposed definition on two points. First, it includes harm as a necessary condition of exploitation; second, it does not require any inequality in wealth, power, or dependency between the exploiter and the individual or group being exploited.

2 "Exploitation necessarily involves benefits or gains of some kind to someone . . . Exploitation resembles a zero-sum game, viz. what the exploiter gains, the exploitee loses; or, minimally, for the exploiter to gain, the exploitee must lose."[14]

According to my definition, the exploitee need not lose, unless being wronged necessarily involves some type of loss, for example, loss of dignity. In addition, on my account, the exploiter might not actually gain. A drug company may take advantage of the illness and poverty of people in a poor country (like Pfizer's trial in Nigeria), and the company may not ultimately gain because there is no resulting successful product. The research subjects have nevertheless been exploited.

3 "Exploitation of persons consists in . . . wrongful behavior [that violates] the moral norm of *protecting the vulnerable*."[15]

This comes close to my definition, as it specifies that exploitative conduct is wrongful; it also includes the idea that exploitees are vulnerable. However, it does not specify the conditions of vulnerability.

4 "There are four conditions, all of which must be present if dependencies are to be exploitable. First, the relationship must be *asymmetrical* . . .

Second, . . . the subordinate party must *need* the resource that the superordinate supplies . . . Third, . . . the subordinate party must depend upon some *particular* superordinate for the supply of needed resources . . . Fourth, the superordinate . . . enjoys discretionary control over the resources that the subordinate needs from him."[16]

The first, second, and fourth conditions of this account are consistent with my proposed definition. However, the third condition need not be present in the account I propose. This is because, in the context of multinational research, individuals or communities in a resource-poor country may never actually get the supply of needed resources – that is, medications they need for their conditions (a study may be placebo-controlled and the experimental drug may not turn out to be effective). Furthermore, research subjects are not dependent on some particular supplier of needed resources. Any international pharmaceutical company will do.

5 "Common to all exploitation of one person (B) by another (A) . . . is that A makes a profit or gain by turning some characteristic of B to his own advantage . . . [E]xploitation . . . can occur in morally unsavory forms without harming the exploitee's interests and . . . despite the exploitee's fully voluntary consent to the exploitative behavior."[17]

This account seems to fit quite well with the situation of some multinational research, since it allows for the exploitee's fully voluntary consent to the exploitative behavior. However, this account does not require that the relationship be asymmetrical, between a subordinate and superordinate, which is a feature of my definition and some of the other accounts mentioned here.

6 "Persons are exploited if (1) others secure a benefit by (2) using them as a tool or resource so as (3) to cause them serious harm."[18]

This definition requires not only that there be harm to those who are exploited, but also that the harm be serious. This account differs from my own definition and that of many others on this list.

7 "A group is exploited if it has some conditionally feasible alternative under which its members would be better off."[19]

This account seems much too broad to constitute a definition of "exploitation," since it embraces many circumstances it would be odd to consider exploitative. For example, all of the uninsured and underinsured people in the United States would be better off if the government provided universal health insurance for its citizens – a "conditionally feasible alternative" to their remaining uninsured. The situation is ethically shameful, but not exploitative. Nevertheless, this is a useful feature to contemplate in the context of multinational research in which a control group is given placebo rather than an established, effective treatment for their condition. Although the subjects who receive placebo are not being made worse off than they would be if they were not enrolled in the research (they have no access to medications), there is a conditionally feasible alternative under which they could be made better off in the research. The research could be conducted with a control arm in which subjects receive an established, effective treatment.

8 "An exploitative exchange is . . . an exchange in which the exploited party gets less than the exploiting party, who does better at the exploited party's expense . . . The exchange must result from social relations of unequal power . . . exploitation can be entered into voluntarily; and can even, in some sense, be advantageous to the exploited party."[20]

This definition can apply to the research context, since sponsors are more powerful than research subjects; the subjects may provide voluntary, informed consent; and some or all subjects in a particular experiment may be benefited, so the situation is advantageous to them. According to my proposed definition, this account would not constitute exploitation because it allows for compensating benefit to the individual or group that is exploited. Perhaps there may be *some* benefit, but not *adequate* compensating benefit.

One novel account distinguishes between *harmful* exploitation and *mutually advantageous* exploitation, where the latter means that the exploitee gains from the transaction as well as the exploiter.[21] This may very well be the case in a substantial amount of research conducted on populations in research-poor countries, where research subjects may actually gain something from being in the research that they would not otherwise gain if not enrolled in the research (for example, better overall health care, diagnosis of an asymptomatic condition for which they can receive treatment, treatment of concurrent illnesses during the research). How, then, can they still be exploited by being enrolled as research subjects? Perhaps they are not. This situation is problematic, and a thorough analysis depends on specific features of the case. Another distinction is that between *consensual* and *nonconsensual exploitation*. The nonconsensual cases are obvious in the context of research, since the absence of properly informed, voluntary consent is at least a *prima facie* instance of exploitation. The consensual cases appear harder to classify as exploitation but they could still qualify, on the definition I propose.

What is exploitation in multinational research?

That it is unethical to exploit vulnerable populations or individual participants in the conduct of research is almost universally accepted. Disagreements emerge, however, with respect to specific examples cited as instances of exploitation. Not everything that is unethical in the design or conduct of multinational research can properly be said to constitute exploitation. One prominent view maintains that different conditions or circumstances in different countries call for different research designs, and those different designs can be ethically justified when they involve providing inferior treatments (or no treatment at all) to research subjects in resource-poor countries, compared to what is provided to subjects in industrialized countries. Others argue that to adopt the standard of what is locally available in the developing country is to exploit nations and people who are economically disadvantaged. According to one physician:

Exploitation by industrialized countries of the human and natural resources of the developing world has a long and tragic history. It has never been difficult for economically wealthy countries to justify their acts by citing, for example, the supposed genetic or moral inferiority of those exploited. Substituting economic inferiority in these old arguments makes the enterprise no less offensive.[22]

Is it exploitative to conduct research in a developing country when it is known in advance that the population will not receive any resulting benefits, which are intended primarily for industrialized countries? The following example is instructive. In the early 1990s, a large-scale trial of hepatitis A vaccine, which involved children aged one to sixteen, was conducted in Northern Thailand. The study found the vaccine to be safe and effective in protecting against hepatitis A for at least a year. Although the Thai Ministry of Public Health welcomed the study because access to such a vaccine was a future public health need, the vaccine was never made widely available to the Thai population. This is because it was determined not to be cost-effective to mount a routine vaccination program for children in Thailand – a calculation that could easily have been made in advance of the trial. In fact, the main reason for doing the trial was to ensure the availability of the vaccine in industrialized countries for people who travel to developing countries. The manufacturer, SmithKline Beecham, licensed the hepatitis A vaccine, and this has been its primary use.[23]

When all this came to light in Thailand, considerable controversy ensued. One author hypothesized two possible explanations for the controversy. One is that people questioned the balance of risks and benefits, since the Thai children who were the subjects bore whatever risks the trial involved but all the benefits accrued to travelers who reside in industrialized countries. The other explanation is a lack of public disclosure and sufficient local discussion that could have justified the decision to conduct the trial in Thailand.[24] The first possible explanation finds the trial unacceptable on grounds of distributive justice, whereas the second criticizes the decision to conduct the trial on procedural grounds – absence of sufficient local input and involvement.

Another instructive example is a breast cancer trial proposed by a US academic researcher to take place in Vietnam. The women were to be randomized into two groups. One group was to undergo mastectomy alone, and the other group was to receive mastectomy and adjuvant treatment. At the time the trial was to take place, mastectomy alone was not standard treatment in the United States, nor was the adjuvant therapy proposed for the trial (mastectomy plus immediate surgical oophorectomy and the drug, tamoxifen, for five years). The researchers contended that they aimed to study treatments that would be relevant to Vietnamese women. However, several ethical problems were apparent. The adjuvant therapy proposed for the Vietnamese women was more risky than what is currently provided as standard treatment in the US. There was little reason to believe that even if successful, the experimental treatment could be widely provided to women with breast cancer in Vietnam. Finally, there is every reason to think that if the treatment proved successful, it would be viewed as relevant to women in the US and other industrialized countries.[25]

The researchers defended the ethics of this study when they ran into difficulties with their IRB. The committee initially stated: "It is exploitative of the women in Vietnam not to provide some systemic adjuvant therapy."[26] The researchers then modified the study by offering to the women in the mastectomy-only group the treatment provided to the women in the other arm of the trial, plus close follow-up, if their cancer recurred.

What guidelines and commentators say

The Declaration of Helsinki does not use the term "exploitation" anywhere in the document. Arguably, the entire declaration can be seen as an attempt to protect human subjects from exploitation, but the same can be said of the other guidelines and reports. These others do make explicit reference to "exploitation." A statement in Helsinki that best expresses the obligation to avoid exploitation is in paragraph 8: "Some research populations are vulnerable and need special protection. The particular needs of the economically and medically disadvantaged must be recognized." One commentator on the draft guidelines posted on the CIOMS website refers to this paragraph in remarking that "The DOH makes clear that the poor are vulnerable and thus must be protected from exploitation."[27]

CIOMS Guideline 10

The most pertinent of the CIOMS guidelines is Guideline 10: Research in populations and communities with limited resources. The commentary under this guideline says:

> Even when a product to be tested in a particular country is much cheaper than the standard treatment in some other countries, the government or individuals in that country may still be unable to afford it. If the knowledge gained from the research in such a country is used primarily for the benefit of populations that can afford the tested product, the research may rightly be characterized as exploitative and, therefore, unethical.

In the preceding chapter, we looked at some comments submitted to CIOMS on Guideline 10. The following additional comments explicitly mention exploitation in endorsing or criticizing this guideline.

Comments that express strong approval of the CIOMS commentary are as follows:

> [This guideline] does a good job in seeing that populations with limited resources are not exploited and receive proper benefits from the research participation.

> Our compliments. Strongly support last sentence in commentary . . . on exploitation.[28]

> The BMA strongly supports the aim of this guideline to prevent exploitation of poor communities for research purposes when the research is unlikely to benefit them.[29]

> It would be exploitative and therefore unethical to use poor communities for research purposes if the research were not responsive to their health needs or otherwise unlikely to benefit them.[30]

One comment expressed support, in principle, of the CIOMS commentary but also pointed out an interesting example of a possible exception to what the guideline says about exploitation:

> The worry, as the commentary on [this] guideline . . . nicely explains, is that if research is not responsive in this way it might be exploitative. However, such research is not necessarily exploitative. To take just one example, there are several cohorts of individuals around the world who are infected with the HIV virus, but have never become symptomatic (so-called long-term non-progressors). For obvious reasons, these individuals are of great research interest. Imagine that such a cohort lived in a poor country where treatment for HIV was unavailable. Further imagine that the cohort members contacted researchers in the US and said: we know that research on us won't help us (given where we live and the low chance of getting treatment for AIDS in our country). Nonetheless, we want to help: if studying us can make a difference in the lives of others who are living with this terrible disease, we want to volunteer. Filled out in the right way, it seems that such a study would not involve exploitation, and CIOMS should not preclude

what could be very important and ethical research. Other examples could be developed that make the same point.[31]

Although this example correctly notes that the research, as described, is not responsive to the health needs of that particular population, the research is an observational study, not a clinical trial from which a successful product might result. This suggests that the type of research to which CIOMS Guideline 10 properly applies is that of clinical trials in which the aim is to test diagnostic, preventive, or therapeutic products, rather than to observe people or do tests that involve minimal risk interventions on healthy individuals.

But it does not automatically follow that purely observational research cannot constitute exploitation. Observational studies can be prime examples of research that is exploitative. After all, the infamous Tuskegee syphilis study was an "observational" study, designed to observe the natural progression of untreated syphilis. Some epidemiologists from developing countries have defended observational studies carried out to ascertain the incidence or prevalence of diseases for which treatments exist in industrialized countries but not for most people in resource-poor countries. Unlike clinical trials, where a product is being tested and the sponsor could be in a position to provide the product, say, at lower cost, epidemiologists do not normally have access to products in the conduct of their research. Is it, therefore, exploitative to do observational studies in populations that have no access to treatments that would be provided for people with the same condition in an industrialized country?

This is a gray area. In some cases, it would be correct to say that researchers are exploiting an unfortunate situation but not exploiting the population being studied. An example might be research on the aftermath of a natural disaster or exposure to radiation, where no remedies can actually be provided to ameliorate disease or suffering. In contrast, a purely observational study, with no intervention, that seeks to determine the rate of HIV transmission in discordant couples (one is HIV-infected, the other is not) could be an instance of exploitation. If the identities of the couples are known, it would be unethical not to provide counseling, not to provide condoms, and not to offer to assist in informing the uninfected partner that he or she is at risk. Whether the researcher has an obligation to disclose that information to the uninfected partner over the objection of the HIV-infected partner remains a matter of considerable controversy. Also controversial is whether researchers from the US who conduct such observational studies have an additional obligation to procure medical treatment for the infected partner. In a similar study in the US, the researcher would refer the infected individual for treatment, and since antiretroviral therapy is readily available, it could be provided. In developing countries where such treatments are not available to the majority of the population, a referral would be meaningless. Those controversies aside, to fail to provide counseling, condoms, and other preventive interventions would surely constitute exploitation of the subjects themselves, and not just their situation.

One comment on CIOMS Guideline 10 expressed support for the general aim of avoiding exploitation in research. Ironically, however, an example of allegedly non-exploitative research mentioned in the comment is open to precisely the opposite charge.

The purpose of this guideline seems to be to prevent exploitation of poor communities for research purposes when the research is unlikely to benefit them. This aim should be supported but at the same time research in developing countries should not be inhibited but encouraged as a means of developing greater international collaboration. The test is whether in the country or territory concerned research subjects would be deprived of an effective intervention solely on account of the proposed research. If so it would be unethical but not otherwise. For example, a randomised trial of an inexpensive and simple method of cervical screening (eg a blood test) could be compared with no screening in parts of India where there was no screening at all.[32]

In this illustration, research subjects are not deprived of a successful diagnostic method to which they would otherwise have access for detecting cervical cancer. This is what prompted the judgment that it would not be unethical to provide no cervical screening to the control group. Nevertheless, there is a striking similarity to the case of the placebo-controlled, short-course AZT to prevent maternal-to-child HIV transmission. None of the women in this study in India would receive the best current method of screening for cervical cancer, some would receive the experimental screening method, and others would not be screened at all. An ethically superior research design would compare the proposed, inexpensive method with the best current method – the pap smear – to determine whether the proposed new method is as good as, or almost as good as, the best diagnostic method. Moreover, from a methodological point of view, if the aim is to find a cheaper method of screening for cervical cancer than the pap smear, it would be necessary to compare the cost of the two methods in the rural area where the new method would be introduced. Finally, in order to fulfill the requirement in the CIOMS guideline, all of the research subjects should be screened with the proven method following completion of the trial. In sum, then, this example of a randomized trial in rural India, seeking a simple and inexpensive method of screening for cervical cancer, is both methodologically unsound and ethically flawed.

Is this randomized trial of a blood test to screen for cervical cancer an unequivocal case of exploitation of poor women in India who do not have access to pap smears, a widely used screening method? Some might argue that the trial does not exploit the women, but it nonetheless exploits a situation in which poor medical practice exists. Even if the women themselves are not exploited, clinical research should not take advantage of poor medical practices but should serve as a means to stimulate better practices.

Two comments submitted on this guideline essentially reject the CIOMS statement regarding what counts as exploitation. First:

> Stating this rule, if anyone observes it, will simply *terminate* the now growing flow of product testing to developing countries which, at present, is generally not accompanied by plans for early marketing in those countries (and would constitute dubious use of their resources if it did). If you think it is "exploitative" to do depression or panic trials in Hungary, Peru, etc., then press on with this. But you'd better mean it, because I believe regulators might be very uncomfortable *accepting* for review such "unethical trials." I doubt very much the people and leaders of Hungary, Peru, India etc., will thank you . . . ['E]xploitative' is a word better omitted from this document. It's just a cuss-word, with no clear meaning or useful purpose.[33]

And second:

> The Guideline appears to be grounded in an assumption that all research carried out in resource-poor settings under the support of external sponsors is equally exploitative. A "one size fits all" approach of requiring advance agreements might prevent a few cases of overt exploitation of a resource-poor country's people, but it is unrealistic, paternalistic, and runs an exceptionally high risk of inhibiting important research in research-poor countries. The emphasis should, instead, be placed on partnership and the criteria for an equitable and just process by which decisions about post-trial availability will be made.[34]

Here again, as in the preceding chapter where comments on this CIOMS guideline were quoted, the strongest objections were from major US federal agencies: the NIH and the FDA. The NIH comment is clearly mistaken in contending that the CIOMS guideline rests on an assumption that all research carried out in resource-poor settings under the support of external sponsors is exploitative. Guideline 10 describes specific circumstances under which such research can properly be characterized as exploitative and does not tar all externally sponsored research in poor countries with the same brush.

As for Dr. Temple's view, it is puzzling why he thinks that the people of Hungary, Peru, and India would be unhappy if the US or industry ceases to sponsor or conduct depression or panic trials there. It is clear why the leaders of such countries might be unhappy. The ancillary benefits that flow to such countries when industry or rich countries conduct research can be considerable. Scientists are trained, laboratories are built or upgraded, state-of-the art equipment is brought in, and new computers are provided. This is all to the good – especially the aspects that help to build the capacity of developing countries to conduct research. But the interest that leaders and scientists in such countries have, in this regard, is not identical to the interests of the population in general. It is, of course, likely that the research subjects themselves in Hungary, Peru, and India would be pleased to have the opportunity to participate in research that may benefit them directly. If, however, there is no guarantee that these same subjects will receive post-trial benefits in the form of continued access to effective products, the subjects will not be so thankful. In that circumstance, the charge of exploitation would be appropriate. As for relatives of the research subjects who may also suffer from depression or panic disorders, and for whom resulting products from the research will be unavailable, they have no reason to thank anyone.

UNAIDS Guidance Document

The UNAIDS Guidance Document for preventive vaccine research mentions exploitation in several places. The first mention occurs in a discussion of the obligation of sponsors of research to engage in capacity-building. Following the observation that disparities in economic wealth, scientific experience, and technical capacity among countries and communities can lead to possible exploitation of host countries and communities, the commentary on Guidance Point 3 offers a list of factors that may increase a country's or community's vulnerability to exploitation:

- level of the proposed community's economic capacity, such as is reflected in the Human Development Index of the UNDP;
- community/cultural experience with, and/or understanding of, scientific research;
- local political awareness of the importance and process of vaccine research;
- local infrastructure, personnel, and technical capacity for providing HIV health care and treatment options;
- ability of individuals in the community to provide informed consent, including the effect of class, gender, and other social factors on the potential for freely given consent;
- level of experience and capacity for conducting ethical and scientific review; and
- local infrastructure, personnel, and technical capacity for conducting the proposed research.[35]

This list is one of the few places in the literature on international research that specifies in considerable detail the factors that make a country or community vulnerable to exploitation.

The Guidance Document discusses exploitation next in Guidance Point 7, addressing vulnerable populations. The Guidance Point states that the research protocol should describe the social context that may create conditions for possible exploitation among potential research participants. The commentary under the Guidance Point then provides a list of factors (in addition to those mentioned in Guidance Point 3) that create conditions for exploitation among the pool of participants selected for the research. Several of these pertain specifically to participants in HIV/AIDS research, but others apply more widely to other areas of research:

- governmental, institutional, or social stigmatization or discrimination on the basis of HIV status;
- inadequate ability to protect HIV-related human rights, and to prevent HIV-related discrimination and stigma, including those arising from participation in an HIV vaccine trial;
- social and legal marginalization of groups from which participants might be drawn, e.g., women, injecting drug users, men having sex with men, sex workers;
- limited availability, accessibility, and sustainability of health care and treatment options;
- limited ability of individuals or groups in the community to understand the research process;
- limited ability of individuals to understand the informed consent process;
- limited ability of individuals to be able to give freely their informed consent in the light of prevailing class, gender, and other social and legal factors; and
- lack of meaningful national/local scientific and ethical review.[36]

The document cautions that conditions affecting potential exploitation may be so severe in some research populations, countries, or communities that adequate safeguards will not be able to be provided, and therefore, HIV preventive research should not be conducted under those conditions.

Guidance Point 8 recommends that early phases of clinical HIV vaccine research should be conducted in communities that are less vulnerable to exploitation. But the guidance document does not rule out the possibility that countries may choose to conduct early phases of research if they are able to ensure sufficient ethical safeguards. In countries or communities that are relatively vulnerable to exploitation, certain conditions must be met in order for the research to be ethically justified. These conditions include: the anticipated effectiveness of the vaccine against the strain of HIV that is an important public health problem in the country; adequate scientific and ethical capability and infrastructure for the successful conduct of the research; and a determination that the population will be adequately protected from exploitation and that the vaccine development program is necessary for and responsive to the health needs and priorities in their country.

As specific and useful as these Guidance Points and commentaries are, the UNAIDS Guidance Document does not venture a definition of "exploitation" or criteria that would distinguish ordinary unethical behavior in the conduct of research from the presumptively more serious violation of the rights of subjects that constitutes exploitation.

NBAC report

The report of the National Bioethics Advisory Commission refers to exploitation in several chapters, again without stipulating a definition. Chapter 1 links the concept with human rights:

> Exploitation in any form can be construed as a human rights violation by virtue of its failure to recognize the inherent dignity of every human being, a precept embodied in the Universal Declaration of Human Rights. It follows that all parties have a fundamental obligation to avoid exploitation when conducting research, especially in poorer, less advantaged countries. In any case, exploitation is a serious moral wrong, and a fundamental obligation exists to refrain from behavior that constitutes or promotes it.[37]

Chapter 3 of the NBAC report, devoted to voluntary, informed consent, states that researchers "must adhere to internationally agreed-upon ethical standards of voluntary informed consent for research, even in the face of cultural diversity. Obtaining adequately informed voluntary consent from individual research participants is a necessary requirement in preventing exploitation."[38] A more explicit statement follows: "The use of human beings as a means to the ends of others without their knowledge and freely granted permission constitutes exploitation and is therefore unethical."[39] This Kantian formulation that exploitation involves treating people as a "means merely" echoes the observation that all research subjects face some risk of exploitation: "They face the possibility that researchers may regard them purely as a means to benefit society or, more subtly, enroll them with the societal benefits to be gained from the research that do not justify the risks that subjects face."[40]

In an entirely different context, NBAC discusses the possibility of exploitation in connection with prior agreements to provide post-trial benefits to the country or community where research is conducted. Although the NBAC report falls far short of requiring such prior agreements as a condition of IRB approval of a proposed research project, it hints that failure to negotiate agreements to provide benefits might be a form of exploitation: "Much-needed research can move forward while, at the same time, these countries are protected from exploitation through arrangements designed to ensure that they receive the benefits of research."[41] Although the implication is evident, NBAC refrains from making a bold statement that failure to provide post-trial benefits constitutes exploitation.

In contrast, two articles in the bioethics literature are unequivocal in alleging that exploitation occurs if successful products are not made "reasonably available." One article states: "[I]f the results of a clinical trial are not made reasonably available in a timely manner to study participants and other inhabitants of a host country, the researchers might be justly accused of exploiting poor, undereducated subjects for the benefit of more affluent populations of the sponsoring countries."[42] And the second states: "If developed countries use inhabitants of underdeveloped countries to create new products that would be beneficial to both the developed and the underdeveloped country, but the underdeveloped country cannot gain access to the product because of expense, then the subjects in the underdeveloped countries have been grossly exploited."[43]

In the final chapter of its report, NBAC includes some general remarks about the importance of avoiding exploitation:

> In the most general terms, it is important that sponsors or investigators from developed nations who are conducting clinical trials in developing countries take steps to ensure that participants are not exploited. Likewise, because there is always a possibility that exploitation might occur when a large disparity in power and wealth exists between the parties involved, it is important to ensure that the host country itself is not exploited and that the rich and powerful do not appropriate an unfair share of the fruits of the research.[44]

These general remarks are salutary, but they fail to give specific guidance on what share of the fruits of research would be fair or unfair. The paragraph is equally unclear on just what NBAC would consider to be exploitation of the less powerful by the more powerful.

Nuffield report

Of all the guidelines and reports devoted to international collaborative research, the Nuffield report contains the most extensive discussion of exploitation. Nuffield elevates the duty to refrain from exploitation to the level of a key moral principle, one of four main principles that provide the framework for the entire report. Nuffield explains the source of this principle by noting that "it can be regarded as a further implication of the principle of respect for persons, for in exploiting others we fail to give proper weight to their interests."[45] The duty not to exploit the vulnerable is especially pertinent in developing countries, and this obligation must be "observed uniformly by all individuals and organizations involved in research, to avoid unfairness and the danger of undermining the principle in practice."[46] From these passages, it is clear that the Nuffield report construes exploitation as arising from harm to individuals or their interests, as well as unfair treatment in the conduct of research.

The Nuffield report's account of the duty to avoid exploitation goes a step further than other accounts. It is not simply a "negative duty," that is, a duty to refrain from harming or wronging people by exploiting them. In addition, some individuals or agencies have a positive duty to seek to bring about changes in institutions and practices in order to reduce the opportunities for exploitation:

Hence, the principle of not exploiting the vulnerable does not mean that we simply take the current context of research related to healthcare in the developing world as unchallengeable and unalterable . . . The wider roles and obligations of all those involved in research, pharmaceutical companies, international organisations, governments, and individuals in reducing global health inequities must always be borne in mind.[47]

In several different chapters, the Nuffield report reiterates its view that "the need to avoid exploitation is imperative."[48] At the same time, the report takes pains to insist that two of the chief circumstances that others have contended are exploitative are not necessarily open to that charge. These by-now familiar circumstances are, first, adherence to the local "standard of care" in determining what may be provided to control groups in clinical trials; and second, failure to ensure the provision of post-trial benefits to the community or country.

With regard to the possibility that research participants might be exploited by not being given an established, effective treatment for their condition, Nuffield says that "insisting upon a universal standard of care may not always be the best way" to respect the principle that researchers and sponsors should not take advantage of the vulnerabilities created by poverty or lack of other resources. Nuffield acknowledges that applying a lower standard of care would take advantage of the vulnerabilities of research subjects in such circumstances. Yet Nuffield maintains that "the principle of equal respect does not imply that we must behave toward others in a uniform manner, since features of individuals and of their circumstances will differ."[49] This account derives from the formal principle of justice – "treat like cases alike, different cases differently" – meaning in this context that circumstances in different countries may vary in relevant respects, thereby permitting a different standard of care based on morally relevant reasons. Nuffield's position also rejects the applicability of justice as *equality* in favor of justice as *equity*.

It is puzzling, however, how Nuffield could imply that this "different standard of care" is not also a *lower* standard of care. If the control group in a clinical trial in an industrialized country is provided with a known, effective preventive or therapeutic method, and the control group in a trial in a developing country in which that method is not generally available gets a placebo, why is the "different" standard of care in the developing country not a "lower" standard of care? It is hard to see how it could be otherwise.

Nuffield directly addresses the second circumstance in which the charge of exploitation has been made – failure to ensure post-trial benefits to the research subjects, the community, or the country where the research is conducted:

Many have voiced the opinion that participants in research should be guaranteed access to interventions shown to be successful once the study is complete, and that to fail to do so is a form of exploitation which is ethically unacceptable . . . However, in some circumstances, the subsequent provision either of interventions shown to be successful or of a better standard of healthcare to participants in research and especially to the wider community is not straightforward.[50]

The report provides several reasons why post-trial interventions may not easily be made available.

One reason is that sponsors of research cannot make unilateral decisions when initiating a trial, since health care is the responsibility of national governments. Although that is certainly true, the proposed solution (as discussed in the previous chapter) is to negotiate prior agreements. The parties to such agreements will include the sponsor and the national government, so the government's authority and involvement are assured from the start. A second reason is that "a new or improved treatment may be expensive."[51] In that case, the health authorities in resource-poor countries will not be able to afford to distribute it to the wider population. About this situation, Nuffield says: "Researchers and sponsors must understand this and justify their decision to conduct research notwithstanding, if they wish to avoid the charge of exploitation."[52]

This conclusion is very close to the NBAC report's position on post-trial benefits: "In cases in which investigators do not believe that successful interventions will become available to the host country population, they should explain to the relevant ethics review committee(s) why the research is nonetheless responsive to the health needs of the country and presents a reasonable risk/benefit ratio."[53] Nuffield and NBAC both maintain that ensuring post-trial benefits to the wider community is a desirable goal. But both fall short of stating that there is an obligation to provide those benefits, failing which the researchers or sponsors could be charged with exploitation.

Some reasons why post-trial benefits may not be able to be provided are obviously sound: the experimental intervention fails and there is no "best current" preventive or therapeutic method. Or the experimental intervention fails and the "best current method" is impossible to provide in the developing country because the infrastructure is not sufficiently developed (e.g., lack of intensive care units in local hospitals throughout the country, absence of refrigeration in rural areas required for drug storage). But the reason that the new or improved treatment is "too expensive" is not one of the reasons that can be considered ethically justifiable if the research proves successful.

The price of drugs is not fixed in stone. The cost of industrial products is not biologically determined. A number of different developments have demonstrated that industry may be willing to lower prices, to donate some products, or to negotiate in advance to make products available following research (see chapter 6, below). Therefore, it seems there can be little excuse in today's world to embark on research without foreknowledge of whether a product of that research will be "too expensive" for wide distribution if the product is shown to be effective. It makes no sense to maintain that research can be justified simply for the sake of contributing to scientific knowledge that is "relevant" to conditions in developing countries. When research involves testing a product whose effectiveness can ameliorate disease conditions but will never be made available in such countries, it cannot be considered relevant to those countries.

For researchers or sponsors such as the NIH or MRC to embark upon research without having a clue whether successful products can realistically be made available is irresponsible. If it does not rise to the level of exploitation, it can nonetheless be considered unethical. Ignorance of the future price to be set by a manufacturer is no excuse. It assumes that free-market pricing decisions made by drug companies are inviolate, unchangeable, or acceptable because that is what industry has to do to maintain its enormous profits.

Candidates for circumstances of exploitation in international research

Based on the tentative definition proposed at the beginning of this chapter, and the comments in guidelines, reports, and other sources, I propose

the following circumstances as leading candidates for research in which exploitation can occur.
1 Studies are carried out without the knowledge or voluntary consent of the individual research subjects.

NBAC clearly states the relationship between voluntary, informed consent and exploitation: "Obtaining adequately informed voluntary consent from individual research participants is a necessary requirement in preventing exploitation," and Nuffield strongly implies the same in chapter 6 of its report. In the Nigerian meningitis study, there was almost certainly a lack of adequate information on the part of parents of the children who received the experimental drug.

2 Basic research is conducted in an industrialized country on a health problem that exists in both the industrialized and a developing country; but clinical trials are done in the developing country because it is simpler or cheaper to do them there. Successful products of the research become available soon afterwards to the industrialized country but become available in the developing country only fifteen to twenty years later, if at all.

This situation exemplifies exploitation because of two features: the decision to do clinical trials in the developing country only because it is simpler or cheaper; and the failure of products to become available in the developing country at the same time as they become available in the industrialized country. This situation fits the definition of "exploitation" since the research serves the ends of the wealthy or powerful (the sponsoring country and the company that realizes the profits) without adequate compensating benefits for the less powerful or disadvantaged individuals and groups in the developing country.

The study conducted by Pfizer in Nigeria has several features resembling this situation. The disease for which the experimental treatment was tested – spinal meningitis – is relatively rare in the US, but it does exist. A spokesperson for the company acknowledged that they could not find the required number of children in the US to do the study, so they "had to move quickly" when they learned of the epidemic in Nigeria.[54] Pfizer sought to justify the study on humanitarian grounds, arguing that if the drug proved to be effective in an oral form, it would be appropriate for use in developing countries because children could simply swallow a pill rather than be injected with the proven form of the medication. But in the absence of a prior agreement containing a realistic plan to make the drug available in Nigeria, there was no indication that the drug, if proven successful, would be accessible to poor families in a poor country in a time of a raging epidemic. And, of course, if the product was approved by the FDA, it would be available for use by American physicians in cases of the disease in the US.

Another example is the depression and panic trials conducted in Hungary, Peru, and India, mentioned by Dr. Robert Temple of the FDA. Temple acknowledged that product testing in developing countries, "at present, is generally not accompanied by plans for early marketing in those countries (and would constitute dubious use of their resources if it did)." In opposition to Temple's view, other commentators on CIOMS Guideline 10 were unequivocal in labeling such situations "exploitative."

3 Clinical trials are conducted in a developing country and could not, for ethical reasons, be conducted in the sponsoring, industrialized country.

There are four variations on this situation:

a The reason the trial cannot be conducted in the industrialized country is that an effective treatment for the condition is already available to the population. The existing product is not available in the poorer country. In a placebo-controlled study conducted in the developing country, a successful new product results from the research, is approved for use in the industrialized country, but is not made available in the developing country where the research was conducted.

This variation fits the criteria for exploitation. The product could not be tested using a placebo control in the industrialized country, the risks of research were borne entirely by the subjects in the developing country, yet the benefits flowed exclusively to the industrialized country.

b A successful product resulting from the research is intended only for the industrialized country and is made available to that country after completion of the study and regulatory approval of the product.

This situation is similar to variation "a," above, but exhibits a higher degree of exploitation than variation "a" because of the intention of the researchers or sponsors. Whereas situation "a" may have hoped or intended that benefits would flow to the developing country, it never happened because no one took the steps to bring about that result. Situation "b" is the one described by Temple of the FDA: "the now growing flow of product testing to developing countries . . . not accompanied by plans for early marketing in those countries." Another probable candidate is the hepatitis A vaccine trial conducted in Northern Thailand (described earlier), in which the product was intended for travelers from industrialized countries, and it could easily have been predicted that the product would be unaffordable for general use in Thailand.

c A successful product resulting from the research is made available to both the industrialized and developing countries.

This situation would not count as exploitation, according to my proposed definition. Although the research subjects in the developing country exclusively bore the risks of the trial, the developing country inhabitants nevertheless receive adequate compensating benefits in the form of the research product. The research may still be considered unethical – even if not exploitative – if a different research design could have been used, one that provided an effective treatment for the control group in the developing country.

d Established, effective treatment in the sponsoring country is not provided to the control group in the developing country; the experimental group receives a regimen thought to be riskier than what is normally provided for subjects in the sponsoring country; there is no plan or evidence of feasibility for providing the results, if successful, to the host country; and the results would nonetheless be applicable to industrialized countries.

This is typified by the breast cancer study in Vietnam, described earlier in this chapter. The control group in the Vietnam study received mastectomy alone, which was no longer standard treatment in the US. The experimental group was to receive mastectomy plus immediate surgical oophorectomy and the drug, tamoxifen, for five years – a regimen considered more risky than what women in the US were normally receiving. As one commentator notes: "[T]here is no reason to expect that the results will not be seen as relevant for hormonal adjuvant therapy anywhere . . . Any arguments that this trial is of particular benefit to Vietnamese women should, therefore, be viewed with suspicion. No data are given to support the claim that this is a treatment that 'could be widely applied in that country'."[55]

4 Randomized clinical trials are conducted in both the industrialized country sponsor and a developing country, with the control group in both countries receiving the best current treatment for the disease. A successful product resulting from the research becomes available only in the industrialized country because neither the government nor the majority of the population in the developing country can afford the product.

In this circumstance, the research subjects are treated equally in the industrialized and developing countries and both groups receive equal benefits during the study. However, the benefits are not provided to the wider population after the study is concluded, for economic reasons. Whether this situation fits the definition of exploitation depends on how the benefits of research are calculated. In this case, there is compensating benefit at least to the subjects who participated in the trial – both the control group and the experimental group. On that basis, the situation might not be construed as exploitative. However, it falls short of the newly recognized requirement for research to be responsive to the health needs of the population, as that requirement is understood in its broader meaning. According to commentators quoted earlier (Glantz et al., Crouch and Arras), this situation would constitute exploitation.

Inducing vulnerable subjects as exploitation

A quite different situation from the exploitation of sick people who are enrolled as research subjects is that of healthy individuals who are vulnerable in other ways. The *Washington Post*'s series on international research sponsored by pharmaceutical companies provides a perhaps unique story in which healthy people were recruited in Estonia and flown to Basel, Switzerland for a variety of experiments. Estonia, formerly a part of the Soviet empire, is a poor country in which the population is not well informed about human subjects research, and informed consent is not a well-established requirement in the practice of clinical medicine or in research. The newspaper article describes a clinic in Basel, operated by Van Tx Research Ltd., a research company that has since gone bankrupt.[56] Many of the beds in the Swiss clinic were filled with refugees from Estonia who were seeking political asylum in Switzerland. Other occupants of the research beds were drug addicts. Both groups were otherwise healthy individuals recruited for experiments. Some of the refugees did not receive adequate information in advance of the trip about the purpose they were to serve in Switzerland. The company flew them to Basel and, in addition, paid them several hundred dollars.

Lacking a sufficient number of potential subjects from Switzerland for clinical trials that were already planned, the company, Van Tx, decided to seek subjects from Estonia. In addition to the refugees seeking asylum and the drug addicts, Estonian students were also recruited for the study. The company enlisted Estonian doctors in the search for potential subjects, paying the doctors well for the individuals they succeeded in bringing. Estonian students were also paid for their assistance in finding other students willing to be subjects. Some of these Estonians were apparently told something about the purpose of their trip to Switzerland; others simply received plane tickets and were told when to arrive at the airport.

As in the case of the Nigerian study and numerous others that have been charged with ethical violations, the Swiss company's study in Basel had seriously flawed procedures for obtaining informed consent. But it is not that feature alone that makes the research open to the charge of exploitation. The recruitment plan and procedures preyed on the vulnerability of at least two groups – the Estonian refugees seeking asylum and the drug addicts – and possibly a third group, the students, who like students everywhere lack money and have a subordinate status during the time they are dependent on continuing their studies in order to complete their education. An offer to be flown free of charge to rich, beautiful Switzerland along with an additional payment of cash, when one is poor and lives in Estonia, begins to look suspiciously like a case of exploitation.

But does it fit my definition – "wealthy or powerful individuals or agencies taking advantage of the poverty, powerlessness, or dependency of others by using the latter to serve their own ends (those of the wealthy or powerful) without adequate compensating benefits for the less powerful or disadvantaged individuals or groups"? The research company was certainly powerful, if not rich; the Estonians were poor, powerless, or dependent; and the ends served were solely those of the company since the subjects were healthy and therefore could receive no direct benefits from participating in the study. The question that remains to be answered is whether they received "adequate compensating benefits," in this case, in the form of monetary payments. Considerable debate continues to surround the practice of paying money to research subjects, and this example perfectly illustrates the dilemma.

On the one hand, an offer of money serves as an inducement to healthy individuals to enroll in research, something most are unlikely to do without some compensation. On the other hand, an offer of too much money may constitute an "undue" inducement – one that is so attractive that it seriously compromises the voluntariness with which the person consents to be a research subject. Since one of the undisputed ethical requirements in research is that subjects must give their voluntary consent – free of force, fraud, deceit, coercion, or undue influence – payment of a large sum of money risks violating this requirement. Opposing views in this debate range from one extreme, which would altogether prohibit monetary payments to research subjects, to the opposite extreme, which justifies not only paying people but paying them more money as the risks of the research increase. Most researchers and ethicists fall somewhere in the middle of this continuum, but others support the extremes.

If the recruitment of these Estonians into the Swiss study is to count as exploitation, it probably requires evidence that the subjects were sufficiently vulnerable to stand in need of safeguards or additional protection, along with knowledge that they lacked sufficient advance information to know what they were getting into in their trip to Switzerland. Absence of adequate informed consent at the time of entry into the research is an uncontroversial condition of exploitation. Lack of sufficient information provided during the recruitment process – which took place in Estonia – is a first step down the path of exploitation, but does not yet fulfill the definition since the subjects still could have refrained from participating in the research once they arrived at the clinic. However, one of the Estonians, who said he knew almost nothing about the drug he took, before or after the trial, was reported as saying: "I didn't like it, but when we were already there, it was too late to change our minds."[57]

Best current treatment and post-trial benefits as undue inducements

There is an interesting twist in the debates over whether an obligation exists to provide the "best current treatment" to research subjects in a control group, and whether post-trial benefits to the wider population in developing countries should be made reasonably available. The twist is whether providing those sorts of benefits to people who would not otherwise have access to them is an "undue inducement" or a "coercive offer," an incentive so great that it compromises their ability to give voluntary informed consent to participate in research. If consent is not voluntary, if it is compromised by an offer that poor people could not meaningfully refuse, then they are exploited in the opposite way from being denied the best current treatment or the successful product following the completion of the research. To enroll participants in research in the absence of adequately *voluntary* consent to research is a prime candidate for an act of exploitation.

It may come as a surprise to those who seek to improve conditions for research subjects during and after clinical trials to learn that proffered or promised benefits can be considered a form of exploitation. This is a no-win situation. If subjects do not receive medical benefits during and after their participation in research, it may be that they are being exploited. On the other hand, if such benefits are offered to potential subjects in the course of obtaining their informed consent, the subjects are allegedly exploited by being presented with an undue inducement.

I find the charge of exploitation in this latter situation to be ridiculous. That charge has been made by those who seek to defend placebo-controlled trials and those who are eager to reject the idea that an obligation exists to provide post-trial benefits to participants or to others. It is, therefore, a counter-charge used to deflect the claim that it is unethical to enroll poor, vulnerable, or disadvantaged subjects in research without providing them with an effective intervention that could be made available using a different design.

The NBAC report makes the following observation about continuing to provide a successful experimental product to subjects who still need it after the trial is over: "the promise to continue to provide a successful intervention after the trial may . . . in certain instances, even amount to an undue inducement to potential participants to enroll in the research."[58] Regarding provision of an effective treatment to members of a control group when they would not otherwise have access to that treatment, NBAC says:

the Commission is interested in exploring whether offering potential participants better care or treatment than they could obtain outside the study would be an undue inducement to potential participants to enroll in a clinical trial. As a general rule, NBAC does not believe this to be the case, but the Commission recognizes that determining the level of treatment that should be provided to participants (including those in a control group, who are not receiving the experimental intervention) is a research design issue with ethical implications that must be addressed.[59]

Thus NBAC recognizes the charge that has been made regarding undue inducements but appears to dismiss it rather easily as not a matter of great concern.

The Nuffield report expresses considerably greater concern about the prospect of healthcare benefits being exploitative of research subjects. The report observes that when research involves medical treatment, that may be an inducement for individuals to enroll. That does not necessarily mean the individual has been exploited. But when research participants have no way of obtaining medical treatment outside of the research context, then the possibility of exploitation is greater.[60] Finally, "guaranteed healthcare . . . offered to individuals on condition that they take part in a research project could be considered to be exploitative if otherwise there is a very low probability of receiving such a benefit."[61]

This results in an unhappy paradox. Exploitation of human beings is a serious wrong. Nuffield voices a concern relating to exploitation when vulnerable subjects are not provided with the universal standard of care; and Nuffield calls upon investigators and sponsors to "justify their decision to conduct research . . . if they wish to avoid the charge of exploitation" in situations where the health authorities in resource-poor countries cannot afford to distribute to the population successful products that result from the research. At the same time, Nuffield appears to say, the poorer the subjects are, and the less they are able to afford during or after their participation in research providing medical benefits, the greater is the possibility that they may be exploited in agreeing to participate. This creates a terrible dilemma for researchers and sponsors who are eager to avoid exploitation of a population and who have the willingness and means to provide health benefits during and after a clinical trial.

Perhaps not surprisingly, the PhRMA discussion paper criticizing paragraph 30 of the Declaration of Helsinki identifies the provision of post-trial benefit as potentially an undue inducement: "The Declaration clearly prohibits coercing individuals to participate in research . . . a prohibition that the research-based pharmaceutical industry fully supports. The act of guaranteeing research participants access to treatments after the conclusion of a trial could constitute undue inducement to participate."[62]

It is a mystery how the provision of potential health benefits during or after participation in research could have come to be viewed as possible coercion, or worse, exploitation of research subjects. Those who sponsor and conduct research take great pains to show that risks of harm are minimized in the conduct of research, that the vast majority of research does not cause harm to subjects, and that they take scrupulous care in the process of informing potential subjects and ensuring that they understand the risks and benefits. To maintain all those views about the low level of harm and the diligence in informing potential subjects of all the risks they may be exposed to, and at the same time to argue that if benefits are considerable then consent is not voluntary, borders on incoherence.

The paradox deepens when we recall that a fundamental principle of research ethics is the obligation to maximize benefits, as well as to minimize harms. The benefits can be benefits to the subjects themselves or benefits to others, such as future patients. However, if there is any merit to the claim that providing health benefits to research subjects during or after their participation constitutes an undue inducement, and is therefore unethical, the only solution is to *minimize* the benefits to the research subjects themselves. The result would be that the only individuals for whom it is appropriate to maximize the benefits are non-participants in the research. That consequence is surely counter-intuitive, if not ridiculous.

The oddest situation in which these arguments regarding undue inducements are made is in the context of preventive vaccine trials for HIV/AIDS. As the UNAIDS Guidance Document stipulates, and as almost everyone in the AIDS vaccine field urges, preventive vaccines demonstrated to be safe and effective should be made available as soon as possible after the research is concluded to the participants in the control group and to others. The UNAIDS document also recommends that care and treatment for HIV/AIDS should be provided to participants who become infected during the trial. Yet some have contended that to make the latter promise would constitute an undue inducement to participate in the trial. That is truly bizarre, since a vaccine trial enrolls healthy people, not people who are already sick and need treatment. What we would have to imagine is that some people would enroll in the trial, then deliberately become infected in order to get the treatment for AIDS. It makes more sense to imagine participants eager to remain healthy or to be protected against acquiring HIV infection by the vaccine. By that token, the possibility of being protected by the vaccine itself is what could possibly be considered an "undue inducement."

The correct way of looking at all this is to acknowledge that yes, the promise of preventive or therapeutic health benefits during or after a trial may be a reason – even *the* reason – why some people choose to enroll in research. But not every incentive counts as exploitation, and not every inducement is "undue."

Conclusion

It is unlikely that agreement will be reached in the debates over what constitutes exploitation in research, any more than agreement is likely on the several other points of controversy. People may well disagree on the definition of "exploitation" suggested here, as they have on other proposed definitions. But most people do take seriously the concerns about exploitation, as evidenced by the numerous comments submitted on the CIOMS draft guidelines, the points elaborated in the UNAIDS Guidance Document, and contributions to the bioethics literature on international research ethics. In contrast, there is the view of the FDA's Dr. Robert Temple: "'[E]xploitative' is a word better omitted from [the CIOMS Guidelines]. It's just a cuss-word, with no clear meaning or useful purpose."

The Nuffield Council report considers the concept of exploitation important enough to discuss at length, and takes great pains to determine which situations in research count as exploitation and which do not. That Nuffield ends up denying that exploitation occurs in the situations the report defends as ethically acceptable is not surprising. It does suggest, however, that the view one already holds on the ethical acceptability of a particular standard of care for research subjects, or on the obligation to provide post-trial benefits to the community or country, predetermines what one judges to be exploitation in research.

In the end, it is worth reflecting on the anti-paternalist sentiment in this comment by a distinguished Indian medical scientist: "[I]t is no use blaming institutions and firms in affluent countries for exploiting us. We are grown up and should look after our own interests. If we are upright and do a thorough job no one stops us in this and all would be well."[63]

NOTES

1. Joe Stephens, "The Body Hunters: As Drug Testing Spreads, Profits and Lives Hang in Balance," *Washington Post* (December 17, 2000).
2. Ibid.
3. Ibid.
4. Ibid.
5. Khabir Ahmad, "Nigerian Government Investigates Pfizer Drug Trial Allegations," *The Lancet*, 357 (2001), 9250, http://www.thelancet.com, accessed May 29, 2003.
6. Joe Stephens, "Doctors Say Trial's Approval Was Backdated," *Washington Post* (January 16, 2001), A1.
7. This definition is almost identical to a comment about exploitation in the NBAC report: "[E]xploitation may be more likely to occur when wealthy or powerful individuals or agencies take advantage of the poverty, powerlessness, or dependency of others to serve their own ends, without a sufficient benefit for the less advantaged individuals or group." National Bioethics Advisory Commission, *Ethical and Policy Issues in International Research: Clinical Trials in Developing Countries* (Bethesda, MD, 2001), 10. As Senior Consultant to the National Bioethics Advisory Commission for its international project, I drafted early versions of chapters of the final report. The wording of the passage quoted here is a slightly altered form of the definition I proposed in early drafts of the NBAC report, but the NBAC comment does not suggest that it should be viewed as a definition of the term.
8. David Orentlicher, "Universality and its Limits: When Research Ethics Can Reflect Local Circumstances," *Journal of Law, Medicine and Ethics*, 30 (2002), 403–410.
9. Ibid., 407.
10. Alan Wertheimer, *Exploitation* (Princeton, NJ: Princeton University Press, 1996).
11. Ibid., 10.
12. The definitions that follow are all taken from Wertheimer, *Exploitation*, 10–12.
13. Allen Buchanan, *Ethics, Efficiency, and the Market* (Totowa, NJ: Rowman and Allanheld, 1985), 87.
14. Judith Farr Tormey, "Exploitation, Oppression and Self-Sacrifice," *Philosophical Forum*, 5 (1974), 207–208.
15. Robert E. Goodin, *Reasons for Welfare* (Princeton, NJ: Princeton University Press, 1988), 147.
16. Robert E. Goodin, "Reasons for Welfare: Economic, Sociological, and Political – But Ultimately Moral," in (ed.) J. Donald Moon, *Responsibility, Rights, and Welfare* (Boulder, CO: Westview Press, 1988), 37.
17. Joel Feinberg, *Harmless Wrongdoing* (New York: Oxford University Press, 1988), 176–179.
18. Stephen R. Munzer, *A Theory of Property* (Cambridge: Cambridge University Press, 1990), 171.

19. John E. Roemer, "An Historical Materialist Alternative to Welfarism," in (eds.) Jon Elster and Aanund Hylland, *Foundations of Social Choice Theory* (Cambridge: Cambridge University Press, 1986), 136.
20. Andrew Levine, *Arguing for Socialism* (London: Verso, 1988), 66–67.
21. Wertheimer, *Exploitation*, 14.
22. Roy J. Kim, Letter to the Editor, NEJM, 338 (1998), 838.
23. Reidar K. Lie, "Justice and International Research," in (eds.) Robert J. Levine and Samuel Gorovitz, with James Gallagher, *Biomedical Research Ethics: Updating International Guidelines: A Consultation* (Geneva: CIOMS, 2000), 27–50.
24. Ibid., 31.
25. Ibid., 34–36. The original article describing the study is discussed in detail in chapter 5: R. R. Love and N. C. Fost, "Ethical and Regulatory Challenges in a Randomized Control Trial of Adjuvant Treatment for Breast Cancer in Vietnam," *Journal of Investigative Medicine*, 45 (1997), 423–431.
26. Lie, "Justice and International Research," 35.
27. Peter Lurie, letter to Dr. Jack Bryant, President, Council for International Organizations of Medical Sciences, dated July 13, 2001.
28. National Committee of Medical Research Ethics (Norway).
29. British Medical Association.
30. Permission was granted to use this quotation without attribution.
31. Dave Wendler.
32. Permission to quote without attribution.
33. Dr. Robert Temple.
34. National Institutes of Health.
35. Joint United Nations Programme on HIV/AIDS (UNAIDS), *Ethical Considerations in HIV Preventive Vaccine Research* (2000), 16.
36. Ibid., 22–23.
37. NBAC, *Ethical and Policy Issues*, 10.
38. Ibid., 36.
39. Ibid.
40. Dave Wendler, "Informed Consent, Exploitation and Whether it is Possible to Conduct Human Subjects Research Without Either One," *Bioethics*, 14:4 (2000), 310–39 at 312.
41. NBAC, *Ethical and Policy Issues*, 68.
42. Robert A. Crouch and John D. Arras, "AZT Trials and Tribulations," *Hastings Center Report*, 28:6 (1998), 29.
43. Leonard H. Glantz, George J. Annas, Michael A. Grodin, and Wendy K. Mariner, "Research in Developing Countries: Taking 'Benefit' Seriously," *Hastings Center Report*, 28:6 (1998), 39.
44. NBAC, *Ethical and Policy Issues*, 77.
45. Nuffield Council on Bioethics, *The Ethics of Research Related to Healthcare in Developing Countries* (London: Nuffield Council on Bioethics, 2002), 52.
46. Ibid.
47. Ibid., 53.
48. Ibid., 90.
49. Ibid.

50. Ibid., 113.
51. Ibid.
52. Ibid.
53. NBAC, *Ethical and Policy Issues*, Recommendation 4.2, 74.
54. Stephens, "Body Hunters."
55. Lie, "Justice and International Research," 36.
56. Sharon LaFraniere, Mary Pat Flaherty, and Joe Stephens, "The Dilemma: Submit or Suffer," *Washington Post* (December 19, 2000), A1.
57. Ibid.
58. NBAC, *Ethical and Policy Issues*, 60.
59. Ibid., 8.
60. Nuffield, *Ethics of Research*, 79.
61. Ibid.
62. Pharmaceutical Research and Manufacturers of America, "PhRMA Discussion Paper on the Declaration of Helsinki as Revised in October 2000" (June 2001), 2.
63. R. Krishnakumar, "Clinical Trials Should Promote Health Care," interview with Dr. M. S. Valiathan, *Frontline*, India's National Magazine, 18:17 (August 18–31, 2001), no page numbers.

5 Providing safeguards: informed consent and review of research

How can human subjects of research be adequately protected against exploitation? What mechanisms exist to protect the rights and welfare of research subjects? The two main safeguards are the requirement of voluntary, informed consent of each individual research subject, and prior review of proposed research by an independent ethical review committee. Both procedures are required by US regulations and international declarations and guidelines for research.[1] Both are discussed at length in the report of the US National Bioethics Advisory Commission and the Nuffield Council's report from the UK. Yet despite the universally acknowledged need for these two safeguards, ample evidence exists that they are at times flawed, often inadequate, and sometimes even nonexistent.

So much has been written about informed consent that it is hard to know where to begin. Even in the United States and Western Europe, both empirical studies and anecdotal evidence make it abundantly clear that a large gap exists between the ideal of informed consent to research and the reality. No one questions the need for subjects of research to be provided with information sufficient to make an informed choice of whether or not to participate. No one questions the importance of conveying that information in terms that potential subjects can understand: in their mother tongue, obviously; free of medical jargon; at a level of language comprehensible to people whose schooling has not gone beyond the eighth grade level. And everyone maintains that consent should be obtained without pressuring potential subjects and without exerting "undue influence" (the term used in the US federal regulations) or coercion.

Empirical studies of informed consent practices have revealed that subjects often do not read the consent documents they are given to sign, because they trust their doctors to act in their best interest.[2] This illustrates the widespread confusion between participating in research investigating new, unproven therapies, on the one hand, and receiving an established, effective treatment for a health-related condition, on the other hand. This confusion is known as "the therapeutic misconception."[3] The trust patients have in their own physicians in the clinical setting relies on the important feature of the physician–patient relationship that physicians should choose the most appropriate treatment for the individual patient. To think that that same obligation applies in the research setting is to fall prey to the confusion between the aims of research and the aim of individualized treatment of patients. The features that characterize the physician–patient relationship should not be assumed to be present in the researcher–subjects relationship.

Even in the United States, complaints are frequent that consent documents are too long, too complex, contain too many technical terms, and are generally off-putting to potential subjects. Drug companies that sponsor research typically provide a model consent form that researchers are expected to adopt. When members of the research ethics committee complain that these consent forms are not comprehensible to the ordinary layperson, researchers reply that the company requires use of their consent form and failure to adopt it will result in refusal of the company to allow the research to proceed.

This brings us to the second purported safeguard: the research ethics committee. How good a job do these committees do in protecting the rights and welfare of human subjects in international research? In the US, research ethics committees (termed Institutional Review Boards, or IRBs) are mandated by federal regulations. All institutions that receive federal funds for research must have such a committee in place and the committee must follow the detailed federal regulations governing research. The activities of IRBs are subject to review by a federal oversight agency, the Office of Human Research Protections (OHRP). But this agency cannot begin to conduct routine, on-site reviews of the operation of such committees, and the agency typically reviews a committee's documents and written procedures only when an alleged violation of the rules comes to light.

The two main charges to research ethics committees are to assess the risks and benefits of proposed research, and to review and approve the consent forms for the study. Although serious harm to subjects as a direct result of research interventions is rare, when it occurs it must be reported to the sponsor of the research, to the institution where the research is conducted, and to one or more oversight agencies. Two episodes resulting in the death of research subjects in prominent medical schools in the United States (the University of Pennsylvania and Johns Hopkins University) led to the temporary closing down of research at those institutions. It also led many people to wonder if the IRBs at those institutions are doing an adequate job of protecting the human subjects of research.

If these concerns exist in the US, which has for decades mandated voluntary, informed consent by research subjects and properly constituted research ethics committees, how are these safeguards working in developing countries? Are the informed consent procedures as good as – or not much worse than – what exists in the US? Do research ethics committees even exist in most developing countries where research is conducted, and if so, are they properly constituted, sufficiently independent, and are their members knowledgeable about ethics in research? Although there have been few systematic studies, there is a growing body of evidence gleaned from various sources to suggest that there is much room for improvement in both of these areas designed to safeguard the rights and welfare of research subjects in developing countries.

Allegations of violations

Reports have come from various sources alleging violations of both of these important safeguards in various studies carried out in developing countries. A total absence of informed consent, or serious deficiencies in carrying out the process, were features of several cases described in detail in the series of articles in the *Washington Post* already referred to in earlier chapters. In recounting these episodes here, I have no independent confirmation of the facts as reported in the *Post* articles. It could well be that researchers involved in those studies would contest some of the allegations, as indeed they have in the stories reported. But given the literacy level of some of the subjects in the studies and the circumstances of their recruitment and participation in the research, there is an inherent plausibility in details of the published stories.

As described in the previous chapter, questions arose regarding informed consent in the clinical trial in Kano, Nigeria, in which children with meningitis were given an experimental drug. The *Post* article said that a laboratory technician alleged that the children and their parents were unaware that they were involved in research. The sponsoring company, Pfizer, maintained that local nurses had explained the research to the families, but that information – even if true – is not sufficient to judge the adequacy of the informed consent process. What did the nurses actually tell the families? Did they make clear that this was medical research, distinguishing research from treatment with proven medications? Did they describe the potential side effects of the drugs and the possibility that the drugs could be harmful and not cure the illness? Did they explain the procedure of randomizing the subjects into different groups? Were the nurses sufficiently knowledgeable about the science and methodology of the study to be able to answer any questions the parents or children may have had? These are essential elements in obtaining informed consent from potential subjects in order to ensure that they understand what they have been told. Without a written consent form, or an information sheet that provided details of what the nurses were supposed to tell the parents and children, there is no documentation of the information given or even whether the consent process occurred at all.

As for prior review of the Nigerian study, conducted by a properly constituted ethical review committee, it is evident that feature was entirely absent. The medical director of the hospital confirmed that the hospital did not have an ethics review committee at the time the research was initiated. When Pfizer requested evidence of approval by a committee, a false document was purportedly created and backdated to include a date six days before the experiment began. So, according to the story published in the *Washington Post*, both of the safeguards that should have been protecting the subjects of research were seriously flawed or missing in the Nigerian meningitis trial.

Another story recounted in the *Post*'s series – the studies in Switzerland for which healthy subjects were recruited from Estonia (described in chapter 4) – indicated inadequate informed consent procedures. In addition to the misleading information provided to the potential subjects while still in Estonia, the actual consent form presented at the time of the study was problematic. One subject interviewed for the newspaper story said he signed a consent form in German, a language he could not read. He eventually got an English translation of the consent form, but the subject complained that he was only shown a copy of the consent form and referred to its contents as "all this mumbo jumbo." Another subject in the same study also said the subjects did not receive copies of the consent forms. The *Post* article contended that this clinical trial in Switzerland is not an isolated or even a rare case of violations of procedures for obtaining adequate informed consent. The article said that these procedures "have been breaking down as drug companies enroll thousands of test subjects at a time in Eastern Europe, the former Soviet Union, Africa, China, Latin America and elsewhere."[4]

Still another article in the series described a case of fraud in the consent procedure in a trial in Buenos Aires, Argentina. This clinical trial involved more serious harms to subjects than other cases in which subjects' right to informed consent was violated. But the main problem uncovered was the discovery of forged consent documents. The family of a subject who died – presumably as a direct result of the experimental procedure, for which he should have been deemed ineligible – was shown the consent document their father had allegedly signed. The family said it was not their father's signature.[5]

What could induce physicians conducting research to perpetrate fraud such as this? One answer is suggested by the payments physicians receive for recruitment. The leader of the research team in the Buenos Aires study was promised $2,700 by the sponsoring company, Hoechst Marion Roussel, for each subject recruited into the trial. Not only is this payment not unusual; it is also lower than the amount often provided per patient recruited in the United States. The more patients a physician recruits into a clinical trial, the more money that goes into that physician's pocket. Especially in developing countries, this incentive can easily lead to short cuts, if not outright violations and fraud in the informed consent process. The Scientific and Ethical Review Group of the human reproduction program at WHO prohibits payments to collaborators in research for subjects recruited. But the committee can approve or disapprove only what it knows from the documents it reviews. What takes place at the actual research site is beyond the purview of this and most other ethics review committees.

Other examples have been reported of researchers' failure to obtain consent, to ensure the required prior review of their research, or both. One highly publicized case involved a clinical trial of a drug to treat oral cancer (the first use of the drug in human beings), conducted in 1999 and 2000 in the state of Kerala in India. The study was reviewed by a local committee in India, but the US researcher, from Johns Hopkins University, failed to seek ethical review and approval by the Hopkins IRB. The researcher's defense was ignorance of that requirement. She was quoted as saying: "because I thought the local IRB in India was sufficient, and none of the Hopkins administrators objected."[6] It is hard to know whom to fault for this lapse: the researcher, a biologist who had been on the faculty at Hopkins since 1965, or the university for failing to make known to all faculty members in all parts of the institution that prior review and approval of research conducted by the faculty must take place at Hopkins, wherever else the research might have been reviewed and approved.

A partial explanation (though not a justification) for ignorance of the rules on the part of the Hopkins scientist was her faculty position in the university's School of Arts and Sciences, rather than in the medical school or the school of public health. It remains the case today at many leading US universities that behavioral scientists fail to submit their research proposals to institutional review boards. Perhaps a similar laxity in adherence to this requirement exists among biological scientists who are not affiliated to medical schools or schools of public health.

But it was not simply in her failure to obtain institutional ethical approval at Hopkins that this researcher violated ethical rules. A Johns

Hopkins faculty committee that investigated the episode also found that the trial failed to meet proper standards for research with human subjects in three further respects. First, there was insufficient prior testing of the cancer drugs in animals (although same animal work was done); second, the informed consent forms used for the study were inadequate; and third, the researcher brought the drugs to India without having first obtained approval from the FDA for use of an investigational new drug or explicit permission from the FDA for export of the drug.[7]

Meanwhile, investigations of the trial in India discovered that the relevant drug approval authority in India (the Drugs Controller-General of India) had not granted prior approval but sanctioned the study only after it was already completed. The Indian drug authority may not have known that the study was already over, and may also have been ignorant of the fact that the US FDA had removed the drug from its "safe" list. Additional problems emerged when one of the subjects in the trial consulted a senior Indian oncologist for treatment. It turned out that this subject and others in the trial had not been properly monitored for their medical condition. Nor were the twenty-six subjects in the trial adequately informed about the risks and benefits of the drug and that their participation was fully voluntary.[8] Most were not aware that they were not simply receiving part of their treatment for cancer but, rather, were involved in a research study.[9]

The Hopkins research team had initially observed the inhibition of growth in tumor cells in animals, and in this study sought to demonstrate the same activity in cancer cells in humans. Phase I data were not available from the US. Why was this phase I study conducted in India and not in the US, where the researchers had done their animal work? Was it because the drugs used in the study in India had been taken off the US FDA's category, "generally regarded as safe," and the FDA would not have approved a phase I study? Or even if the FDA might have approved a phase I study in the US, was it because – as the director of the center where the research was conducted in India said – there was a "dearth of patients in the US" compared with those who could be enrolled in India?[10] It is certainly the case that cancer research is responsive to the health needs of the population in the United States.

Inadequacies of safeguards

Despite the layers of committees, drug approval authorities, and other mechanisms in place to safeguard the rights and welfare of human subjects of research, the episodes described above demonstrate that the gaps in such protections are unacceptably large. The Johns Hopkins study in

India is especially troubling because of the stature of the sponsoring US research institution, the level of research ethics and drug controls already well established in India, and the high literacy rate in the population in the state of Kerala where the trial took place.

Granted, the episodes reported in the *Washington Post* series and elsewhere are individual anecdotes. They are no substitute for systematic investigation into the nature and extent of violations of informed consent procedures in research conducted in developing countries. But the major concerns regarding informed consent and review by research ethics committees in multinational research are not limited to these reported cases of blatant, intentional wrongdoing. My own experience serving as a reviewer of research on international committees and study teams confirms the suspicion that a huge problem exists and needs rectifying.

As a member of the Scientific and Ethical Review Group in the human reproduction program at WHO since 1989, I have reviewed hundreds of consent forms. Virtually all of these were too complex and contained medical jargon that even the educated layperson could not understand. Many of these forms omitted significant information about the research: in some case physical risks of the experimental procedures, in other cases pain or discomfort from the research maneuvers, and in still other cases important features related to privacy and confidentiality, such as home visits by the researchers and interview questions dealing with intimate questions like subjects' sexual behavior.

This WHO review committee requires "evidence of local or national ethical approval" for the proposed research. Such approval must be provided by a properly constituted ethical review committee, sufficiently independent of the researcher so as to avoid conflicts of interest. While it is true that the committee has received much in the way of excellent documentation from institutions in many developing countries, including some in Africa and Asia, in numerous instances it is clear that no review by a committee ever took place. Officials from the government or local institution attest to the acceptability of research, but they appear to be one administrative official's judgment, without evidence that an independent committee has reviewed the research. This practice was confirmed by one US researcher who conducted studies in a developing country where no IRB existed and the Ministry of Health did not believe that ethics review was important. The researcher said that "our approval came in the form of a letter from the Director of the Division of Epidemiology and no IRB review process was undertaken."[11]

In a study to be conducted at several different sites throughout one Asian country, documents were submitted to the WHO Scientific and Ethical Review Group with the letterhead of each institution involved, purporting that ethical review had taken place at that institution. However, the wording in all of the letters was identical and the official seal and the signature on every letter was that of the coordinating center for the research. It was obvious that the documents had all been prepared at the central location and submitted to WHO as if they came from the individual centers.

That it will take some time for researchers and research ethics committees to get up to speed in developing countries is completely understandable. There is no acceptable excuse, however, when researchers from industrialized countries prepare consent forms that are completely incomprehensible in developing countries to all but the doctors who are the local collaborators in the research. There may be no excuse, but there is an explanation: the same poorly worded, complex, jargon-filled consent forms are prepared for research conducted in the US.

Fraud and corruption

Clearly, also, there can be no excuse for fraud, either in the documentation of informed consent or in the documents submitted as evidence of local or national ethical review of research. If the explanation for cases of fraud that have been uncovered has anything to do with the large monetary payments given to developing country researchers for each subject they succeed in recruiting, it requires a serious look at these financial incentives. Pharmaceutical companies want their studies to be completed as quickly as possible, so they can submit their data for regulatory approval and begin marketing their products. When they do not succeed in meeting target enrollments fast enough, they offer bonuses to the physicians for every patient recruited over and above the initial quota.

In one such case in my own institution, a cardiologist received a letter from the sponsor promising an additional $5,000 for every patient recruited into the study by a certain date because the pace of recruitment had fallen behind schedule (this study was conducted in the US). When researchers from academic institutions are provided with such incentives, the money goes into the medical school department rather than into their pockets. For physicians in developing countries, however, who generally are paid much less than their industrialized country counterparts, the money goes directly to them. Sufficiently large sums can be a corrupting influence on physicians charged with recruiting potential research subjects and obtaining their informed consent.

In an effort to gather much-needed empirical data on an array of topics to be included in its international report, the National Bioethics Advisory Commission conducted a survey of US researchers who carry out studies in developing countries, along with developing country researchers who collaborate with US-sponsored researchers. NBAC sought to extend the study to researchers from pharmaceutical companies that carry out research in developing countries, but PhRMA, the US trade association that represents the industry, effectively blocked NBAC's attempt to involve drug company researchers.[12]

One researcher who responded to the NBAC survey remarked on the corrupting influence of money and other inducements on developing country researchers:

Some of the potential risks/ethics violations or cutting of corners can be perpetrated by collaborating investigators in other countries because the incentives to them (status, publications, foreign travel) to get the data collected are substantial enough as to be coercive. I don't know how policies and regulations could be written around this problem but I think it is not a trivial issue.[13]

It is evident that at least some of the problems that arise in attempting to provide adequate protection for the rights and welfare of human subjects can be traced to the way research is promoted by industry, with attractive financial inducements to governmental officials, developing country researchers, and local institutions. A problem of a different sort is the deeply rooted, widespread corruption in developing countries. In both situations, there is little that well-intentioned researchers can do by themselves when they embark upon research aimed at improving the health conditions of populations in resource-poor countries.

Informed consent: standards and practices

Although informed consent requirements have been introduced in the research setting in many developing countries, it is much less common for physicians to obtain consent from patients for medical treatment in those parts of the world. Some of the same problems persist in industrialized countries, despite their long experience with human subjects research. Still, particular problems pertaining to the process and documentation of informed consent appear especially difficult to resolve in countries where cultural features differ considerably from those common to most Western nations.

The challenge of cultural differences

How to deal with cultural practices that depart from the requirements of informed consent embodied in international ethical guidelines and many national laws and regulations remains a challenge for researchers who conduct clinical trials in developing countries. Ethical relativists have defended two prominent situations that constitute departures from widely accepted ethical standards for informed consent. The first is the perceived need to withhold key information from potential research subjects; the second is the cultural custom of requiring husbands to sign consent forms for research in which their wives are participants. Supporters cite three different considerations in defense of these departures.

The first is that the departures are justified by the cultural context in the country or community where the research is carried out. This is the view that cultural relativity justifies ethical relativism.[14] Second, researchers contend that it would be impossible to conduct research without these deviations from what they call "Western" requirements of informed consent. This is the pragmatic defense. The third consideration follows from the second: requiring adherence would result in a loss of contributions to medical science and lack of consequent benefits to the population in those countries or communities. This is an appeal to justice, citing the consequences of not conducting the research in the developing country.

There is a common confusion between two very different types of relativism. The first is the need to adapt the form and content of procedures for obtaining informed consent to the educational level and understanding of the potential subjects of research. This is necessary because the methods and type (written or oral; pictures and visual aids) of informed consent must be relative to the literacy level of the subjects, their comfort with signing documents, and perhaps other cultural circumstances.

The second type of relativism is an unacceptable ethical relativism that could permit community leaders to grant permission for an entire village to be enrolled in research without the need for individual consent by each participant.[15] In many cultures it is necessary to approach a tribal or community leader in order to gain permission to embark on research in that setting. Respect for the authority of the leader is necessary as a first step in the process of informing the community and eventually obtaining consent from individual members. But the idea of "community consent" as a substitute for individual consent is ethically unacceptable. The NBAC report puts the matter clearly and correctly in its Recommendation 3.6:

Where culture or custom requires that permission of a community representative be granted before researchers may approach potential research participants, researchers should be sensitive to such local requirements. However, in no case may permission from a community representative or council replace the requirement of a competent individual's voluntary informed consent.[16]

Cultural factors are sometimes used to justify departures from the accepted standard of disclosure of information in the informed consent process. Practices in developing countries include withholding diagnoses from patients who become research subjects[17] and not disclosing key elements that comply with the substantive ethical standard of informed consent, such as the use of placebo controls, the process of randomizing subjects into different groups in a clinical trial, and the expected efficacy (or lack of efficacy) of a method being tested.[18]

One article describes the problems a researcher encountered concerning informed consent in a randomized clinical trial of adjuvant treatment for breast cancer conducted in Vietnam[19] (see chapter 4 for a detailed account of the study and the question of whether the study can properly be considered exploitative). The investigator "found himself uncertain about the application of American standards of informed consent in the Vietnamese setting."[20] After consultation with Vietnamese persons and cultural experts, he concluded that "American standards would not be acceptable to Vietnamese physicians, political leaders in Vietnam, or the vast majority of Vietnamese patients."[21]

A key reason for this unacceptability is the paternalistic practice of medicine in Vietnam, in which patients do not participate in medical decision-making, but look to their physicians to tell them the appropriate treatment. As a result, the researcher contended that it was necessary to withhold from potential subjects any elements of the consent process that would convey uncertainty by the treating doctor. Specific items that were to be left undisclosed were alternative therapies and an explanation that the subject's proposed treatment had been determined by randomization. The investigator requested that the IRB in his American medical school "waive the requirement for informed consent, at least with respect to the subject of randomization."[22] After many months of deliberation and considerable negotiation, the final version of the consent form did include the key elements of informed consent, "though with somewhat less detail than is typical in a US consent form."[23] Yet the authors acknowledge that it is unclear whether the women in the study understood that their treatment was determined by randomization.

Multinational research requires adherence to internationally accepted standards, one of which is disclosure to research subjects even if similar disclosure is not made to patients in the clinical practice of medicine. The example of reluctance to disclose a physician's uncertainty about the best treatment rests on customary medical practice in such countries. The authors of the article describing the breast cancer study in Vietnam argue that "trying to force [the US mode of] consent on the physicians [in Vietnam] risked losing their cooperation with the project because of the tone of cultural imperialism that it would convey."[24] Yet even if it would be inappropriate to force a non-customary process on physicians in the practice of clinical medicine in their own country, research is not medical practice. To withhold information from potential research subjects who are unfamiliar with the research enterprise is to actively foster the therapeutic misconception and thereby fail to promote the subjects' ability to understand the distinction between clinical practice and research.

In meetings of its international project, the National Bioethics Advisory Commission discussed the Vietnam breast cancer study. The Commission also heard testimony and gained additional evidence from the literature confirming that in many cultures, a diagnosis of cancer is not made to the patient but instead to the patient's family. The question that arises from this cultural context is whether practices common in the clinical setting should be acceptable in the research setting, especially when the local or national cultural practices depart significantly from international standards of informed consent in research.

The NBAC report contains two recommendations that address this issue:

Recommendation 3.1: Research should not deviate from the substantive ethical standard of voluntary informed consent. Researchers should not propose, sponsors should not support, and ethics review committees should not approve research that deviates from this substantive ethical standard.[25]

Recommendation 3.2: Researchers should develop culturally appropriate ways to disclose information that is necessary for adherence to the substantive ethical standard of informed consent, with particular attention to disclosures relating to diagnosis and risk, research design, and possible post-trial benefits.[26]

The second of these two recommendations is intended to show respect for cultural differences and at the same time adhere to the fundamental principle of respect for persons that underlies the requirement for gaining adequately informed, voluntary consent in research. The Nuffield Council report is in essential agreement with the NBAC recommendations, affirming that "obtaining genuine consent to research from participants is vital in ensuring that respect for persons is promoted."[27]

Even if the custom of routinely withholding complete information from patients with certain diseases might be defended in ordinary medical practice, it poses a severe challenge to the need to adhere strictly to the substantive ethical standard of disclosure required for research involving human subjects. Potential subjects cannot make an informed decision to participate without knowing that they may not receive a proven treatment that will benefit them. To enroll individuals in research who are not provided with these key items of information is an unacceptable departure from the substantive ethical standard of disclosure required for informed consent.

Spousal authorization for research

The tension between adherence to the requirement of respect for persons, on the one hand, and the cultural traditions that treat women as less than full persons, on the other, raises even more profound problems for research conducted in such places. In a workshop devoted to building capacity for ethical review of reproductive health research in Zimbabwe, participants from several African countries were sharply divided over whether permission from a woman's husband should be sought for her participation in research.[28] People on both sides of the issue included women as well as men. Perhaps not surprisingly, the younger women were opposed to any need to obtain the husband's consent while older women at the workshop expressed the more traditional view that permission from the women's husbands would be appropriate, if not necessary. In a similar workshop held in Bangkok for reproductive health personnel from Asia, most of the women subscribed to the need for spousal authorization. However, one male participant, an obstetrician/gynecologist from Vietnam, argued that the requirement violates the woman's autonomy.

The commissioners on NBAC had heated debates regarding the role of husbands or fathers of adult women who were potential research subjects. Some commissioners argued that cultural sensitivity required adherence to the norms and customs in non-Western countries. Others replied that to permit husbands to continue to exercise power over their wives' choices is to perpetuate a system that oppresses women and subordinates them to men. The Commission did eventually make an important distinction between the totally unacceptable situation in which a husband or father of an adult woman may place her in research without an opportunity for her to refuse, and the marginally acceptable (to many commissioners) situation in which a husband's or father's permission is granted in addition (usually prior) to the informed consent of the woman. A gray area in this debate is whether the researcher should first gain the man's permission to approach the woman before she can be asked to provide her informed consent. Some people contend that the man's permission is required in some cultures before the next step can be taken, and it would be a serious violation of cultural norms to try to circumvent the custom. It was even suggested that a researcher who sought to do so might be placed at some risk.

Eventually, NBAC agreed on a position that became Recommendation 3.9 in its final report:

Researchers should use the same procedures in the informed consent process for women and men. However, ethics review committees may accept a consent process in which a woman's individual consent to participate in research is supplemented by permission from a man if all of the following conditions are met:

a it would be impossible to conduct the research without obtaining such supplemental permission; and

b failure to conduct this research could deny its potential benefits to women in the host country; and

c measures to respect the woman's autonomy to consent to research are undertaken to the greatest extent possible.

In no case may a competent adult woman be enrolled in research solely upon the consent of another person; her individual consent is always required.[29]

The Nuffield Council report, here again, is in essential agreement with NBAC. Nuffield requires that genuine consent be obtained from each participant, but also acknowledges the need to obtain assent from the community or a senior family member before approaching individuals. Nevertheless, Nuffield says: "If a prospective participant does not wish to take part in research this must be respected. Researchers must not enrol such individuals and have a duty to facilitate their non-participation."[30]

I have a lingering ambivalence with regard to the allowable exception that could require researchers to approach a woman's husband or father before speaking to her. Although I strongly favor not allowing any exceptions, my ambivalence stems from two different yet related considerations. The first is a degree of uncertainty about the nature of evidence provided in support of the contention that the research could not be conducted without spousal authorization of women's participation. This may simply be a claim made by researchers or consultants without genuine evidence. Claims about what customs will allow are sometimes based on mere surmise rather than on hard evidence. On the other hand, it may actually be true that some research would be disallowed if spousal authorization were prohibited. If that is so, it gives rise to the second consideration.

The second consideration lies in the tension between the adequacy of the utilitarian justification and the strength of a leading ethical principle. The principle of individual informed consent is normally thought to be inviolate, with only the rarest of exceptions permitted – if at all. Opening the door to spousal consent in those parts of the world where adult women are subordinated to men perpetuates a practice that violates the principles of respect for autonomy and equal respect for women. But what if the only condition enabling women in a Muslim country to have access to, say, a long-acting injectable contraceptive would be the successful completion of research in that country, with the proviso that husbands grant permission for participation of their wives? That is the utilitarian justification for bending the rule and creating the exception. The negative consequences for women in the country of *not* conducting the research might be sufficiently great to override the prohibition of spousal authorization in that situation.

The 2002 CIOMS international ethical guidelines include a guideline entitled: "Women as research participants." The guideline itself does not mention spousal authorization, but the topic is introduced in the commentary, under the subheading "Individual consent of women." The text of the commentary says:

[O]nly the informed consent of the woman herself is required for her participation. In no case should the permission of a spouse or partner replace the requirement of individual informed consent. If women wish to consult with their husbands or partners or seek voluntarily to obtain their permission before deciding to enrol in research, that is not only ethically permissible but in some contexts highly desirable. A strict requirement of authorization of spouse or partner, however, violates the substantive principle of respect for persons.[31]

This statement is stronger in defense of women's autonomy than the NBAC recommendation. CIOMS permits the woman to make the choice to consult with her husband or partner, but does not allow the loophole created by NBAC, in which the research ethics committee can allow for spousal authorization if the researcher requests it, along with the relevant evidence. The difference between these two documents is interesting, in light of the fact that the NBAC commissioners were all from the US, whereas the drafting group for the CIOMS guidelines included two persons from developing countries in Latin America, one from Asia, and one from Africa, in addition to two from the US. The all-US NBAC was more inclined to ethical relativism in the matter of respect for women's autonomy than was the international group that drafted the CIOMS guidelines.

Adherence to US rules: universal standards or ethical imperialism?

US federal regulations require that research conducted by US researchers or using US funds outside the United States must be reviewed by a US IRB as well as by a local, regional, or national committee in the country where the research is carried out. Some people contend that this is precisely the right mechanism for adequate protection of human subjects, others argue that approval of proposed research by a US IRB should be sufficient, and still others argue that a research ethics committee in the developing country should suffice. In between these positions is a variety of views about how flexible US regulations should be when research is conducted elsewhere, and whether requiring strict adherence to US rules governing ethical review of research is a form of "ethical imperialism" or "colonialism" in the conduct of research. A study commissioned by the National Bioethics Advisory Commission reported that 77 percent of US and 85 percent of developing country researchers surveyed recommended the use of international guidelines instead of US regulations to cover joint projects.[32]

In 2002 the US Office of Human Research Protections issued new rules for non-US institutions seeking to register with the US government in order to be authorized as sites for research by US investigators or others using US funds. (The technical name for this authorization is Federalwide Assurance for International [non-US] Institutions.) The foreign institution must indicate on the application which statement of ethical principles governs the institution in fulfilling its responsibilities for the protection of the rights and welfare of human subjects in research. The application states that international institutions may elect the Declaration of Helsinki as their statement of ethical principles for the protection of human subjects in research. If the box marked "Other" is checked and other principles are named, a copy of those principles must be submitted with the application.

Adherence to the statement of ethical principles is not sufficient, however. A much more burdensome requirement is compliance with US federal regulations or an accepted equivalent. If the institution applying for this authorization intends to comply with regulations other than those required in the United States, the alternative regulatory standards must be those considered to be generally consistent with the US Common Rule (the US Federal Policy for the protection of human subjects in research). The list of accepted international regulations and those of other countries includes the national regulations of Canada (1998) and the Indian Council of Medical Research Ethical Guidelines issued in 2000.[33]

It is much easier to agree to comply with ethical principles than to succeed in conforming to detailed regulations governing research. This is because ethical principles are always stated in general terms and often require interpretation for each situation to which they are applied, whereas regulations are very specific and cover a wealth of topics in minute detail. To appreciate the difference between principles and regulations, it is important to recall the distinction between substantive ethical standards – the domain of principles – and procedures for ethical conduct, stipulated by specific rules or regulations. There is, however, a gray area where procedures become so important they shade into ethical principles. An example is the requirement for due process in legal or ethical proceedings, where the rights of accused individuals are protected by procedural safeguards.

Leading controversies in research ethics can be traced to this confusion between ethical principles and specific rules of procedure, in particular, rules governing the informed consent process and the need for prior review of research by an independent committee. Confusion surrounding this distinction with regard to informed consent exists in several areas: whether research subjects should be required to sign the consent document; how much information must be included in the consent form and the legalistic language in which the forms are written; whether the consent process may be conducted orally or whether a written form is necessary; and the methods for obtaining proper informed consent from illiterate subjects. About some of these topics there is widespread consensus; about others, sharp disagreements. Most researchers appear to agree that strict adherence to US regulations is not only unnecessary, but can be counterproductive in seeking to safeguard the rights of research subjects. The following is a sample of responses by international researchers to the survey commissioned by NBAC.

Signing consent forms

One respondent said:

In [Latin American country] particularly those with limited reading ability, are very hesitant about signing things. This is also not a procedure typically followed by native researchers. Our insistence on informed consent was seen as culturally insensitive but was accepted out of understanding of our needs to satisfy our funding agency and government regulations (bureaucracy was certainly understood).[34]

And another commented:

In some places, in some cultures, you don't sign an informed consent. It really freaked them out . . . once I wanted to enroll the patient for a tuberculosis treatment protocol. And I explained to him that it was very straightforward . . . And I could see he was profoundly disturbed to sign the informed consent. And then he asked me, "When am I going to die?" I said, "Why are you saying that?" "Well, you asked me to sign all these papers." And to him, it was a sign that he was so ill that the written thing in the Muslim culture is something very strong: it's the will. It's the testimony at the end.[35]

Oral versus written consent documents

According to some US researchers who responded to the NBAC survey, the requirement of written informed consent documents is meaningless. One researcher said:

So we get it translated into [local language] and back translated and it's delivered. And we field test it and we check it for its understandability, and we negotiate back and forth with [name of institution] here first to make sure it's acceptable to them. Then we send it out into the field and we get lots of thumb prints and signatures on that page. And everybody at [institution] is very happy . . . and the OPRR [Office for Protection from Research Risks] is happy with the way it's read to the patients verbatim . . . But the process is not clearly obtaining consent.[36]

Unfamiliarity with modern science

There is, however, a more serious problem than whether research subjects should be required to sign consent forms, whether the consent process may be entirely oral rather than written, and whether the consent document may depart from the detailed, legalistic format typically created by pharmaceutical sponsors and found in US institutions. That is the lack of familiarity with or understanding of the nature of scientific research or the basic concepts of modern science. A couple of comments from researchers attested to this problem. The first comment virtually dismisses the meaningfulness and necessity of seeking informed consent in such situations.

Informed consent is a joke. It is not possible to claim a person who has never heard of a bacteria or virus is informed about what a vaccine or drug is doing or how their participation fits into any such study. The protection these people have is only from 1) the ethics of the investigators and 2) developing country review boards.[37]

The second comment makes essentially the same point, but urges that groups not be precluded from serving as research subjects in this situation:

In many African languages, there is no word for "research" or "science". The word used is generally the same as the word for "medicine". There is no concept of an experiment, placebos, etc. and despite the best translation of the most simply worded consent form, many adult subjects still have no understanding of the difference between being a research subject and receiving medical treatment. This should not be a reason to exclude these people from research; in fact they are often the population who will benefit most from the research and the only population in whom the studies can be done, e.g. persons at risk of naturally acquired malaria or other tropical diseases.[38]

The NBAC report acknowledges that unfamiliarity with modern science is a formidable obstacle to obtaining meaningful informed consent to research from potential subjects. Yet the report notes that "if they are willing to devote the time and effort to do so, researchers often are able to devise creative measures for overcoming these barriers."[39] One example provided is an explanation of the concept of an immune response. The researcher obtaining consent made an analogy with people who guard houses, describing cells in the immune system as a sort of "watchman in your blood."[40]

The dilemma that arises when a population lacks familiarity with modern scientific concepts and with the very notion of scientific research is profound. Either the research should not be conducted because of the impossibility of obtaining genuinely informed consent, with the likely result that the population will have no chance of realizing the potential benefits of the research; or the research should go forward in violation of the cardinal principle that requires understanding and voluntary consent on the part of each adult subject invited to participate. One possible solution is to place strict limits on the type of research conducted in such situations. My own view is that at least the following requirements should be met:

1 it would not be possible to carry out the study on a population capable of understanding the nature of research and scientific concepts that are carefully explained to them;
2 the disease or condition being studied is a major health problem in the population; and
3 prior agreements are in place to make successful products or other benefits of the research available to the population at the conclusion of the study.

Adherence to these conditions would rule out conducting certain types of research in some places. For example, the amount of genetic research being conducted around the world is greatly increasing, with significant interest in the genetic characteristics of relatively isolated populations. The likelihood of any benefits accruing to these groups is remote, although the research may contribute to scientific knowledge. The risks of the research are minor, usually only those of taking a blood sample. Many people defend genetic studies on the grounds of the low risk to participants, and there is some merit to that position. That justification relies solely on an assessment of the risks to subjects and the judgment that those risks are reasonable in light of the expected contributions to scientific knowledge.

The problem with the justification arises with the next step: concluding that the benefit–risk ratio is sufficient to override the requirement of adequate informed consent of the subjects of research. This is a point on which reasonable people disagree. That disagreement is understandable, as there is no fixed order for ranking the two applicable ethical principles: *respect for persons*, which underlies the informed consent requirement, and *beneficence*, which requires a favorable balance of benefits over harms in research.

Research ethics committees: do they provide adequate protection?

If informed consent is the first safeguard for the protection of human subjects of research, the second is prior review by a properly constituted, independent research ethics committee. But this mechanism can serve as a safeguard for protecting subjects only if researchers submit proposed studies to such committees in the first place, and beyond that, the committees have all the relevant information about the studies. A significant complication arises when the researcher provides the US institutional committee responsible for approving the research with inadequate information or even fails to submit a research proposal.

Two cases that attracted media attention when they were uncovered demonstrate that this can be a complicated business in international collaborative research. One case involved a researcher from the Harvard School of Public Health, who had originally come from China and maintained contact with his former colleagues in the region where the research was carried out. The research, a series of epidemiologic genetic studies, was conducted in a rural province in China and included subjects who were poor and relatively uneducated. The studies involved taking blood samples from participants, and in some cases, performing lung function tests and x-rays. Following an allegation that Harvard researchers were conducting unethical research in China, the US Office of Human Research Protections investigated and found numerous violations. One violation was the researcher's failure to submit some studies to the IRB at the Harvard School of Public Health and to obtain the committee's approval prior to initiating the study. Another violation was making changes in the research in some studies that had received prior approval, but without obtaining approval for the changes (one of which was an increase in the amount of blood drawn from the participants).

OHRP also found the informed consent documents inadequate, not only because they were too complex for rural Chinese farmers to understand, but also because they lacked information about subjects' right to refuse to participate. An additional concern was that the research participants could have been placed at risk of job discrimination if their employers found out about health problems diagnosed in the studies. There was no information about the degree to which confidentiality of the subjects could be adequately protected in China.

In public statements, both the Dean of the Harvard School of Public Health and Harvard's President acknowledged the researcher's wrong-doing, as well as some shortcomings in the process of ethical review of research at the school. Steps have since been taken to improve the quality of the review process. In addition, the Dean reprimanded the researcher for seeking to suppress reports of the episode that had begun to appear in Chinese media and for attempting to interfere with criticisms of his research.[41]

A second case also involved research carried out in China. In this instance, however, the problem lay in the failure of a professor of microbiology to seek IRB approval at the University of California at Los Angeles (UCLA) for analyzing data and blood samples obtained by a collaborating researcher in China whom the US professor had trained. This might seem like a minor infraction of the rules were it not for the fact that the research maneuvers in China involved injecting malaria-infected blood into Chinese AIDS patients. This so-called "malariotherapy" is based on a discredited theory, viewed by most scientists as medical quackery. The malaria injections would never have been approved in the US, and therefore, the failure of the UCLA professor to obtain IRB approval for his part in the research was compounded by the unscientific and unethical procedures that yielded the blood samples.[42]

These episodes at Harvard and UCLA occurred at highly respected US institutions that have had rules and procedures governing human subjects research for decades. Although some developing countries are still in the process of establishing committees and issuing regulations or ethical guidelines for research, other countries have had longer experience. Even in the latter places, there is evidence that noncompliance persists. A scientist in India complained about the failure of researchers and sponsors to comply with the rules in his country:

A serious problem arises when medical investigators and companies go about clinical trials without paying the slightest attention to the Ethical Guidelines for Biomedical Research on Human Subjects issued by the Indian Council for Medical Research (ICMR) ... I cannot understand why this document is ignored by investigators and companies.[43]

This scientist responded to an interviewer's question about whether there is a lack of awareness among Indian medical professionals about ethical requirements, saying "Yes, there is a serious lack of awareness of ethical guidelines among health care professionals – not doctors alone, administrators, politicians, media, etc. . . . Of course, guidelines are not laws . . . However, it is a fact that in practice the guidelines are not often observed."[44]

Numerous questions surround the mechanism of committee review, including at least the following: Must committees in developing countries have the same composition and rules of procedure as stipulated in the US regulations for IRBs? When research is sponsored by the US government and conducted entirely by developing country researchers, is review by a properly constituted local or national committee in that country sufficient? Or must the research proposal also be reviewed by a US IRB? When research proposals are reviewed by an IRB in each country, how should any disagreements between the two committees be resolved?

Available evidence suggests that at least in the US, IRBs rarely, if ever, try to communicate with host-country ethics review committees. US IRBs do not seek pertinent information from the developing country committee, or even ascertain whether a qualified committee exists. One article that discusses review of international clinical research makes a specific recommendation in this regard:

IRBs from a wealthy sponsor country should ensure that a viable local ethics committee in the proposed host country will review the protocol . . . A viable local IRB should be viewed as a critical resource for IRBs in sponsor countries . . . Better communication between the sponsor country IRB and the local IRB could help resolve [any] disagreements . . . Further, the sponsor country IRB and the local IRB may possess complementary expertise and may be able to carry out a better review working together than either could working alone.[45]

If US IRBs were to adopt this novel recommendation, it could succeed in raising the review of multinational research to a new level, improving both the quality of the review process and protection of the rights and welfare of research subjects in developing countries.

What the guidelines say

All of the international guidelines contain provisions regarding ethical review of research. Paragraph 13 of the Declaration of Helsinki lists among its Principles for All Medical Research:

The design and performance of each experimental procedure involving human subjects should be clearly formulated in an experimental protocol. The protocol should be submitted for consideration, comment, guidance, and where appropriate, approval to a specially appointed ethical review committee, which must be independent of the investigator, the sponsor or any other kind of undue influence . . . The committee has the right to monitor ongoing trials. The researcher has the obligation to provide monitoring information to the committee, especially any serious adverse event. The researcher should also submit to the committee, for review, information regarding funding, sponsors, institutional affiliations, other potential conflicts of interest and incentives for subjects.

This is probably the most detailed provision in the Declaration of Helsinki. It specifies what information researchers must submit to the committee and includes a monitoring function for the committee, but does not stipulate anything about membership requirements or detailed rules of procedure.

The UNAIDS Guidance Document for research on preventive vaccines for HIV/AIDS contains a succinct but strong provision regarding ethical review of proposed research: "HIV preventive vaccine trials should only be carried out in countries and communities that have the capacity to conduct appropriate independent and competent scientific and ethical review."[46] According to the commentary under this guideline, the sponsor is responsible for ensuring that the country's capacity for review is adequate. If it is not, the sponsor should be responsible for ensuring that adequate structures for review are in place before initiating any research. The UNAIDS guidance includes the same provision as the CIOMS guidelines, requiring membership on review committees from the country and community where the research is conducted in order to ensure that the research is analyzed by individuals familiar with the prevailing conditions.

The NBAC report generally concurs with the position taken by other guidelines and reports. Recommendation 5.2 is as follows:

The US government should not sponsor or conduct clinical trials in developing countries unless such trials have received prior approval by an ethics review committee in the host country *and* by a US Institutional Review Board. However, if the human participants protection system of the host country or a particular host country institution has been determined by the US government to achieve all the substantive ethical protections outlined in Recommendation 1.1, then review by a host country ethics review committee alone is sufficient.[47]

The second half of the guideline permits a waiver of the requirement for US review just so long as the host country can provide "equivalent protection" of the rights and welfare of human subjects.

This statement is one of the few international guidelines that explicitly allows ethical review only in the host country as sufficient for the protection of human subjects. In making this recommendation, NBAC attempted to strike a balance between ensuring that research subjects in developing countries are adequately protected and refraining from an "imperialistic" imposition of US committee review. The OHRP is the US agency that must determine whether the host country has equivalent protections. The criteria for determining whether the protections in the host country are equivalent will depend on whether the country complies with one of the items stipulated on the OHRP list of accepted international and national regulations.[48]

The Nuffield Council report is, for the most part, again in basic agreement with the NBAC report. The Nuffield report notes that review by ethics committees may be ineffective for various reasons, including lack of training of members, lack of experience, and lack of financial resources. Unlike NBAC, however, Nuffield does not mention the possibility of a waiver of review by a committee in the sponsoring country. It requires ethical review of research in both the host and the sponsoring country: "We recommend that externally-sponsored research projects should be subject to independent ethical review in the sponsor's country(ies) in addition to the country(ies) in which the research is to be conducted." In case of disagreement between committees in the developed and developing countries, the report suggests that negotiation between the committees may be required. Finally, if irreconcilable differences remain, "a committee may choose not to approve the research."[49]

The CIOMS debates

The CIOMS draft guidelines posted on its website for comments contained two separate guidelines on ethical review committees. Guideline 2 included a wealth of details about the operation and function of ethical review committees in general. A different guideline, entitled "Ethical review of externally sponsored research," contained the following text:

An external sponsoring agency and individual investigators should submit the research protocol to ethical and scientific review in the country of the sponsoring agency, and the ethical standards applied should be no less exacting than they would be for research carried out in that country. Appropriate authorities of the host country, including an independent national or local ethical review committee *or its equivalent* should ensure that the proposed research is responsive to the health needs and priorities of the country and meets the requisite ethical standards [emphasis added].

At the CIOMS consultation convened to review and comment on that version of the draft guidelines, sharp disagreements arose. Some participants questioned why the guideline is needed at all, arguing that it is paternalistic and imperialistic. This group contended that responsibility for review should lie entirely with the host country. Although no one in this forum argued that it would be sufficient for ethical review to take place only in the industrialized country sponsoring the research, strong views were expressed that ethics review committees are required in both the sponsoring and host countries. Some objected to the idea that there could be a satisfactory "equivalent" to an independent national or local ethical review committee, arguing that those words should be struck from the guideline. It was not clear what would constitute an "equivalent" or who would have the ultimate say over whether the alternative mechanism would, in fact, be equivalent. In the final version of the guidelines issued in 2002, the words "or its equivalent" were dropped from this guideline.

Substantial debate also occurred over a statement in the commentary under the draft guideline that full, detailed committee review by the sponsoring country may not be necessary, but may be limited to "ensuring compliance with broadly stated ethical standards." The reasoning for this position is that members of the host country's committee are familiar with matters relevant to the conduct of the research in the local context, whereas members of an IRB in the sponsoring industrialized country are likely to be wholly ignorant of such matters.

It is surely true that most members of US IRBs are woefully ignorant of circumstances in developing countries. But it remains unclear precisely what familiarity with the local context is meant to ensure. It is one thing if the local committee has knowledge of a situation that is relevant to the protection of the rights and welfare of prospective subjects, for example, a context in which women may be subordinated to men's dominance and therefore rendered vulnerable, or whether prospective subjects would have adequate understanding of the information to be provided in the informed consent process and document. Such items are appropriate and necessary for the committee to ascertain. But it is quite another thing if the local committee would act to perpetuate customs such as spousal authorization of women's consent to participate in research. Members of research ethics committees could seek to apply universal ethical standards, or they could be adherents of cultural customs that may depart from international standards.

One commentator on the draft guideline cited statistics from the NBAC report indicating that ethical review of research in many developing countries is either nonexistent or less than adequate. The commentator concluded that "full review by IRBs in all involved countries is therefore necessary."[49] Objections to the division of labor specified in the commentary under the CIOMS draft guideline were sufficiently strong to warrant revision in the final version of the guideline. Instead of limiting the role of committee review in the sponsoring country, the roles of the respective committees are made a matter of emphasis:

Committees in the external sponsoring country or international organization have a special responsibility to determine whether the scientific methods are sound and suitable to the aims of the research; whether the drugs, vaccines, devices or procedures to be studied meet adequate standards of safety; whether there is sound justification for conducting the research in the host country rather than in the country of the external sponsor or in another country; and whether the proposed research is in compliance with the ethical standards of the external sponsoring country or international organization.

Committees in the host country have a special responsibility to determine whether the objectives of the research are responsive to the health needs and priorities of that country. The ability to judge the ethical acceptability of various aspects of a research proposal requires a thorough understanding of a community's customs and traditions. The ethical review committee in the host country, therefore, must have as either members or consultants persons with such understanding; it will then be in a favourable position to determine the acceptability of the proposed means of obtaining informed consent and otherwise respecting the rights of prospective subjects as well as of the means proposed to protect the welfare of the research subjects.[50]

Written comments submitted in response to the draft version posted on the CIOMS website took opposing sides on key provisions. Both the international trade association representing the pharmaceutical industry and US PhRMA questioned why ethical review by a committee in the sponsoring country is necessary. The comment submitted by US PhRMA said:

We understand that there is a strong movement to ensure that consistent ethical standards are applied to research globally. However, requiring ethics committee review in the sponsor's country as well as local ethics committee review would impose the standards of the sponsor's country on the host country. Moreover, we are not confident that ethics committees in sponsoring countries will have the resources to be involved routinely in such activity, given the demands already placed on such committees for review of protocols to be conducted in their own country.

This comment by PhRMA could be interpreted as a stance against the alleged ethical imperialism of adopting the industrialized country's standards. However, it could also reflect the recognition that ethical review in developing countries is less well developed and committees have had considerably less experience in reviewing the ethical aspects of research than is the case in the US and Western Europe. Consistent with the frequent observation that it is easier and faster to initiate and conduct research in developing countries than in industrialized countries, representatives of the pharmaceutical industry clearly have an interest in limiting the role of industrialized-country research ethics committees in research that industry sponsors in developing countries.

From a procedural point of view, CIOMS used a transparent, iterative process in developing these guidelines. Posting two successive versions of the draft guidelines on its website, and inviting critical commentary from all interested parties, was about as fair a procedure as could be carried out in arriving at a set of guidelines intended to have universal application.

As noted above, some commentators on the CIOMS draft guidelines expressed the strong view that it is paternalistic to require review by sponsoring countries, since it presumes – without any evidence – that developing countries lack the capacity for adequate ethical review. The survey of US and developing country researchers commissioned by NBAC contained comments on this same issue and included especially useful quantitative and qualitative information about ethical review in developing countries.

More disagreements: the NBAC survey

Quantitative results included the information that US IRBs reviewed 91 to 96 percent of the studies described by US researchers responding to the survey; 87 percent of studies also were reviewed by an ethics review committee in the host country. In 29 percent of studies reported by US researchers, the host country ethics review committee was established because of US regulations. On the qualitative side, respondents to the survey reported varying experiences with host country IRBs. Some researchers remarked on the evolution of committees from mere rubber stamps to a more rigorous process of review. Others said that host country research ethics committees needed to learn more about ethics. Still others expressed more critical views, such as the following:

[Local IRB members] may be people that are not all equipped intellectually, culturally, scientifically to deal with the issues you are asked to deal with. And therefore, you introduce a false sense of security and conformity with the rule, with the letter, when the spirit is actually vacant.

And another:

In some cases, the developing country ethical review is actually a process of seeking permission to conduct research, and no ethical questions are raised at all. Developing country review boards are often more concerned about the financial aspects of the study than about ethics.[51]

A more disturbing finding was that host country ethics committees are likely to have conflicts of interest when it comes to approving a study because "research generates desperately needed resources that often provide an incentive to host country governments, ethics committees, and local researchers to accept such projects."[52] This indicates that it is not only some researchers in developing countries who are prey to the financial and other rewards resulting from their collaboration in research sponsored by industrialized countries or drug companies; ethical review committees may also fall prey to such influences.

Comments by researchers critical of the requirement that US regulations should govern the work of research ethics committees in developing countries express a range of views from one extreme to the other. The following views were expressed by researchers surveyed by one of the studies commissioned by NBAC:

The United States dictating how another sovereign nation should behave in the operation of medical research is a bit arrogant and colonialistic.

And:

Rigid enforcement[s] of US regulations in another country or culture, however well-meaning or politically correct, are a form of cultural imperialism and are often resented by [the] local population.

And:

It is humiliating to ask bodies in other countries to accept US rules.[53]

An even stronger view was that:

The formation of an IRB board according to US standards does nothing to assure appropriate review . . . The check of having the Board look like a US board seems to be designed to assuage consciences here rather than to get at the real issue of whether the protocol will be reviewed by members who are truly objective and include a "member of the community" who can provide input into the study.[54]

Several respondents said it would be preferable to use international ethical guidelines for multinational studies instead of insisting on adherence to the detailed federal regulations from the United States. But some did believe that US research regulations go a long way toward protecting the rights and welfare of subjects when US researchers conduct studies in other countries.

Conclusions

What is a reasonable way to try to resolve the profound differences expressed both by researchers who responded to the NBAC survey and by the various commentators on the CIOMS draft guidelines? A first step is to determine just what these commentators disagree about. One view contends that imposing US regulations on developing countries is "colonialistic" or a form of "ethical imperialism." This implies a rejection of universally applicable ethical principles for research, leading to the conclusion that ethical relativism in the conduct of research is perfectly acceptable since each country should be permitted to fashion and apply its own ethical rules. A more nuanced interpretation of this view would not reject the ethical principles underlying the US or any other industrialized country's regulations, but would hold that some of the specific procedures are unnecessarily rigid or even ridiculous. This latter interpretation properly distinguishes between substantive and procedural ethical concerns, whereas the former position seems merely to be a slogan that labels a practice as "ethical imperialism" without an accompanying analysis.

A different disagreement exists between those who say that adherence to an industrialized country's regulations or procedures does not succeed in protecting the rights or welfare of research subjects in developing countries, and their opponents who say that those regulations or equivalent international guidelines are the only mechanism that can ensure such protections. To adjudicate this disagreement would require a great deal of empirical evidence, facts, and information that are not readily at hand. It would require much more than the anecdotal information contained in the *Washington Post* series and the other reports of malfeasance in research sponsored by some of the most prestigious US institutions and by industry.

NBAC's survey of US researchers who conduct studies in developing countries is an additional source of information, but the study was somewhat limited in scope, as well as highly selective. As noted earlier, PhRMA, the US pharmaceutical industry trade association, used its influence to prevent the attempt by NBAC to extend its survey beyond university-based researchers to include drug-company researchers. When spokespersons for industry refuse to cooperate with efforts to bring information to the public, one can only wonder what they are worried about and whether they have something to hide.

An additional area of disagreement appears in the comments of some researchers in the NBAC survey who said that studies were delayed or even thwarted by bureaucratic rules and the detailed provisions of US regulations. To the extent that such delays or blockage of research prevented much-needed health benefits from reaching the population in a timely manner or at all, improvement in the process of ethical review of research is clearly needed. If, on the other hand, the only ones who lost out were the researchers themselves or the drug companies eager to begin marketing successful products of research, then it is not the interests of the developing country that have been adversely affected. This serves as a reminder that it is not the research itself that confers benefits on the population in poor countries, but the availability of the fruits of the research once products are demonstrated to be safe and effective.

NOTES

1. Department of Health and Human Services, 45 CFR 46 (1991); Council for International Organizations of Medical Sciences, *International Ethical Guidelines for Biomedical Research Involving Human Subjects* (Geneva: CIOMS, 2002); World Medical Association, Declaration of Helsinki, 2000; International Conference on Harmonization (ICH), *International Conference on Harmonization: Harmonized Tripartite Guideline*, Guideline for Good Clinical Practice (1997).
2. Final Report of the Advisory Committee on Human Radiation Experiments, *The Human Radiation Experiments*, chapter 16 "Subject Interview Study" (New York: Oxford University Press, 1996), 459–481.
3. Paul S. Appelbaum, Loren H. Roth, and Charles W. Lidz, "The Therapeutic Misconception: Informed Consent in Psychiatric Research," *International Journal of Law and Psychiatry*, 5 (1982), 319–329; Nancy M. P. King, "Experimental Treatment: Oxymoron or Aspiration?" *Hastings Center Report*, 25 (1995), 6–15.
4. Sharon LaFraniere, Mary Pat Flaherty, and Joe Stephens, "The Dilemma: Submit or Suffer," *Washington Post* (December 19, 2000), A1.
5. Karen DeYoung and Deborah Nelson Washington, "Latin America is Ripe for Trials, and Fraud; Frantic Pace Could Overwhelm Controls," *Washington Post* (December 21, 2000), A1.
6. *Science*, 293:5532 (August 10, 2001), 1024.
7. "Scientist Sanctioned Over Drug Trial in India," *The Gazette Online*, the Newspaper of the Johns Hopkins University, 31:12 (November 26, 2001). Available at http://www.jhu.edu/~gazette/2001/26nov01/26india.html.
8. K. M. Seethi, "Clinical Drug Trials: Bioethics Under Siege," EPW Commentary, *Economic and Political Weekly*, India (August 25–31, 2001), no page numbers.
9. R. Krishnakumar, "Drug Trials and Ethics," *Frontline*, India's National Magazine, 18:17 (August 18–31, 2001), no page numbers.
10. Seethi, "Clinical Drug Trials."
11. Nancy Kass and Adnan A. Hyder, "Attitudes and Experiences of US and Developing Country Investigators Regarding US Human Subjects Regulations," in NBAC, *Ethical and Policy Issues in International Research*, II (2001), B-51.
12. There is no written documentation of this successful stonewalling by the trade association. However, as the senior consultant to NBAC on this project, I was privy to information provided by NBAC staff and other consultants regarding the responses of industry to this and other requests from NBAC.
13. Kass and Hyder, "Attitudes and Experiences," B-52. For a condensed version of the report by Kass and Hyder, see Nancy Kass, Liza Dawson, and

Nilsa I. Loyo-Berrios, "Ethical Oversight of Research in Developing Countries," *IRB: Ethics and Human Research*, 25:2 (2003), 1–10.

14. For criticism of this position, see Ruth Macklin, *Against Relativism: Cultural Relativism and the Search for Ethical Universals in Medicine* (New York: Oxford University Press, 1999).

15. For a full discussion of acceptable and unacceptable forms of ethical relativism, see Macklin, *Against Relativism*.

16. NBAC, *Ethical and Policy Issues*, 43.

17. Jeremy Sugarman, Benjamin Popkin, Judith Fortney, and Roberto Rivera, "International Perspectives on Protecting Human Research Subjects," NBAC, *Ethical and Policy Issues*, II (2001), E-1-11; Kass and Hyder, "Attitudes and Experiences of Investigators."

18. Sugarman et al., "International Perspectives."

19. R. R. Love and N. C. Fost, "Ethical and Regulatory Challenges in a Randomized Control Trial of Adjuvant Treatment for Breast Cancer in Vietnam," *Journal of Investigative Medicine*, 45 (1997), 423–431.

20. Ibid., 424.

21. Ibid.

22. Ibid., 429.

23. Ibid., 430.

24. Ibid.

25. NBAC, *Ethical and Policy Issues*, 38.

26. Ibid., 40.

27. Nuffield Council on Bioethics, *The Ethics of Research Related to Healthcare in Developing Countries* (London: Nuffield Council on Bioethics, 2002), 73.

28. Workshop conducted by the Reproductive Health and Research program of WHO in November 2000 in Zimbabwe.

29. NBAC, *Ethical and Policy Issues*, 45.

30. Nuffield, *Ethics of Research*, 77.

31. CIOMS, *International Ethical Guidelines*, 73.

32. NBAC, *Ethical and Policy Issues*, 80.

33. All US federally supported human subject research will comply with the requirements of any applicable US Federal regulatory agency as well as one or more of the following:

    a The US Federal Policy for the Protection of Human Subjects, known as the Common Rule (e.g., Subpart A) or the US Department of Health and Human Services (DHHS) regulations at 45 CFR 46 and its Subparts A, B, C, and D;

    b The May 1, 1996, International Conference on Harmonization E-6 Guidelines for Good Clinical Practice (ICH-GCP-E6), Sections 1 through 4;

    c The 1993 Council for International Organizations of Medical Sciences (CIOMS) International Ethical Guidelines for Biomedical Research Involving Human Subjects;

    d The 1998 Medical Research Council of Canada Tri-Council Policy Statement on Ethical Conduct for Research Involving Humans;

    e The 2000 Indian Council of Medical Research Ethical Guidelines for Biomedical Research on Human Subjects; or

f Other standard(s) for the protection of human subjects recognized by US
Federal Departments and Agencies which have adopted the US Federal
Policy for the Protection of Human Subjects, http://ohrp.osophs.dhhs.gov/
humansubjects/assurance/filasurt.htm/, accessed May 29, 2003.

34. Kass and Hyder, "Attitudes and Experiences," B-24.
35. Ibid.
36. Ibid.
37. Ibid., B-27.
38. Ibid.
39. NBAC, *Ethical and Policy Issues*, 41.
40. Ibid.
41. This episode was reported in a number of articles, including the following:
Joe Stephens, "Harvard Research in China is Faulted: Safety, Ethics Problems of Tests Noted," *Washington Post* (March 30, 2002), A6; Josh Gerstein,
"Harvard President Laments China Study," *Boston Globe* (May 15, 2002),
A12.
42. Rebecca Trounson and Charles Ornstein, "Researcher Violated Rules,
UCLA Says," *Los Angeles Times* (April 16, 2003).
43. R. Krishnakumar, "Clinical Trials Should Promote Health Care," interview
with Dr. M. S. Valiathan, *Frontline*, India's National Magazine, 18:17 (August
18–31, 2001), no page numbers.
44. Ibid.
45. Daniel W. Fitzgerald, Angela Wasunna, and Jean William Pape, "Ten Questions Institutional Review Boards Should Ask when Reviewing International
Clinical Research Protocols," *IRB: Ethics and Human Research*, 25:2 (2003),
14–18 at 14.
46. Joint United Nations Programme on HIV/AIDS (UNAIDS), *Ethical Considerations in HIV Preventive Vaccine Research* (2000), 21.
47. NBAC, *Ethical and Policy Issues*, 83.
48. See above, n. 33.
49. Nuffield, *Ethics of Research*, 141.
50. Peter Lurie, comments submitted to CIOMS.
51. CIOMS, *International Ethical Guidelines*, 31
52. Kass and Hyder, "Attitudes and Experiences," B-51.
53. NBAC, *Ethical and Policy Issues*, 82.
54. Kass and Hyder, "Attitudes and Experiences," B-54.
55. Ibid., B-52.

6   Making drugs affordable

An underlying premise in arguments defending recent clinical trials is that the chief way of providing medical benefits to populations in resource-poor countries is to develop cheaper drugs – presumably affordable, but probably less effective than those considered to be the "best current treatments" in industrialized countries. It is no doubt true that some newly developed drugs may turn out to be as good as or even better than the best current preventive or therapeutic methods, while at the same time being much cheaper and therefore more affordable to the governments or the people in developing countries. Nevertheless, the controversy that has raged over the use of placebo controls in research aimed at finding cheaper drugs relies on one formulation of the research question: Is the intervention being studied better than nothing? (when nothing is what the majority of such populations normally get).

Defenders of the placebo-controlled methodology insist that a different research question would be inappropriate: Is the experimental drug as good, or almost as good, as the best treatment used in the industrialized world? One line of defense contends that because the healthcare system currently provides nothing, a placebo-controlled design is ethically acceptable and contextually relevant. Another line of argument maintains that the answer obtained by comparing the experimental drug with the best current medication is less scientifically reliable than results obtained from a design using placebo controls.

The most persuasive argument in defense of the HIV maternal-to-child transmission studies is that no reliable data existed regarding the rate of HIV transmission from mother to child without any intervention in the settings where the trials were conducted; therefore, there could be no way of knowing whether the experimental drug lowers the rate of transmission beyond what occurs naturally. This claim becomes less persuasive in those settings where some data about the natural rate of transmission were available. Whatever explanation lies at the bottom of the insistence on the placebo design, the quest for an "affordable" treatment is the fundamental rationale for doing the research in the first place.

Aside from the ethical problem of using placebos in a control group instead of an existing, effective treatment for the condition being studied, there are two additional shortcomings of this approach to finding affordable drugs. The first is that people in the poorest countries still may not be able to afford the newly developed drugs. This was certainly true of the placebo-controlled AZT trials initiated in African countries. The second is that the newly developed drugs may not be nearly as good as the best current methods, but may nonetheless be considered "good enough" for people who would otherwise get nothing in these countries. If placebo-controlled clinical trials conducted in resource-poor countries are one manifestation of a double standard – one for the rich and one for the poor – a second example is the search for second-rate treatments. If a second-rate treatment could make people better off than they would be if they got no treatment, the justification is analogous to that of giving placebos to the control group who would get no treatment outside the clinical trial. Nevertheless, the justification that "something not-so-good is better than nothing at all" has to be taken seriously. This illustrates the complexity of arguments that invoke the concept of "double standards."

These questions have to be examined against a much larger backdrop in many developing countries. First is the enormous difficulty of actually getting necessary drugs to the population. This requires a reasonably efficient system of distribution, as well as assurance that the medications are safe, in addition to being affordable. Guaranteeing affordable prices is only one factor among several that impede access to drugs by large numbers of poor people in developing countries. Another requirement is rational selection of drugs by governments that purchase them for use in the country. A study by the World Bank revealed that the selection and purchase of drugs in many African countries was inefficient and wasteful. Drugs are chosen and purchased in the absence of a national list of essential drugs and without treatment guidelines that aid in choosing the best treatment for common diseases in the most cost-effective manner. Other important factors are reliable supply systems for drugs and appropriate infrastructure in the country to ensure proper distribution of medications where they are needed.[1]

The cost of preventive and therapeutic methods is not fixed in stone. Prices have historically been determined almost entirely by market forces, with few exceptions such as arrangements by co-sponsors of research, for example the World Health Organization, to make successful products available to the public sector in developing countries following the research. The Joint United Nations Programme on HIV/AIDS (UNAIDS) has been instrumental in negotiating lower prices for drugs to treat HIV/AIDS in resource-poor countries. Given an array of recent developments, it is no longer credible to insist that the only or best way of providing affordable drugs for resource-poor countries is to conduct placebo-controlled trials of newer, presumably cheaper medications.

What reasonable alternatives exist that could make effective drugs currently used in industrialized countries affordable and therefore accessible to poor countries? This chapter explores four ways, with considerable overlap among them, especially the first three. They are categorized separately, primarily to elucidate their respective features. The four pathways are:

1 differential pricing and financing of essential drugs;
2 negotiations followed by prior agreements before research is initiated;
3 collaborative efforts among international agencies and the creation of public–private partnerships;
4 manufacture of generic copies of patented drugs in developing countries and sale of such drugs to other poor countries.

One additional prospect is worth mentioning. Several pharmaceutical companies have made outright donation of free drugs, chiefly for medications to treat or reduce the incidence of HIV. Boehringer-Ingelheim offered to provide a free supply of Nevirapene, a relatively inexpensive drug demonstrated to be effective in reducing maternal-to-child HIV infection, for a period of five years to countries that have an adequate system to administer the drug properly. Pfizer agreed to provide a drug in South Africa to AIDS patients affected by cryptococcal meningitis.[2] In 2001, the pharmaceutical giant, Novartis, pledged to donate Glivec, a new cancer drug, to people who could not afford to purchase it.[3]

On the one hand, these companies can be commended for their charitable acts, as "they represent an assumption of moral agency and moral responsibility."[4] At the same time, a critical view holds that "dependence on charity morally degrades the individual, by fostering dependence, promoting an attitude of humility toward the giver, and relieving the recipient of the ability to set terms and negotiate the terms of receipt."[5] Despite the apparent good will demonstrated by these charitable acts, and even setting aside the above criticism, this approach cannot possibly meet the needs of the populations in resource-poor countries.

An article criticizing the traditional approach that has relied on the United States providing aid to poor countries refers to "the perennial and stale aid debate: Should we give more? Does it work?"[6] This critique contends that the term "aid" is patronizing and divides the world into "donors" and "recipients." The preferred approach, according to the article, is the formation of genuine partnerships. On this model, "rich countries should pay their fair share, based on their privileged place in the world economy," while developing countries would take responsibility for implementing and monitoring plans to improve the health status of their populations, and play a role in decision-making, as well. This model is best exemplified by several of the public–private partnerships described below.

Differential pricing

Differential pricing (also called "equity pricing" or "preferential pricing") is defined as follows: "setting the price of essential drugs in a way that reflects countries' ability to pay, as measured by their level of income."[7] The concept of differential pricing must be distinguished from the situation throughout the world in which different countries charge different prices for the same drugs. The latter situation results from the policies that individual countries have established to regulate the drug market for their own people. Variations also are traceable to taxes, import duties, wholesale and retail mark-ups, and other factors. Different prices for drugs in various countries are typically not the result of a deliberate and systematic international policy, whereas "differential pricing" has precisely that aim and structure.

The aim of a policy of differential pricing is obvious: to enable low-income countries to gain access to essential drugs for their populations.[8] In low-income countries, both the government and the majority of the population are unable to afford drugs that are needed for a variety of treatable conditions. In most higher income countries, public funding is the major source of health financing, ranging from over 95 percent in the UK, more than 90 percent in Norway, to a low of less than 50 percent in the US. Most high-income countries finance 70 percent or more of the healthcare costs for the population. In contrast, public funding accounts for considerably less than 40 percent of healthcare financing in almost all low-income countries, with India, Myanmar, Georgia, and Cambodia among the lowest, contributing less than 20 percent of the healthcare costs. In effect, out-of-pocket payments, rather than prepaid insurance, are the primary mechanism in most poor countries.

Although the US ranks lowest among the industrialized countries in public funding for health care, the percentage of out-of-pocket payments is still somewhat lower than in several of the high-income countries (Norway, Japan, and France are leading examples). The consequence of this pattern of financing is that the poorest people are burdened with the largest percentage of out-of-pocket expenses, with drugs being the main expenditure.

The World Health Organization has defined "essential drugs" in a statement that includes a prescriptive element: "Essential drugs are those drugs that satisfy the health care needs of the majority of the population; they should therefore be available at all times in adequate amounts, and in the appropriate dosage forms, and at a price that individuals and the community can afford."[9] WHO contends that public budgets for essential drugs could be increased, as governments of developing countries are responsible for the performance and regulation of the health system. At the same time, prices are set by manufacturers, based largely on what the market will bear. This is primarily the case when pharmaceutical products are under patent protection for a defined period. During that period, there is little or no competition and prices are higher than when there are five or more competing products. Companies make most of their money from the sale of drugs in high-income countries, a pattern that has led to much less investment in research and development of products that would primarily be used in developing countries, such as much-needed anti-malarial drugs.

It may come as a surprise to learn of considerable variations in the retail price of a single drug, both within and among countries. Pharmaceutical products are often not priced lower in low-income countries, and several factors beyond the manufacturer's selling price contribute to differences in the cost of drugs. These factors include import duties, taxes, and wholesale and retail mark-ups. WHO has called for "equity pricing" or "differential pricing," which would result in much lower manufacturers' selling prices for certain drugs in low-income countries.[10] Since about 1994, experience with differential pricing of vaccines has resulted in a successful reduction of the cost in low-income countries – as low as 1 percent of the price charged in the US. Another area in which successful agreements have been made to lower prices for low-income countries is that of contraceptives. This has occurred with the help of an international United Nations agency (United Nations Fund for Population Activities [UNFPA]), a nongovernmental organization (International Planned Parenthood Federation), and a US-based private foundation (the Rockefeller Foundation).

It is not surprising, however, to discover that the pharmaceutical industry is generally opposed to anything that would remove the pricing of drugs from the free market. A statement by PhRMA, the US pharmaceutical industry trade association, is a classic defense of free-market capitalism:

Competitive market forces, which promote innovation and help to control expenditures for pharmaceutical products in the US, have never been allowed to operate freely in most other parts of the world. In most European countries and Japan, the government is the largest purchaser of pharmaceuticals. Governments use their power to negotiate directly or to indirectly control the prices of pharmaceutical products; in some cases, they also compel companies to make investments in their country. While the mechanics of each price-control system differ widely from country to country, the end result is the same. Research-based pharmaceutical companies are prohibited from charging a free-market price for the products they discover and develop. These price controls distort the market for pharmaceuticals and undermine the vitality of the European and Japanese pharmaceutical industries.[11]

One need not be a thoroughgoing critic of the capitalist system to question whether there ought to be some exceptions to the rule that everything has a price, and the price should be set by the free-market economy. The sale and purchase of some things is altogether prohibited: human babies, for example. Until the accelerating trend in the 1990s toward privatization, European countries considered the healthcare system to be exempt from the free-market system that operated for other commercial products. The US government has always treated health care as a commodity, except for the two government-financed programs, Medicare for the elderly and Medicaid for the poor – programs that are underfinanced and destined for further cuts. What the PhRMA association criticizes as a system that "distorts the market," others praise as a system that enables people even in industrialized countries of Europe and Japan to obtain drugs at more affordable prices than residents of the US are required to pay.

Early efforts to reduce the high price of AIDS drugs were made by UNAIDS. In 1997, UNAIDS began a collaborative effort that involved three pharmaceutical companies and health officials in Chile, Côte d'Ivoire, Uganda, and Vietnam. Despite this initiative, prices for antiretroviral drugs remained too high for most people in these countries. This marked the beginning of a trend, however, with manufacturers of antiretrovirals beginning a successive lowering of prices.

It is hard to pinpoint the exact moment when the campaign began to convince drug companies to reduce the price of life-prolonging, health-preserving AIDS drugs for poor countries. In February 2001, Oxfam, a charity based in Oxford, England, began a campaign to force multinational drug companies to cut prices in poor countries. The charity did not limit its appeal to HIV/AIDS, but included other drugs such as powerful antibiotics. In addition, Oxfam attacked the patent laws that have not permitted poor countries to import cheap, generic drugs from other countries without fear of retaliation.[12]

Merck, one of the largest pharmaceutical companies, offered in early March 2001 to sell two of the AIDS drugs it manufactures to developing countries at much lower prices than it charges in the US. The company offered to sell Crixivan for $600 per patient per year and Stocrin for

$500 per patient per year. (At the time, the US prices for these drugs were $6,000 and $4,700, respectively.) Shortly thereafter, Merck agreed to cut the prices of these same two drugs in Brazil, but at higher prices than it had offered to the other developing countries ($1,029 for Crixivan and $920 for Stocrin). The company said it based its decision on which countries would qualify for its lowest price on the United Nations Human Development index. The company's decision for Brazil was described as "bowing to pressure from that country's government, which was threatening to develop generic copies of one of the drugs." The Brazilian government also exerted pressure on Hoffmann-La Roche, a manufacturer of another AIDS drug, to lower its price.[13]

In May 2001, still another company took the step of lowering the price of a drug for developing countries, in this case, a powerful medicine to treat malaria. Novartis, a Swiss drug company, agreed to cut the price of Riamet for sale to the World Health Organization. Priced at about $12 in industrialized countries, Novartis agreed to sell the drug to WHO for $2 for a full treatment. Altogether, between March and May 2001, the companies that agreed to sell their AIDS drugs at significantly reduced prices in developing countries were Merck, GlaxoSmithKline, Bristol-Myers Squibb, and Abbott Laboratories.[14]

Pharmaceutical companies have traditionally opposed tiered pricing for drugs, even when it enables poor countries to purchase medications that would otherwise not be affordable for their populations. The worry is that the phenomenon known as "parallel trade" or "parallel importing" will undermine the profits of the companies. The pharmaceutical industry's trade association has this to say:

Parallel trade refers to the purchase of trademarked or patented goods in one country, and the subsequent export of those goods to another country, without the consent of the patent or trademark owner. The practice of parallel importation is driven by price differences among markets. In many countries, the government fixes the prices at which medicines can be sold or are reimbursed; it is this government interference in free markets that can encourage parallel trade. Parallel imports are generally exported from a low-price market and resold at a higher price in another country . . . Some may believe that parallel trade that results from government price controls will lead to lower prices of medicines for patients. However, recent evidence demonstrates that this does not necessarily happen. Often only the middleman benefits from buying low and selling high. In the end, patients on both ends of the unfair parallel trade process lose.[15]

If it is indeed true that parallel trade arrangements do not result in lower prices for consumers, it demonstrates only that some form of regulation is required to ensure that the people who need the medications benefit from this cost-saving measure.

Increasingly, individual companies have taken the step of voluntarily lowering the price of drugs in some of the poorest countries. According to the International Federation of Pharmaceutical Manufacturers Associations (IFPMA), the following are examples:

Abbott offers its two antiretrovirals medications, Ritonavir and Kaletra, and its HIV test, Determine, in Africa at no profit to the company.

Bristol-Myers Squibb provides the patent for Zerit [d4T] at no cost to treat AIDS in South Africa. It offers full transparency in pricing for drugs in Africa and offers to sell ddI and Zerit below cost.

GlaxoSmithKline offers discounted HIV/AIDS to developing nations, including all of sub-Saharan Africa. The preferential pricing policy is expanded to include additional AIDS-fighting drugs.[16]

United Nations agencies devoted to public health are helping to facilitate and promote these new developments. In May 2000, WHO and UNAIDS together launched a program called the Accelerated Access Initiative, which called for improved access to antiretroviral drugs to treat HIV/AIDS. Several major companies responded to this call, providing evidence that industry had begun to accept plans to lower prices to ensure equity pricing, as well as to collaborate with other partners to increase availability of their products. International public–private partnerships have also resulted in companies making drug donations to poor countries for other diseases, such as African sleeping sickness, malaria, and leprosy.[17]

Some people have voiced skepticism – or even cynicism – about the motivation of drug companies in reducing their prices and for giving away free medications. Physicians in India viewed the motives of Novartis – the company that promised to give away its new cancer drug to poor people – with suspicion. The Indian doctors suspected that the company sought to establish a firm foothold in the large drug market in their country, the population of which is predicted soon to surpass that of China.[18] Still, it is worth recalling the words of the nineteenth-century British philosopher, John Stuart Mill: "[U]tilitarian moralists have gone beyond almost all others in affirming that the motive has nothing to do with the morality of the action, though much with the worth of the agent. He who saves a fellow creature from drowning does what is morally right, whether his motive be duty or the hope of being paid for his trouble." If reducing the prices of manufactured drugs or giving them away free of charge can succeed in making beneficial treatments affordable and accessible to the world's poor, then it matters little if industry's leaders make such decisions in order to enhance their image and prestige, or whether they do so from the motive of unalloyed altruism.

The approach of reducing prices can be faulted for some of the same reasons that donations of free drugs are ethically problematic: "such offers are fraught with conditions, time and quantity based limitations and a continuing dependence of the developing country's health care planning on the good-will of commercial organizations."[19] In the case of Glivec, the cancer drug that Novartis promised to make available to people all over the world, the initial offer came with strings attached. The company said that if a generic version of the drug were to be developed and made available in India, a country with manufacturing capability, the company would cease to provide it. That is, in fact, what happened when India approved a generic version for sale in 2003. Novartis withdrew its program, leaving it to Indian companies to provide the drug to patients in that country.[20] Ethical criticism aside, this piecemeal approach is hardly sufficient to meet the demand for drugs in the many developing countries whose populations need them but cannot afford them. Big, international pharmaceutical companies are significant actors in the field of medicine and health, but acting alone they could not realistically be expected to shoulder the burden.

Nevertheless, differential pricing is a big step in the right direction. A WHO report concludes that the most feasible approach would be to have two broad price bands – one for low-income countries, the other for the rest of world.[21] Many questions remain unanswered and details need to be addressed: How should priorities be set, both for health problems and particular products? Which countries should benefit from the scheme? What should be the role of international agreements? Who would be responsible for financing differentially priced drugs? How can developed countries be persuaded not to demand the same low prices?[22] Even if adequate answers can be given to these questions, it is likely that efforts in addition to equity pricing will have to move ahead simultaneously in order to meet the challenge of fighting the global burden of disease.

Prior agreements

Negotiating prior agreements to make successful products of research available following clinical trials is a further step beyond that of individual, voluntary efforts by industrial sponsors to donate or lower the price of drugs. Prior agreements (also known as "community benefit agreements") are "arrangements made before research begins that lay out a realistic plan for making effective interventions or other research benefits available to the host country after the study is completed."[23] The parties involved in making prior agreements will typically include the industrial sponsor of the research and the host-country government. Others that may be involved are international agencies such as the World Health Organization, governmental agencies that sponsor research, such as the NIH in the US and the Medical Research Council (MRC) in the UK, representatives from communities from which research subjects are drawn, and nongovernmental agencies such as the International AIDS Vaccine Initiative (IAVI). IAVI describes its mission as follows: "[W]orking to speed the development and distribution of preventive AIDS vaccines . . . IAVI's work focuses on four areas: mobilizing support through advocacy and education; accelerating scientific progress; encouraging industrial participation in AIDS vaccine development; and assuring global access."[24] One of IAVI's efforts in seeking to ensure global access is working with the World Bank, the European Community, and other partners to establish Vaccine Development and Purchase Funds. These funds are designed to encourage companies that manufacture vaccines to invest in the global AIDS vaccine enterprise. IAVI funds research and development of AIDS vaccines only under contracts stipulating that resulting products must be made available in developing countries rapidly after licensure, at reasonable prices and in sufficient quantities.[25]

On a rather pessimistic note, the NBAC report says that few prior agreements had been negotiated at the time the report was in preparation. The report cites as a rare example a letter of intent from VaxGen, the US biotechnology company that sponsored a phase III HIV/AIDS vaccine trial conducted simultaneously in Thailand and the US. The letter promised assistance to the government of Thailand to produce and distribute the vaccine there if the vaccine proved effective. Although few details were spelled out in the letter of intent, and agreements of this sort are not legally binding, this development was an encouraging sign of the willingness of at least some industry sponsors to enter into such agreements.

There has been considerable skepticism about the feasibility of negotiating prior agreements, and critics have objected to making such negotiations a condition of approval of proposed research in resource-poor countries.[26] The following are the main reasons that have been cited by way of objection:

- It would serve only to delay or prevent new drug research in developing countries.
- There are financial, logistical, and other formidable obstacles to the use of prior agreements.
- It is not the prevailing international standard.
- It would go far beyond the influence one can reasonably expect researchers to have to effect changes in a country's health policy.

- It would create a double standard with regard to clinical research conducted in the United States.
- Prior agreements can always be breached.[27]

Some of these objections are more difficult to reply to than others, but all of them invite a response.

A reply to the first objection is that even if it is true that research will be delayed or prevented altogether, the population will have lost nothing because the benefits of the research would not be available to them anyway.[28] The second objection envisages an array of obstacles to negotiating prior agreements. Here again, although the observation is true, such things as payments, royalties, subsidies, technology, and intellectual property, as well as distribution costs, are matters that should be discussed before any research is initiated. The parties to these negotiations should be representatives of all stakeholders, including relevant officials from the host country and members of the communities from which research subjects are drawn.

The third criticism – that an obligation to negotiate prior agreements is not and has not been the prevailing international standard – is factually true but irrelevant to efforts to improve the current situation. Ethical judgments are not descriptive statements about what is, in fact, the case but rather, prescriptive statements about what ought to be the case. A requirement to negotiate prior agreements should be seen as a move in the direction of moral progress when industry or developed countries sponsor and conduct research in developing countries.

Another criticism is that an obligation to negotiate prior agreements would go far beyond what researchers can be expected to accomplish in the countries in which they conduct studies. Of course this is true if one expects researchers to bear the burden by themselves. As already noted, however, the parties to prior agreements will be numerous stakeholders, and should include individuals and agencies with more power and authority than the medical scientists who actually conduct clinical trials. Research ethics committees rarely, if ever, have considered post-trial benefits as part of their deliberations in reviewing research proposals. Since one of the tasks of such committees is to ensure that the burdens and benefits of research are equitably distributed, an assessment of post-trial benefits should be an integral part of their review of proposals.

When the US National Bioethics Advisory Commission discussed this topic, some commissioners criticized the requirement that prior agreements be negotiated for research conducted in developing countries, on the grounds that the requirement does not currently exist for research conducted in the United States. Critics argued that it would create a

double standard. Although it is true that negotiating such prior agreements for research conducted in developing countries would privilege
the poor people in those countries, that points to a shortcoming in the
United States rather than a flaw in the idea that prior agreements should
be negotiated. To the extent that patients in the United States have ready
access to the fruits of research through private insurance, health maintenance organizations, or government-sponsored insurance, the need to
ensure access through prior agreements does not exist. For those individuals in the US who either lack insurance or have inadequate insurance to
grant them access to the results of successful research, the shame lies with
the healthcare system – or lack of it – in the richest country in the world.
It is lack of political will in the US that leaves millions of people with no
health insurance or insufficient insurance. If requiring prior agreements
for research in resource-poor countries would constitute a double standard, it is the responsibility of political leaders and policy-makers to raise
the standard in the US.

The final criticism is that any of the parties to prior agreements might
breach their obligations to make effective interventions available after the
conclusion of a trial. This is true, of course, so long as such agreements
are not legally binding. But the very fact that people can and do break
agreements of all sorts – including promises and legal contracts – does not
mean that the practice of making such agreements and contracts should
be altogether abandoned. That people break laws does not constitute a
reason for not having laws in the first place. The same can be said for
ethical obligations and informal agreements. The fact that some people
do not honor them is not a good reason for eliminating such obligations
and agreements.

An obligation to undertake negotiations to make the products of
research available in developing countries where the research is conducted
is a relatively new idea. But it is not the only new idea at a time when
the impetus to provide relief from disease and the benefits of medical
progress is gaining momentum.

International collaborative efforts and public–private partnerships

The 1990s witnessed a large growth in the formation of public–private
partnerships, as well as a variety of collaborations among international
agencies. The alliances described below are some of the leading examples
of this current trend, which includes the Global Alliance for Vaccines and
Immunization (GAVI), the International AIDS Vaccine Initiative (IAVI),

and the Global Fund to Fight AIDS, Tuberculosis, and Malaria. Others established since 1996 include the Consortium for Industrial Collaboration in Contraceptive Research; International Partnership for Microbicides; Malaria Vaccine Initiative; Medicines for Malaria Venture; and Pediatric Vaccine Initiative. These organizations operate by using funds to support research directed at products. They work more like investments than like grants, the projects being managed much as they would be in an industrial portfolio. The industrial partners in these ventures benefit by using patents that result from their collaboration to develop products they can sell more profitably in industrialized countries. The commitment they make by entering into the partnership is to provide products to developing countries at reasonable prices.[29]

These developments are a response to the failure of reliance on industry and market forces alone to bring health benefits in the form of drugs, vaccines, and other medical products to poor people in developing countries. A related factor contributing to the establishment of public–private partnerships has been the restrictions imposed by intellectual property rights, discussed later in this chapter.

The Concept Foundation

An early entrant into the field of public–private partnerships was the Concept Foundation. This organization opened its first office in November 1989 in Bangkok, Thailand, with the aim of bringing improvements in reproductive health services to developing countries. The Concept Foundation owes its existence to an initiative taken by the Special Programme of Research, Development and Research Training in Human Reproduction (HRP) of the World Health Organization. HRP has been a leader in seeking to create public–private partnerships for the development and distribution of affordable contraceptives throughout the developing world. In preparation for establishing the Concept Foundation, HRP's 1988 report said:

With the realization that large commercial pharmaceutical companies are not interested in sponsoring several of WHO/HRP's new contraceptive technologies, WHO/ HRP is faced with immediate problems in completing development of these products. After much deliberation within the World Health Organization, United Nations Population Fund and the World Bank, and as a direct response to the need of the WHO Special Programme, a decision has been taken to create an independent non-profit entity for the management of intellectual property relating to products required for the public sector in developing countries.[30]

As early as 1990, the foundation began to be involved in different public–private partnerships with pharmaceutical companies. Its first and most important product has been the injectable contraceptive, Cyclofem, which the Concept Foundation licenses for use in various countries. In fact, the Concept Foundation was initially established for the purpose of managing intellectual property for this product and for licensing it out. The Foundation embarked on an intensive program of technology transfer to its licensees in order to develop manufacturing capabilities in several countries. Cyclofem began to be available following that process.[31]

The vaccine gap

The failure of market forces to meet the health needs of developing countries is strikingly illustrated by the lack of availability of vaccines for children in resource-poor countries. This failure is especially noteworthy since vaccines have traditionally been cheaper to manufacture and distribute than most other medications. The pharmaceutical industry has apparently had little interest in vaccines, despite their great public health value. As of 2000, vaccine sales constituted only 4 percent of the more than $400 billion per year of the pharmaceutical market. According to WHO, one in four children throughout the world did not receive routine immunization with the six basic vaccines against polio, diphtheria, whooping cough, tetanus, measles, and tuberculosis in 1998. The proportion of children immunized each year against these six diseases actually declined between 1990 and 1998.[32] Moreover, the "vaccine gap" between children in industrialized countries and those in resource-poor countries has widened. Until a few years ago, children in Africa and in Europe received the same childhood vaccines. Today, children in industrialized countries typically receive eleven or twelve vaccines, whereas children in developing countries receive six or seven. This gap is likely to continue to widen due to the higher costs of newly developed vaccines.

Traditional vaccines have been relatively inexpensive. Products based on old technologies have typically cost only a few cents to manufacture. The total cost of vaccines in the past was around US $1 to $2 per vaccine. Newer vaccines, such as *Haemophilus influenzae* type b, meningococcal conjugate, and pneumococcal conjugate vaccines, are now being introduced into the childhood immunization programs of many industrialized countries at a cost of tens of dollars per vaccine. For example, the cost of a pneumococcal conjugate vaccine in the US is around $50 per dose, and three or four doses are needed. Newer vaccines use techniques of biotechnology and, as a result, will be much more expensive to manufacture and consequently to purchase. Poor countries where these vaccines are most needed cannot now afford them and will be unable to afford them in the future without assistance from wealthier nations or international organizations. If a gap already exists between vaccines that are widely available in industrialized countries and those accessible to people in resource-poor countries, the newer technologies provide a reason why the gap is likely to increase.[33]

In 1999 the Global Alliance for Vaccines and Immunization was established to ensure the protection of children against diseases that can be prevented by vaccines. GAVI promotes new vaccine development, coordinates existing immunization programs, and works at international, regional, and national levels. A special concern is to accelerate research and development of vaccines for developing countries.

According to GAVI:

Intent on increasing child immunization around the globe, GAVI and its financial arm, The Vaccine Fund, act as a fuel energizing the efforts of poorer countries to provide children with basic access to life saving vaccines. Using a revolutionary performance based approach to funding, The Vaccine Fund motivates national governments to secure a more promising future for their children. Simultaneously, the alliance aims to stimulate the vaccine industry to develop and supply vaccines vital to low-income countries.[34]

GAVI has succeeded in attracting numerous public and private partners for this effort, including: the United Nations agencies, WHO, the World Bank, and UNICEF; private foundations, the Bill and Melinda Gates Children's Vaccine Program and the Rockefeller Foundation; the industry group, International Federation of Pharmaceutical Manufacturers Associations as well as public health and research institutions and national governments. One of the mechanisms GAVI has established is the Vaccine Fund, which provides direct support to countries in two forms. The first is provision of new and under-used vaccines, accompanied by safe immunization equipment; the second is in the form of funds to assist governments in strengthening their immunization services. GAVI is a good illustration of a successful alliance among public and private partners that has already demonstrated the ability to raise funds and provide them directly for necessary vaccine products and services.

Combating malaria

One of several public–private partnerships actively combating malaria is Medicines for Malaria Venture (MMV). This was among the first of these public–private partnerships established to tackle a major global disease. The initiative arose from discussions between the World Health

Organization (WHO) and the International Federation of Pharmaceutical Manufacturers Associations (IFPMA). Other partners in the early, exploratory discussions were the Global Forum for Health Research, the Rockefeller Foundation, the World Bank, the Association of the British Pharmaceutical Industry, and the Wellcome Trust, a British philanthropic foundation. According to MMV:

> The countries today that are most affected neither have the resources nor the money to combat malaria. The figures justifiably raise alarm bells. It is estimated that every 30 seconds one child dies from the disease. Vaccines remain for the moment a distant dream and medicines are at present our only effective option, continuing to be the major tool in the cure and prevention of malaria. However with growing resistance to existing drugs, there is urgency to discover new drugs at affordable prices for poor disease endemic countries. The major obstacle to the discovery of new antimalarials is the lack of global investment in drug R&D. The enormous costs and time needed for R&D, with little or sometimes no prospect of return upon investment once a drug is fully registered and on the market, are dissuasive to the large pharmaceutical groups. MMV therefore finds its origins in the failure of the market system to provide the required incentives for wide scale R&D in new medicines to treat malaria.[35]

Another global partnership to fight malaria was established in November 1998. This organization, called Roll Back Malaria, was founded by several international agencies, including the World Health Organization, UNICEF, and the World Bank.[36] According to Roll Back Malaria, the existing antimalarial drugs (which are generally cheap and most readily available) are becoming increasingly ineffective. Where evidence shows that existing drugs are no longer working, WHO urges countries to switch to combination therapy as a strategy to minimize resistance. The partnership formed by Roll Back Malaria acts to support governments in seeking to provide adequate supplies of materials and drugs, as well as new sources of financing and training of personnel.

The approach taken by public–private partnerships in forging plans to help developing countries has considerable overlap with the approach calling for prior agreements to make products available. One illustration is an agreement between Bayer AG, the German pharmaceutical company, and MMV, seeking to develop and test a new malaria medicine for which Bayer holds the patent rights. The manufacturer says that previous studies of the new substance show that the drug is twenty to thirty times more effective and takes effect more rapidly than other malaria medications. The first clinical trials were scheduled to begin in 2003. According to the agreement, the drug company will develop and supply the finished product, while WHO/MMV will monitor and distribute the product in developing countries through their health systems. The price is to be set at a level permitting treatment of all segments of the population who suffer from malaria in these countries. Bayer will market the product in industrialized countries, in an example of two- or multi-tiered pricing.

The goal of MMV in this partnership is eventually to eradicate malaria. The means to that goal is to have a new malaria drug available and accessible approximately every five years to countries where malaria is endemic. The objective of making malaria drugs affordable is secured by the cooperative agreement with Bayer, which is one of the first such alliances for developing a new medicine for use in developing countries.[37]

Another public–private partnership involving MMV as one of the partners was announced in October 2001, this time with the pharmaceutical company, GlaxoSmithKline, and researchers at the University of California at San Francisco (UCSF). Under this three-way agreement, MMV provides the funding for research and development of a malaria drug, with the industrial and academic partners providing substantial in-kind contributions. UCSF is involved in this collaboration because its scientists have studied the mechanism by which the malaria parasite attacks and degrades red blood cells to obtain basic nutrients. The mechanism involves an enzyme, which may provide a clue to developing medications that inhibit the enzyme. Scientists at the company, GlaxoSmithKline, have also worked on finding inhibitors for closely related enzymes, and the company has agreed to contribute what it has learned along with laboratory facilities and other services. GlaxoSmithKline holds patent rights to inhibiting compounds specifically in the area of malaria treatment and prophylaxis, and the company has agreed to contribute certain of these patent rights under the new partnership.

The Global Fund

One of the newest and most promising developments is the initiative taken by several United Nations agencies to forge public–private partnerships aimed at making needed drugs available in poor countries that are unable to afford them. The leading example is the establishment of the Global Fund to Fight AIDS, Tuberculosis, and Malaria. The call for creation of a huge fund to combat diseases that kill or disable millions of people in poor countries came from both Gro Harlem Brundtland, the former Director General of the World Health Organization, and Kofi Annan, the Secretary General of the United Nations. Both leaders envisaged the need for commitments from governments in rich and poor countries alike, as well as from private foundations, nongovernmental agencies, and the private sector, to mount this effort. It would require funds not only for the purchase of drugs from manufacturers, but also to mount better educational and prevention programs, build new clinics or enhance existing ones, train healthcare workers, and strengthen the infrastructure in other ways.[38]

Secretary General Kofi Annan called for the establishment of a global fund on AIDS and health at the Organization of African Unity summit in Abuja in April 2001. In his "Call to Action," Annan urged greater coordination among nations and a strong political and financial commitment to support efforts to combat AIDS.[39] Soon thereafter, pledges to the fund began coming in, with the United States initially pledging $200 million and the UK an equal amount. A United Nations General Assembly Special Session on HIV/AIDS took place in New York in June 2001, and the UN adopted a declaration of commitment that set out clear goals for a global battle against HIV/AIDS. As of April 2003, pledges to the Global Health Fund totaled more than 3 billion US dollars. The majority of the pledges were from governments, including contributions from rather poor African countries (Uganda and Zimbabwe). Pledges from governments and multilateral institutions amounted to $3,366,786,167. Other donors included corporations, foundations, other nongovernmental organizations, private individuals, and the Bill and Melinda Gates Foundation, which contributed $100 million.[40]

The first grants awarded under the Global Fund were announced in November 2002. The grants, made to Ghana, provided $6.5 million for HIV/AIDS and TB prevention and treatment. This was to provide HIV/AIDS drugs to 2,000 Ghanaians and TB treatment to 20,000 people in the country. An award announced in December 2002 to Tanzania provided a voucher program to enable pregnant women to buy insecticide-treated mosquito nets to protect their infants against malaria. As this agreement involved the collaboration of private industry that produces and distributes the treated bednets, it is a prime example of the innovative public–private partnerships now being promoted and established.[41] By January 2003, agreements had been signed with China, Haiti, Honduras, Malawi, Morocco, and Sri Lanka.

On January 30, 2003 the fund announced eight new awards to countries around the world: Argentina, Cambodia, Madagascar, Ukraine (two agreements), Indonesia, Panama, and the Lutheran World Federation (the first nongovernmental agency to receive funds), for a total of $66 million. These were part of the first round of proposals approved by the Board of the Global Fund, which committed $616 million over the subsequent two years. The money for Argentina, Cambodia, and Ukraine was for AIDS programs, the funds to Indonesia and Panama were for tuberculosis programs, and those to Madagascar were to reduce malaria-related mortality. The total amount the

Global Fund had committed by the end of January 2003 was nearly $220 million.

In the second round of approvals for funding, the Global Fund awarded ninety-eight separate grants to countries throughout the developing world. Some of these awards targeted only one of the three diseases covered by the fund, whereas others included programs directed at all three. Among the many recipients of grants during the second round were Afghanistan, Cuba, East Timor, Iran, Kazakhstan, Mongolia, Nepal, Pakistan, and Yemen. The Global Fund issued its third call for proposals in March 2003. By that date, the fund had approved two rounds of proposals with a total commitment of $1.5 billion over two years to eighty-five countries (more than one individual award was made to quite a few countries).[42]

The Global Fund formally adopted the stance of encouraging poor countries to purchase generic drugs instead of the more costly brand-name drugs still under patent protections by the big pharmaceutical companies. This approach was designed to enable manufacturers of generics in countries like Brazil and India, which have that capability, to sell their products to other resource-poor countries. Since the role of the Global Fund is to provide grants to countries that apply for them, requiring countries to buy the lowest priced drugs of guaranteed quality will be a more efficient and effective use of the fund's money.[43] However, the World Trade Organization's intellectual property agreement remains a barrier to full access by poor countries to generic copies of medications that are still under patents held by the huge pharmaceutical companies.

Despite the promise inherent in the creation of the Global Fund, some people have expressed extreme disappointment at the level of contributions, especially from the United States. In February 2002, the *New York Times* reported that donations to the fund had fallen far short of the amount initially sought by Secretary General Kofi Annan – at least $7 billion a year – when the fund was established. Advocates for the fund blame the White House, claiming that the $200 million pledge by the US sets a poor example for other countries.[44] However, much to the surprise of many people, in January 2003 President George W. Bush proposed the Emergency Plan for AIDS Relief. Bush asked Congress to commit $15 billion over the subsequent five years, including nearly $10 billion in new money. The money was slated for the most afflicted nations of Africa and the Caribbean. It was not clear precisely how much of those funds would go to the Global Fund. A top fund official was quoted as saying that the administration was committed to $400 million, whereas the amount the fund needed over the subsequent two years was $6.3 billion.[45]

One of the latest entrants into this field of public–private partnerships is the International HIV Treatment Access Coalition (ITAC), aimed at increasing access to antiretroviral (ARV) drugs to the growing number of people with HIV/AIDS in low- and middle-income countries who need them. According to the announcement posted on its website the day the initiative was launched in December 2002:

> ITAC currently unites more than 50 partners including NGOs, donors and governments, people living with HIV/AIDS and their advocates, the private sector, academic and research institutions and international organisations working to overcome the challenges of expanding ARV access. These include more efficient sharing of information and technical data about what works in successful programmes, setting up reliable drug procurement systems, and training health-care workers. The group also aims to galvanise and coordinate donor action and provide much-needed technical assistance to national HIV treatment programmes.[46]

In a report commissioned by the World Health Organization, the Commission on Macroeconomics and Health proposed as the next step forward a joint agreement among pharmaceutical companies and low-income countries, in collaboration with WHO, to set guidelines for pricing and licensing of production of drugs for the low-income countries. These guidelines would work as follows. They would "provide for transparent mechanisms of differential pricing that would target low-income countries . . . and identify a designated set of essential medicines . . . at the lowest viable commercial prices."[47] Although the proposed arrangements would be voluntary, they would have to be backed up by safeguards in order to ensure implementation. The only safeguard currently in place is the mechanism of "compulsory licensing" specified in the World Trade Organization's agreement on intellectual property rights, known as TRIPS.

Manufacture of generic copies of patented drugs and compulsory licensing

This brings us to the fourth pathway designed to make drugs affordable in developing countries. In addition to the failure of market forces to ensure access to drugs, another significant factor contributing to the establishment of public–private partnerships has been the restrictions imposed by intellectual property rights. Although the stated purpose of intellectual property rights – patents, in particular – is to encourage commercial investments in research and development, a current assessment contends that the increasing restrictions in this domain have resulted in stagnation. According to one account: "private ownership of scientific processes and materials and the fragmentation of these ownership rights have resulted in the economically sub-optimal use of assets."[48] Perhaps surprisingly, a former chairman of the giant pharmaceutical company, GlaxoSmithKline, said that "just as science is increasing exponentially, we're getting fields of research that are ring-fenced by patents, and people can't move."[49]

The international trade agreements that protect the financial interests of patent-holders in world markets have begun to come under increasing scrutiny in the health arena. These patent protections are provided by the World Trade Organization (WTO) through its division on Trade-Related Aspects of Intellectual Property Rights (TRIPS). The WTO TRIPS Agreement, which became operative in January 1995, requires all member countries to respect the patents held by pharmaceutical and biotechnology companies, and to pass laws respecting medical patents. Although the patent system serves the interests of manufacturers by guaranteeing a return on their research and development costs, the system is viewed by many to be in the public interest, as well as a benefit to the financial interest of industry. One description of the TRIPS Agreement describes it as "an attempt at the multilateral level to achieve the difficult task of balancing the public health interest in providing incentives for research and development into new drugs with the public health interests of making existing drugs as accessible as possible."[50]

There is one provision in this agreement that enables countries to make an exception to the rule that requires respecting the patent rights of pharmaceutical companies. That provision permits countries to manufacture copies of patented drugs in case of a "national emergency." The mechanism for this is to obtain a "compulsory license" to make a generic copy of a drug, and the patent-holder is paid a reasonable royalty under this arrangement. Somewhat less certain under this provision has been the ability of a country to import a generic copy of a patented drug. An obvious question is what constitutes a "national emergency"? Arguably, the AIDS epidemic in countries with a high prevalence rate would qualify. Does the same hold for countries with a high incidence and prevalence of malaria and tuberculosis?

Drug companies and their international umbrella organization, IFPMA, have long resisted efforts to invoke the provision that would allow countries to make or import generic copies of patented drugs under the compulsory licensing clause. Over a four-year period, the United States came to soften its initial strong opposition to allowing South Africa (and by implication, other countries) to seek compulsory licensing for AIDS drugs.

In 1997 South Africa amended its laws to allow compulsory licensing, and an array of pharmaceutical companies brought suit against the country. At the time, the United States supported industry's position. Congress passed a law in 1999 that contained the following provision, referring to the 1997 South African law:

None of the funds appropriated under this heading may be available for assistance for the central Government of the Republic of South Africa, until the Secretary of State reports in writing to the appropriate committees of the Congress on the steps being taken by the United States Government to work with the Government of the Republic of South Africa to negotiate the repeal, suspension, or termination of section 15 (c) South Africa's Medicines and Related Substances Control Amendment Act No. 90 of 1997.[51]

In a remarkable exhibition of crass endorsement of the interests of the pharmaceutical industry, the Clinton administration initially exerted pressure on the South African government to withdraw or modify this law.[52] However, as a result of bad publicity for taking this position against a poor African country with a raging AIDS epidemic, the Clinton administration eventually withdrew its opposition. However, the pharmaceutical manufacturers' lawsuit continued.

Although many observers expected a reversal of the softened US stance with the arrival of the pro-business Bush administration, that did not happen with respect to South Africa. In fact, the thirty-nine drug multinational companies that had brought suit against South Africa began to negotiate to settle the lawsuit, especially after the European Union, the World Health Organization, and the National AIDS Council in France publicly supported South Africa's position.[53] In April 2001, the companies withdrew their suit, thus allowing South Africa to import cheaper anti-AIDS drugs and other medications.

This move did not end other ongoing battles, however. Since 1998, Brazil has been a major challenger to the international pharmaceutical industry by copying and manufacturing AIDS drugs. State-owned laboratories in that country have produced generic copies of several patented AIDS drugs. Another country in the forefront of this development is India, where private companies have been manufacturing generic drugs. The most prominent of these companies is Cipla Ltd.

In May 2001, the Bush administration threatened trade sanctions against Brazil. The head of the Brazilian HIV/AIDS program called the US position "unacceptable."[54] In a surprising reversal, in June 2001 the US withdrew the complaint it had made against Brazil in the World Trade Organization, agreeing to settle its dispute out of court. This decision by the US was announced on the first day of a three-day meeting at the United Nations General Assembly devoted to the global AIDS crisis.

The agreement between Brazil and the US proposed to establish a joint panel that would deal with patent cases.[55]

With the annual, controversy-provoking Ministerial Conference of the World Trade Organization due to take place in November 2001, there was a general expectation that the WTO would reiterate its firm stance on the TRIPS Agreement, thereby continuing to make it extremely difficult for countries to obtain compulsory licenses to manufacture or import needed drugs for which patents are held by industry. Unexpectedly, however, the anthrax scare in the United States in October prompted a rethinking of the existing structure of patent protections. According to one report:

The US was suddenly faced with a situation where there was a perceived need for immediate access to a product still on-patent, where the exclusive owner of that patent, Bayer in this case, appeared unable or unwilling to offer enough supplies to meet immediate demand. The US government's first instinct was to consider the compulsory license option and seek out alternative manufacturers.[56]

Although the United States eventually resisted overriding the patent for Cipro, held by Bayer AG, the Canadian government did just that by ordering a million tablets of a generic version of the drug from a Canadian company. A spokesperson for Health Canada justified the action by saying: "These are extraordinary and unusual times. Canadians expect and demand that their government will take all steps necessary to protect their health and safety." Bayer, the manufacturer of Cipro, condemned Canada's action, saying that the company was able to meet the demand for Cipro.[57] For its part, the US managed to strike a deal with Bayer.[58]

With these developments as a backdrop, it was natural to wonder what would transpire at the WTO meeting in November 2001. Advocates of compulsory licensing have argued that it is the best alternative among the various efforts designed to provide essential drugs to developing countries, especially for treating HIV/AIDS. The authors of one article argue that "making use of the . . . TRIPS provision or even breaking international trade agreements might be a given developing country's most effective means of providing life-saving medication time-efficiently to its people."[59] A prominent bioethicist concurs:

When developing countries choose not to respect product patents as their only effective means of making available pharmaceuticals necessary to save lives and protect the health of their citizens, doing so is arguably a step forward to greater justice between the developed and developing world; this may be a case where two wrongs make a right, that is where existing global injustices make not respecting product patents, which in the absence of those injustices would be wrong, all things considered, morally justified.[60]

Others have leveled strong criticism at the US for supporting the WTO agreement and imposing or threatening to impose trade sanctions on developing countries that have sought to produce or import inexpensive generic copies of drugs. Oxfam International issued a Briefing Paper early in November 2001, entitled "Eight Broken Promises: Why the WTO Isn't Working for the World's Poor."[61] Broken promise 6, "Global patent rules that safeguard public health in poor countries," accuses the US and other industrialized countries not only of threatening the health of vulnerable communities in developing countries, but also of adhering to double standards:

The US and Canadian governments have shown themselves willing to threaten to override patents at home when faced with bio-terrorist threats to their own citizens. Although no compulsory licences for patented antibiotics were eventually issued, the threat of purchasing low-cost generics was successfully used to bargain down prices.

The Oxfam recommendations in this Briefing Paper include the following statements:

- The social and developmental objectives of TRIPS should be paramount.
- Health obligations should take precedence over intellectual property rights.
- Governments should have an absolute right to introduce compulsory licences in order to meet pressing public-health needs, and to import patented drugs from the cheapest source.

The Declaration on the TRIPS Agreement and Public Health, issued at the WTO Ministerial Conference on November 14, 2001, was not the best that might have been achieved. Nevertheless, it was an improvement over the previous situation, which not only left much uncertainty, but also held a strong presumption against the right of developing countries to gain access to much-needed drugs. Paragraph 4 of the 2001 Declaration states:

We agree that the TRIPS Agreement does not and should not prevent Members from taking measures to protect public health. Accordingly, while reiterating our commitment to the TRIPS Agreement, we affirm that the Agreement can and should be interpreted and implemented in a manner supportive of WTO Members' right to protect public health and, in particular, to promote access to medicines for all.[62]

In light of the statement in paragraph 4, the document goes on to say in paragraph 5 that "Each Member has the right to grant compulsory licences and the freedom to determine the grounds upon which such licences are granted;" and "Each Member has the right to determine what constitutes a national emergency or other circumstances of extreme urgency, it being understood that public health crises, including those relating to HIV/AIDS, tuberculosis, malaria and other epidemics, can represent a national emergency or other circumstances of extreme urgency." These statements make it explicit that the developing countries themselves are the ones to make determinations regarding compulsory licensing and national emergencies, surely an improvement over the previous situation. What, then, are the shortcomings of the Declaration on the TRIPS Agreement?

The Declaration does not go far enough, since it still contains a prohibition against importing inexpensive, generic drugs from countries that have the capability of manufacturing them. Paragraph 6 states:

We recognize that WTO members with insufficient or no manufacturing capacities in the pharmaceutical sector could face difficulties in making effective use of compulsory licensing under the TRIPS Agreement. We instruct the Council for TRIPS to find an expeditious solution to this problem and to report to the General Council before the end of 2002.[63]

In effect, the Ministerial Conference sent this important issue back to committee.

The net effect of paragraph 6 was that only a small group of developing countries would be able to manufacture affordable generic medications for their own populations. Argentina, China, India, Mexico, and South Korea are among the developing countries in which the level of development of their pharmaceutical industries is sufficiently high to have innovative capabilities. Countries at the next lower level (having pharmaceutical industries with reproductive capabilities – active ingredients and finished products) include Brazil, Cuba, Egypt, Indonesia, and Turkey. There is a long list of countries with no pharmaceutical industry, including many in Africa with high rates of HIV/AIDS: Botswana, Burkina Faso, Burundi, Central African Republic, Congo, Rwanda, and Senegal.[64]

The end of 2002 marked the deadline for finding an expeditious solution to the problem posed by paragraph 6 of the TRIPS Agreement. In March 2002, the European Commission (EC) and member states submitted a proposal at a session of the Council for TRIPS. The EC proposal contained two possible options:

1) An amendment to Article 31 of the TRIPS Agreement, which would create an exception to allow for exports under compulsory licenses, under certain conditions, for products needed to combat serious public health problems;
2) An interpretation of a clause of Article 30 of TRIPS that would allow production for export, to certain countries and under certain conditions, of products needed to combat serious public health problems.[65]

At the same session of the TRIPS Council, the US made a very different proposal. It called for a moratorium on bringing a WTO complaint against countries that export some medications to countries in need, subject to two conditions. First, any solution to the prohibition against export in paragraph 6 would apply only to HIV/AIDS, tuberculosis, and malaria; and second, it would apply only to countries that lack sufficient pharmaceutical manufacturing capability or have no such capability at all. These restrictions marked a significant difference between the US proposal and that of the European Commission.

Alternative proposals were made on behalf of a group of developing countries. Kenya suggested, as one possible option, the elimination of the provision in the TRIPS Agreement requiring that a compulsory licensee predominantly supply the domestic market, since that provision prevents a compulsory license from being granted mainly to export to a country in need of certain medicines. The other possible option would be to develop what is known as an "authoritative interpretation" of a different provision, which would grant countries the right to allow the production of drugs to address public health needs in another country, without the consent of the patent holder.

The year 2002 came and went without a solution. In late December, the United States led other industrialized nations in refusing to accept the draft accord because it covered more drugs and more diseases than the US was willing to accept. As in the March 2002 meeting, the US insisted on limiting the drugs to those needed to combat HIV/AIDS, tuberculosis, and malaria, "or other infectious epidemics of comparable gravity and scale."[66] The other countries joining the US in its opposition were Canada, the European Union, Switzerland, and Japan. All were seeking to protect the patents of the pharmaceutical industry, while still making available medicines to treat HIV/AIDS, malaria, and TB.

These countries balked at broadening the scope of any exceptions to paragraph 6 of the TRIPS Agreement to include diseases like cancer and asthma. The US and its industrial allies argued that allowing countries like China, Brazil, and India to manufacture generic copies of patented drugs for export without the consent of the patent-holders would "open the door to copying Viagra as well as ointments for baldness."[67] The United States and its industrial allies care more about protecting the pharmaceutical companies from inroads into their profits from remedies for sexual dysfunction and baldness than they care about the suffering of millions of developing country inhabitants who have diseases other than the big three: AIDS, malaria, and tuberculosis.

These circumstances prompt well-meaning researchers to offer a rationale for the type of questionably ethical trial of breast cancer proposed in Vietnam: mastectomy alone (the control group) was the only treatment the majority of women with breast cancer in Vietnam would ever receive. Moreover, this situation enables pharmaceutical companies to use placebo-controlled trials to study experimental medications for childhood asthma with the blessing of the FDA: these African children would not have access to any treatment for their asthma outside the trial, so they are not being made worse off if they get a placebo in the trial.

The TRIPS Agreement becomes fully operative after 2005. It remains uncertain just what will happen if member WTO nations that have manufacturing capability seek to export generic copies of patented drugs to the much larger number of developing countries without that capability (most of which are also much poorer). An executive of India's largest pharmaceutical company was said to have predicted that multinational drug companies would strongly resist any attempt on the part of generic drug makers like those in India to export their copies of drugs for which the big manufacturers in the West hold patents.[68]

Even more dismaying is the fact that the poorest countries would not be able to afford even these much less expensive drugs for the large numbers of inhabitants in need of medications to treat HIV/AIDS and tuberculosis. In countries such as Uganda, for example, the per capita governmental expenditure on health care is estimated as being between US $8 and $12 per year. Taken together, the new Declaration on TRIPS, the Global Health Fund at its present level of pledges, and the charitable donations and price reductions of the big US and multinational drug companies will still not be able to provide for the needs of many developing countries. Nevertheless, this bleak picture does not compel the conclusion that it is useless even to attempt reforms and part-way solutions that would improve the situation. A good first step would be repeal of the TRIPS prohibition against the export of generic copies of patented drugs and vaccines.

NOTES

Portions of this chapter are excerpted from my chapter entitled "Affordable and Accessible Drugs for Developing Countries: Recent Developments," to appear in (eds.) George Andreopoulos, Zehra Arat, and Peter Juviler, *Looking Beyond the State but not Ignoring It: Non-State Actors and Human Rights*. Excerpts reprinted with permission from the editors.

1. Jayashree Watal, "Background Note," prepared for WHO–WTO workshop on differential pricing and financing of essential drugs, Hosbjor, Norway, April 8–11, 2001.
2. Udo Schüklenk and Richard E. Ashcroft, "Affordable Access to Essential Medication in Developing Countries: Conflicts Between Ethical and Economic Imperatives," *Journal of Medicine and Philosophy*, 27:2 (2002), 179–195.
3. Stephanie Strom and Matt Fleischer-Black, "Drug Maker's Vow to Donate Cancer Medicine Falls Short," *New York Times* (June 4, 2003), A1.

4. Schüklenk and Ashcroft, "Affordable Access," 186.
5. Ibid., 187.
6. Salik Booker and William Minter, "Aid – Let's Get Real," *The Nation* (July 8, 2002).
7. WHO secretariat, "More Equitable Pricing for Essential Drugs: What Do We Mean and What Are the Issues?" background paper for WHO–WTO secretariat workshop on differential pricing and financing of essential drugs, Hosbjor, Norway, April 8–11, 2001.
8. Ibid.
9. "The Use of Essential Drugs," WHO Technical Report Series 895 (Geneva: World Health Organization, 2000).
10. WHO secretariat, "More Equitable Pricing."
11. Accessed from the PhRMA website, http://www.phrma.org, May 20, 2002.
12. Donald G. McNeil Jr., "Oxfam Joins Campaign to Cut Drug Prices for Poor Nations," *New York Times* (February 13, 2001), A6.
13. Melody Petersen and Larry Rohter, "Maker Agrees to Cut Price of 2 AIDS Drugs in Brazil," *New York Times* (March 31, 2001), A4.
14. Melody Petersen, "Novartis Agrees to Lower Price of a Medicine Used in Africa," *New York Times* (May 3, 2001), C1.
15. Accessed from the PhRMA website, September 14, 2002.
16. Accessed from the IFPMA website, http://www.ifpma.org, September 14, 2002.
17. World Health Organization, Report of the Commission on Economics and Health, *Macroeconomics and Health Investing in Health for Economic Development* (2001), available at http://www.who.int/whosis/cmh/cmh_report/e/report.cfm?path=cmh,cmh_report&language=english, accessed February 13, 2002.
18. Strom and Fleischer-Black, "Drug Maker's Vow Falls Short."
19. Schüklenk and Ashcroft, "Affordable Access," 188.
20. Strom and Fleischer-Black, "Drug Maker's Vow Falls Short."
21. WHO secretariat, "More Equitable Pricing."
22. Ibid. These and other questions are posed, with some answers suggested.
23. Alice K. Page, "Prior Agreements in International Clinical Trials: Ensuring the Benefits of Research to Developing Countries," *Yale Journal of Health Policy, Law, and Ethics*, 3:1 (2002), 35–64 at 38.
24. http://www.iavi.org/about/overview.htm.
25. http://www.iavi.org/vaccinedev/ip.htm.
26. Reidar K. Lie, "Justice and International Research," in (eds.) Robert J. Levine and Samuel Gorovitz, with James Gallagher, *Biomedical Research Ethics: Updating International Guidelines: A Consultation* (Geneva: CIOMS, 2000), 27–50; Nuffield Council on Bioethics, *The Ethics of Research Related to Healthcare in Developing Countries* (London: Nuffield Council on Bioethics, 2002).
27. Page, "Prior Agreements."
28. Leonard H. Glantz, George J. Annas, Michael A. Grodin, and Wendy K. Mariner, "Research in Developing Countries: Taking 'Benefit' Seriously," *Hastings Center Report*, 28:6 (1998), 38–42; Page, "Prior Agreements."

29. Gordon Conway, "Biotechnology and the War on Poverty," in (eds.) I. Serageldin and G. J. Persley, *Biotechnology and Sustainable Development: Voices of the South and North* (Wallingford, Oxford: CABI, 2003), 1–25.
30. http://www.conceptfoundation.org/AboutConcept.html.
31. Ibid.
32. WHO Vaccine Preventable Diseases Monitoring System, 1999 Global Summary.
33. This paragraph is excerpted from Ruth Macklin and Brian Greenwood, "Ethics and Vaccines," in (eds.) Barry Bloom and Paul-Henri Lambert, *The Vaccine Book* (San Diego: Academic Press, 2002), 123–124, with permission from Elsevier.
34. http://www.vaccinealliance.org/home/General_Information/About_ alliance/Governance/whatisgavi.php, accessed January 30, 2003.
35. http://www.mmv.org, accessed August 28, 2002.
36. http://Mosquito.WHO.int, accessed August 28, 2002.
37. http://www.news.bayer.com, accessed August 29, 2002.
38. Barbara Crossette, "A Wider War on AIDS in Africa and Asia," *New York Times* (April 30, 2001), A6.
39. http://www.aegis.com/news/unaids/2001/UN010625.html.
40. http://www.globalfundatm.org/files/pledges&contributions030416.rtf, accessed April 29, 2003.
41. http://www.globalfundatm.org/journalists_journalists/pr.html, accessed January 8, 2003.
42. http://www.globalfundatm.org/proposals.html, accessed April 29, 2003.
43. Donald G. McNeil Jr., "UN Disease Fund Opens Way to Generics," *New York Times* (October 16, 2002), A6.
44. Sheryl Gay Stolberg, "AIDS Fund Falls Short of Goal and US is Given Some Blame," http://query.nytimes.com/gst/abstract.html?res= F30813F934580C708DDDAB0894DA404482, accessed February 13, 2002.
45. Sheryl Gay Stolberg and Richard W. Stevenson, "Bush AIDS Effort Surprises Many, But Advisers Call it Long Planned," *New York Times* (January 30, 2003), A19.
46. http://www.itacoalition.org/content.html?folder= 4&envelope=5&page=13, accessed December 16, 2002.
47. WHO, Report of the Commission on Economics and Health, *Macroeconomics and Health Investing*, 89.
48. Conway, "Biotechnology and the War on Poverty," 15.
49. Ibid.
50. Watal, "Background Note," 7.
51. Carlos M. Correa, "Implications of the Doha Declaration on the TRIPS Agreement and Public Health," WHO, Essential Drugs and Medicines Policy, EDM Series No. 12, Annex 2 (Geneva: World Health Organization, 2002), 1, n. 5.
52. Tina Rosenberg, "Look at Brazil," *New York Times Magazine* (January 28, 2001).

53. Rachel L. Swarns, "Companies Begin Talks with South Africa on Drug Suit," *New York Times* (April 18, 2001), A3.
54. Barbara Crossette, "Brazil's AIDS Chief Denounces Bush Position on Drug Patents," *New York Times* (May 3, 2001), A5.
55. Barbara Crossette, "US Drops Case Over AIDS Drugs in Brazil," *New York Times* (June 26, 2001), A4.
56. Hannah E. Kettler and Chris Collins, "Using Innovative Action to Meet Global Health Needs through Existing Intellectual Property Regimes," study paper prepared for the Commission on Intellectual Property Rights, available at http://www.iprcommission.org/papers/.
57. Amy Harmon and Robert Pear, "Canada Overrides Patent for Cipro to Treat Anthrax," *New York Times* (October 10, 2001), A1.
58. Kettler and Collins, "Using Innovative Action."
59. Schüklenk and Ashcroft, "Affordable Access," 191.
60. Dan W. Brock, "Some Questions About the Moral Responsibilities of Drug Companies," *Developing World Bioethics*, 1:1 (2001), 33–37 at 37.
61. http://www.Oxfam.org/what_does/advocacy/papers/8broken.rtf.
62. World Trade Organization, Declaration on the TRIPS Agreement and Public Health, Ministerial Conference, WT/MIN/01/DEC/W/2 (November 14, 2001).
63. Ibid.
64. Correa, "Implications of the Doha Declaration."
65. Ibid., 25.
66. Elizabeth Becker, "Trade Talks Fail to Agree on Drugs for Poor Nations," *New York Times* (December 21, 2002).
67. Ibid.
68. Celia W. Dugger, "A Catch-22 on Drugs for the World's Poor," *New York Times* (November 16, 2001), W1, 7.

7 Respecting, protecting, and fulfilling human rights

It is not uncommon to hear people refer to all sorts of bad situations as violations of human rights. The term "human rights" is often used quite loosely, divorced from its narrow yet correct meaning that refers to provisions in various international declarations and treaties issued under the auspices of the United Nations. As one public health lawyer observes:

> The fields of ethics and human rights share an abiding belief in the paramount importance of individual rights and interests, but beyond that, their perspectives diverge. While legal scholars stress the importance of treaty obligations, ethicists seldom refer to international law doctrine.[1]

It is, of course, true that there are all sorts of legal rights, as well as moral rights, that pertain to human beings in general, as well as in the specific context of research. But this wide array of general rights are only *human* rights in the sense that they apply to humans and not, say, animals. The strict meaning of "human rights" refers chiefly to those rights stipulated in documents such as the Universal Declaration of Human Rights (1948), the International Covenant on Civil and Political Rights (1966), the International Covenant on Economic, Social, and Cultural Rights (1966), and the Convention on the Elimination of All Forms of Discrimination Against Women (1979).[2] In addition, human rights lawyers maintain that human rights can be identified in international custom and treaties, the decisions of treaty bodies, and organizations that contain human rights as a central aspect of their mandate. Treaty laws may become customary international law if widely enough observed.[3] The discussion of human rights in this chapter accords with this meaning of the term, as elucidated by human rights lawyers.

The United Nations makes a further distinction regarding human rights terminology:

> A distinction has to be made between Charter-based and treaty-based human rights bodies. The former derive their establishment from provisions contained in the Charter of the United Nations, hold broad human rights mandates, address an unlimited audience and take action based on majority voting. The latter derive

their existence from provisions contained in a specific legal instrument (i.e., the Covenant on Civil and Political Rights), hold more narrow mandates (i.e., the set of issues codified in the legal instrument involved), address a limited audience (i.e., only those countries that have ratified the legal instrument in question) and base their decision-making on consensus.

The leading Charter-based body is the Commission on Human Rights, whereas the various treaty-based bodies were established to supervise the implementation of the various UN treaties and conventions.[4]

Still another important distinction is that between human rights declarations and human rights treaties. The former are not legally binding, whereas the latter are legally binding on the nations that have signed and ratified them. The Universal Declaration of Human Rights, notable for being the first human rights statement issued by the United Nations, is a declaration, whereas the International Covenant on Civil and Political Rights and the International Covenant on Economic, Social, and Cultural Rights are treaties.

The nations that ratify these human rights treaties are referred to as "states parties" to the treaties. Some countries may sign and then not ratify, in which case they are not parties. For others the act of signing is equivalent to ratification. States parties are bound to *respect*, *protect*, and *fulfill* the rights embodied in the treaties they have committed themselves to uphold.

The two major human rights treaties differ in several important respects. As the name implies, the International Covenant on Civil and Political Rights (ICCPR) deals mainly with the rights of citizens in civil society to be free from certain restrictions or impositions by government. So, for example, Article 1 states that all peoples have the right of self-determination, Article 6 establishes the "inherent right to life of every human being," Article 8 prohibits slavery, and Article 9 states that everyone has a right to liberty and security of person. For the most part, the rights in this treaty state what governments must refrain from doing to their citizens. At the same time, however, governments must take some positive actions to ensure that individuals have the requisite self-determination, freedom, and liberty stipulated in the various provisions.

It is often thought that the International Covenant on Economic, Social, and Cultural Rights (ICESCR) requires somewhat more proactive steps on the part of governments. Article 9 says that the "States Parties recognize the right of everyone to social security, including social insurance"; Article 11 requires the states parties to "recognize the right of everyone to an adequate standard of living for himself and his family, including adequate food, clothing and housing, and to the continuous improvement of living conditions"; and most notably in the present context, Article 12 requires that "The States Parties . . . recognize the right of everyone to the enjoyment of the highest attainable standard of physical and mental health." Although it is obvious that governments must take active steps to implement these rights, the same is also true of many of the rights embodied in the International Covenant on Civil and Political Rights.

One chief difference between the two covenants lies in the way in which rights are to be achieved. The ICCPR requires states to be in immediate compliance with its provisions, whereas the ICESCR allows for a "progressive realization" of the rights embodied in the treaty. A General Comment from the Office of the High Commissioner for Human Rights explains the difference:

> The concept of progressive realization constitutes a recognition of the fact that full realization of all economic, social and cultural rights will generally not be able to be achieved in a short period of time. In this sense the obligation differs significantly from that contained in article 2 of the International Covenant on Civil and Political Rights which embodies an immediate obligation to respect and ensure all of the relevant rights. Nevertheless, the fact that realization over time, or in other words progressively, is foreseen under the Covenant should not be misinterpreted as depriving the obligation of all meaningful content.[5]

In addition, the ICESCR explicitly mentions the involvement of international assistance and cooperation as a means of achieving progressively the full realization of the rights.

The dominant perception has been that the human rights enunciated in the International Covenant on Civil and Political Rights are fundamentally different from those discussed in the International Covenant on Economic, Social, and Cultural Rights. The former set of rights has traditionally been termed "negative rights," requiring governments to refrain from interfering with individuals' freedoms, while the economic, social, and cultural rights have been considered "positive rights," requiring governments to engage in some affirmative obligatory actions.[6] However, many critics have questioned and sought to dispel this distinction, among them the treaty bodies that interpret the human rights obligations of nations. A rationale for challenging the distinction between these two allegedly different types of rights points out that freedom requires both types of rights and equality must be assured in both, as well as the fact that the realization of both types of rights requires the investment of resources.[7]

That governments have to refrain from interfering as well as to play an active role with regard to both types of rights is evident from the different types of obligations human rights impose on states parties – the obligations to *respect*, *protect*, and *fulfill*. In the case of the right to health, these obligations are elucidated as follows:

The obligation to *respect* requires States to refrain from interfering directly or indirectly with the enjoyment of the right to health. The obligation to *protect* requires States to take measures that prevent third parties from interfering . . . Finally, the obligation to *fulfil* requires States to adopt appropriate legislative, administrative, budgetary, judicial, promotional and other measures towards the full realization of the right to health.[8]

It may appear that the very idea of a "right to health" is meaningless because health cannot be guaranteed by governments or laws, be they nationally or internationally recognized. That criticism rests on a confusion between the right to health and the right to be *healthy*. As the Committee on Economic, Social, and Cultural Rights[9] explains, the right to health includes the following freedoms: "the right to control one's health and body, including sexual and reproductive freedom, and the right to be free from interference, such as the right to be free from . . . non-consensual medical treatment and experimentation." In addition, the right to health embodies entitlements: the right to a system of health protection. In turn, the system of health protection must provide "equality of opportunity for people to enjoy the highest attainable standard of health."[10] This latter concept – the highest attainable standard of health – recognizes genetic, environmental, and behavioral limitations to the attainment of perfect health, and the consequent inability of states to guarantee that people remain healthy.

Human rights and the concept of dignity

All of the United Nations human rights instruments rely on and explicitly invoke a vague concept that has gained currency in much discourse in European bioethics but not among UK and US bioethicists: the "dignity" of the human being. This locution, prominent in the Kantian tradition in continental philosophy, is expressed in numerous United Nations documents. The first of these is in the first sentence of the Preamble to the Universal Declaration of Human Rights, which states that "recognition of the inherent dignity and of the equal and inalienable rights of all members of the human family is the foundation of freedom, justice and peace in the world."

The Preamble to the ICCPR repeats the phrase: "Considering that, in accordance with the principles proclaimed in the Charter of the United Nations, recognition of the inherent dignity and of the equal and inalienable rights of all members of the human family is the foundation of freedom, justice and peace in the world;" and "Recognizing that these rights derive from the inherent dignity of the human person." Whether rights derive from inherent dignity or something else is a profound philosophical question that is not answered by the mere assertion that rights derive from dignity.

The Council of Europe is another body whose documents include dignity as a central feature. The Council's leading document in bioethics is entitled "Convention for the Protection of Human Rights and Dignity of the Human Being with Regard to the Application of Biology and Medicine."[11] Following introductory clauses in the Preamble (for example, "Conscious that the misuse of biology and medicine may lead to acts endangering human dignity"), Article I of this Convention begins with the statement: "Parties to this Convention shall protect the dignity and identity of all human beings."

Who could be opposed to respect for dignity? No one is likely to contend that human beings should *not* be treated with respect for their dignity. However, the concept is so vague it is nearly devoid of meaning without further elucidation. That makes appeals to human dignity especially problematic in the context of understanding and applying claims that invoke human dignity as a basis for actions or policies of various sorts. Neither scholars nor drafters of national, regional, or international guidelines or declarations appear to have analyzed the concept of human dignity in a way that yields clear criteria for its application. Yet much discourse from the United Nations organizations and European bodies relies on the vague and imprecise notion of human dignity in formulating guidelines and declarations.

"Respect for human dignity" has in some contexts become a mere slogan, as in the case of debates over human reproductive cloning. Opponents claim that cloning is "contrary to human dignity" and even "a violation of the dignity of the human species." An example is the additional protocol to the Council of Europe's Convention for the Protection of Human Rights and Dignity of the Human Being with Regard to the Application of Biology and Medicine, which asserts that "the instrumentalisation of human beings through the deliberate creation of genetically identical human beings is contrary to human dignity and thus constitutes a misuse of biology and medicine."[12] When challenged to explain precisely how producing a child by means of nuclear transplantation constitutes a violation of human dignity, those who make this claim turn on the challengers and accuse them of some sort of moral blindness in failing to recognize the dignity inherent in all human beings. The International Bioethics Committee of the United Nations Educational, Scientific, and Cultural Organization (UNESCO) issued a consensus statement declaring that reproductive cloning of human beings should not be permitted. The third of three reasons in support of the ban stated that cloning "could reduce human beings to the level of a tool, and as such would be contrary to human dignity."[13] This is clearly a Kantian formulation, and could be expressed more clearly by omitting reference to dignity altogether, and saying that it is unethical to use human beings merely as a means.

The pioneering work of Jonathan Mann in human rights and public health relied on the concept of human dignity in support of a human rights basis for public health obligations.[14] In the words of one commentator who gives well-deserved praise to Mann's contributions in this area: "Mann set two conditions for developing an ethics of public health: that it use the vocabulary of dignity rather than biomedicine and that it apply a human rights framework."[15] With all due respect to Jonathan Mann, I maintain that he was on the right track in the second of these two conditions, and misguided with regard to the insistence on appeals to the all-too-vague concept of human dignity. The vocabulary of bioethics could very well be used in developing an ethics of public health, with a gain in precision and clarity.

If it is problematic to seek to derive human rights from the concept of dignity, it is a more manageable philosophical task to try to derive rights from fundamental ethical principles. The final section of this chapter explores the relationship between human rights and leading principles of bioethics. There remains the problem of where these foundational principles of ethics come from and how they are to be justified, but that is beyond the scope of this book. Other scholars have competently tackled that task.

The United States and human rights

In its report on ethics in international research, the National Bioethics Advisory Commission mentions human rights exactly twice. A single sentence (cited previously in chapter 4) identifies exploitation as a human rights violation: "Exploitation in any form can be construed as a human rights violation by virtue of its failure to recognize the inherent dignity of every human being, a precept embodied in the Universal Declaration of Human Rights."[16] The second occurrence is in NBAC's chapter on informed consent, noting that the requirement of voluntary, informed consent appears in "a major international human rights instrument – the International Covenant on Civil and Political Rights – to which the United States is a party."[17] NBAC omits any mention of the fact that the United States is not a party to the International Covenant on Economic,

Social, and Cultural Rights, the human rights treaty that includes the right to health.

Although two human rights lawyers were invited to testify at meetings of the Commission, commissioners rejected the idea of making human rights a significant feature in its report. As one commissioner said, "It's too controversial to deal with human rights in this report. We'll lose credibility." This might seem puzzling. Why should linking ethics in international research with human rights be so controversial as to risk a loss of credibility in a report issued by a presidential commission? The answer can lie only in the failure of the United States to ratify most of the international human rights treaties – not only the International Covenant on Economic, Social, and Cultural Rights, but also the Convention on the Elimination of All Forms of Discrimination Against Women, and the Convention on the Rights of the Child.

Despite the self-proclaimed role of the United States as a champion of human rights, the abysmal record of the US in its failure to adopt this array of treaties and conventions ratified by many nations throughout the world is shameful. The United States recognizes human rights as existing mainly in the sphere of civil and political rights, the convention that the US has ratified and uses in criticizing the human rights records of other countries. It is evident why conservative US presidents and legislators reject the provisions of the International Covenant on Economic, Social, and Cultural Rights. Conservative politicians in the United States view the kinds of rights enumerated in that document as "entitlements" and therefore unacceptable to those who reject the presuppositions of the welfare state and the role of government in providing health and economic benefits to its citizens. The persistent failure of the US government to provide for universal health insurance demonstrates the hostility legislators continue to manifest when it comes to economic and social rights.

In the case of the Convention on the Elimination of All Forms of Discrimination Against Women, it is somewhat puzzling to learn that the US has not formally adopted a treaty ratified by 170 countries – almost 90 percent of the members of the United Nations, including Algeria, Bangladesh, Haiti, Malawi, Rwanda, and Saudi Arabia. The United States is one of three countries that have signed (but not ratified) the treaty, binding themselves not to contravene the treaty's terms. On the other hand, perhaps it is not surprising after all, when one considers the steady march of the US Congress over the past three decades to erode the reproductive rights of American women and the failure of the states collectively to pass an equal rights amendment to the Constitution.

The equal rights amendment was first proposed in 1923; it has been ratified by thirty-five of the thirty-eight states necessary for passage. The federal government's "War Against Women" (the title of a *New York Times* editorial[18]) reached a feverish pitch by January 2003. President George W. Bush took a variety of steps that not only put American women's right to safe, legal abortions in jeopardy, but also elevated the status of a fertilized egg to that of a person "with rights equal to, or perhaps even exceeding, those of the woman."[19] The Bush administration tried to limit women's access to contraception; reinstated the infamous "gag rule" first established by Ronald Reagan, which prohibits family planning clinics outside the US that receive US funds from counselling women about abortion, even with the clinics' own money; opposed a United Nations effort to help young girls who have been raped in the commission of war crimes; and at a United Nations population conference in Bangkok, sought to block an endorsement of the use of condoms to prevent transmission of HIV/AIDS, among other anti-women actions. If a double standard exists anywhere, it has been in the stance of the administration of George W. Bush to lower the reproductive rights of women to a level below that of all industrialized nations and many developing countries.

It is not nearly as clear, however, why US legislators have refused to ratify the Convention on the Rights of the Child. Despite the way their conservative social ideology seeks to diminish the reproductive rights of women and rejects any form of welfare rights, such as the right to health care for citizens, right-wing legislators and members of the executive branch of US government have not traditionally been anti-child. One supposition is that these conservative politicians are loath to grant any rights to adolescents, especially adolescent girls, in the reproductive area. Nevertheless, these conservatives appear to have succeeded in privileging the rights of embryos and fetuses above those of women and children in both legislation and the courts.

Another possible explanation could be the incorporation of both major types of human rights within the same treaty: "The Convention on the Rights of the Child, the first human rights treaty to be opened for signature after the end of the Cold War, is the only one so far to include civil, political, and economic and social rights considerations not only within the same treaty but within the same right."[20] Given the continued refusal of US government officials and legislators to recognize the legitimacy of economic and social rights, it is perhaps not surprising that the US would refrain from ratifying a treaty that combines these rights with the acceptable civil and political rights.

Human rights in the conduct of research

At first glance, the connection between human rights and international research involving human subjects may appear rather narrow. It is tempting to construe the connection as confined to the application of human rights to actions or omissions that occur in the actual conduct of research involving human subjects. However, a human rights analysis can also apply to the aftermath of research, as illustrated in the provisions in the Declaration of Helsinki and the CIOMS international ethical guidelines that address what should happen when research is completed. With regard to the global health situation beyond the context of research, a human rights approach can apply to matters such as access to care and treatment, availability of health-related goods and services, and environmental factors that contribute to health and disease. This applicability is apparent from the text of Article 15 of the International Covenant on Economic, Social, and Cultural Rights:

1. The States Parties to the present Covenant recognize the right of everyone:
   (a) To take part in cultural life;
   (b) To enjoy the benefits of scientific progress and its applications;
   (c) To benefit from the protection of the moral and material interests resulting from any scientific, literary or artistic production of which he is the author.
2. The steps to be taken by the States Parties to the present Covenant to achieve the full realization of this right shall include those necessary for the conservation, the development and the diffusion of science and culture.
3. The States Parties to the present Covenant undertake to respect the freedom indispensable for scientific research and creative activity.
4. The States Parties to the present Covenant recognize the benefits to be derived from the encouragement and development of international contacts and co-operation in the scientific and cultural fields.

The main justification for adopting a broader human rights analysis is that conducting biomedical, epidemiological, and social research is a necessary condition for being able to develop programs to fulfill the health needs of populations throughout the world. Without research on tropical diseases, there can be no preventive vaccines or therapies for those conditions. Without research directed at the forms that a global disease such as HIV/AIDS takes in resource-poor countries, there can be no effective programs to control and treat such diseases. And without research in countries where poverty is endemic and the population suffers from malnutrition and its consequences, the results of research conducted in wealthier countries may be inapplicable in the poorest countries.

Subsequent sections in this chapter focus on the broader human rights analysis, which links human rights and public health in ways begun in the work of Jonathan Mann and continued by scholars and activists working in the intersection between public health and human rights. We begin in this section with the direct application of human rights principles and instruments to the conduct of research involving human beings.

Probably the most straightforward reference to research in any of the human rights instruments is Article 7 of the International Covenant on Civil and Political Rights: "No one shall be subjected to torture or to cruel, inhuman or degrading treatment or punishment. In particular, no one shall be subjected without his free consent to medical or scientific experimentation." This statement could be taken to imply that involving human beings in research is to subject them to "inhuman or degrading treatment or punishment," a description evocative of experiments conducted by doctors in Nazi Germany rather than the research commonly carried out under the supervision of research ethics committees in developing as well as industrialized countries. Still, it is worth recalling the charges levelled at the research carried out by Pfizer in Kano, Nigeria (described in chapters 1 and 4) as a reminder that the perception, if not the reality, of some contemporary research fits this description.

A closer look at Article 7, however, reveals that it refers to any research conducted *without the free consent of the individual subject*. So it is the absence of voluntary, informed consent that constitutes "inhuman or degrading treatment," and not medical or scientific experimentation itself. The original Article 7, quoted in its entirety in the previous paragraph, was replaced in 1992 with an expanded version in a General Comment issued by the Human Rights Committee established under the ICCPR (see below, pp. 216–217 and 219).

Right to health care, right to health

Scholars in human rights and public health have identified several different provisions in human rights instruments as a basis for the claim that there exists a right to health care, as well as the right to health.[21] The relevant human rights provisions begin with Article 25 of the Universal Declaration of Human Rights (UDHR), which explicitly recognizes a claim to health: "Everyone has the right to a standard of living adequate for the health and well-being of himself and his family, including food, clothing, housing and medical care and necessary social services, and the right to security in the event of unemployment, sickness, disability, widowhood, old age or other lack of livelihood in circumstances beyond his control." Article 27 of the UDHR identifies another pathway to a right to health: "Everyone has the right freely . . . to share in scientific advancement and its benefits." To share in the benefits of scientific advancement "underscores the rights of the general public,"[22] and can be interpreted to mean that the fruits of biomedical research must be made available to everyone who needs information or products developed in such research.

Article 12 of the International Covenant on Economic, Social, and Cultural Rights addresses "the right of everyone to the highest attainable standard of physical and mental health," requiring states to take certain defined steps, including "the prevention, treatment and control of epidemic, endemic, occupational and other diseases" and "the creation of conditions which would assure to all medical service and medical attention in the event of sickness." The wording of Article 12 recalls the preamble of the 1946 constitution of the World Health Organization, a member of the United Nations family of organizations and the international organization devoted to public health: "The enjoyment of the highest attainable standard of health is one of the fundamental rights of every human being without distinction of race, religion, political belief, economic or social conditions."[23]

How can these fundamental human rights claims regarding health care and health be realized in the poorest countries in the world today, given the prevalence of diseases that are difficult to prevent and costly to treat? And which actors should play a role in the progressive realization of these rights? As noted in chapter 1, establishing and strengthening scientific and technological capacity in developing countries was stated as an obligation in a United Nations declaration more than a quarter of a century ago.[24] Although this obligation has recently been affirmed and taken seriously by governmental and industrial sponsors of research in developing countries, it cannot by itself begin to meet the vast health needs of the large numbers of people suffering from malaria, tuberculosis, HIV/AIDS, parasitic diseases, and other causes of sickness and death.

One of the tasks of the committees established to monitor the implementation of the human rights treaties is the ongoing review of progress in light of changing circumstances. This process results in the periodic issuing of General Comments. One pertinent example is a Comment issued by the Committee on Economic, Social, and Cultural Rights in 2000 when it revisited Article 12 of the International Covenant on Economic, Social, and Cultural Rights: the right to the highest attainable standard of health.[25] The committee observed that much has changed in the world health situation since the ICESCR was adopted in 1966, noting that more determinants of health are now recognized, such as resource distribution and gender differences.

The Comment identifies *accessibility* as one of the essential elements required for fulfilling the right to health. This includes accessibility to health facilities, goods, and services with four overlapping dimensions: non-discrimination (accessibility to everyone), physical accessibility, economic accessibility, and information accessibility. In addition to enumerating various detailed actions that states parties must undertake in order to respect, protect, and fulfill their obligations regarding this right, the Comment includes a section on international obligations. It refers states parties to a declaration that "proclaims that the existing gross inequality in the health status of the people, particularly between developed and developing countries . . . is politically, socially and economically unacceptable and is, therefore, of common concern to all countries."[26] Compliance with their international obligations requires countries with available resources to "facilitate access to essential health facilities, goods and services in other countries, wherever possible, and provide the necessary aid when required."[27]

It is clear from this detailed commentary on the right to the highest attainable standard of health that wealthier countries (among those that have ratified the ICESCR) have international obligations to assist in providing access to health facilities, goods, and services to resource-poor countries. Although only states parties are accountable to fulfill this and other human rights obligations, the Comment also addresses non-state actors. It states that all members of societies have responsibilities regarding the right to health, including intergovernmental and nongovernmental organizations, civil society, and the private business sector. The Comment specifically identifies the World Trade Organization (WTO), a member of the United Nations system, as one of the organizations that should cooperate effectively with states parties regarding the implementation of the right to health. Yet as we saw in the preceding chapter, the WTO Ministerial Conference at Doha did not go far enough in permitting the poorest countries to gain access to inexpensive, generic drugs. Later in this chapter we revisit the TRIPS Agreement and its relation to the right to the highest attainable standard of health.

The role of WHO

WHO has sought to strengthen the links between health and human rights. A report to the Commission on Human Rights of the UN Economic and Social Council notes that WHO's newly adopted Corporate Strategy "sets out human rights as a new emphasis of work."[28] WHO cites the following complex linkages between health and human rights:

• Violations or lack of attention to human rights can have serious health consequences;
• Health policies and programmes can promote or violate human rights in the ways they are designed or implemented;
• Vulnerability and the impact of ill health can be reduced by taking steps to respect, protect, and fulfil human rights.

In its report to the Commission on Human Rights, WHO outlined specific areas in which it has begun to strengthen its focus on human rights. These include the following areas and WHO's activities within them:

- Racism, racial discrimination, xenophobia, and all forms of discrimination. In September 2001 a World Conference against Racism, Racial Discrimination, Xenophobia, and Related Intolerance was held in Durban, South Africa. The Programme of Action agreed at the conference encouraged WHO and other international organizations to devote attention to this area of work, "including the HIV/AIDS pandemic, and access to health care, and to prepare specific projects, including research to ensure equitable health systems for the victims."[29] WHO welcomed the Durban Declaration, and identified several ongoing programs that are responsive: in particular, the WHO program on indigenous health.

- The right to development. WHO observed that Article 8 of the Declaration on the Right to Development states that "States should undertake, at the national level, all necessary measures for the realization of the right to development and shall ensure, inter alia, equality of opportunity for all in their access to basic resources, education, health services, food, housing, employment and the fair distribution of income."[30] WHO has been a strong partner in the transitional working group of the Global Fund to Fight AIDS, Tuberculosis, and Malaria since the inception of the Global Fund. In its efforts to improve the health conditions associated with poverty around the world, WHO has contributed to the mission of the Global Fund. The report of the Commission on Macroeconomics and Health documented that poverty is both a cause and a consequence of ill health. Citing this report, WHO noted that "investments in health would not only support governments in fulfilling their human rights obligations but may also generate up to a six-fold return on investment."[31]

- Economic, social, and cultural rights. This area represents what is probably the major contribution of WHO in establishing the link between health and human rights. WHO has developed training models and other educational materials to increase awareness and application of the right to health. The organization has also begun a global study to assess the extent to which the right to health is embodied in national constitutions and legislation. Another important activity, already described in the previous chapter, is the effort WHO has made, along with other UN organizations, in lowering the cost of AIDS drugs. One such mechanism is the Accelerated Access Initiative, designed to increase access to antiretroviral treatments.

- Human rights of women and gender perspective. WHO has been gathering evidence about how all aspects of women's health are related to the manifestation, severity, and frequency of diseases, as well as social and cultural responses to disease. Efforts to integrate gender and gender perspective into WHO's work have long been a feature of its Human Reproduction Programme. More recently, the scope of attention to gender has widened to include other WHO programs. One area of focus directly related to human rights is the prevention of violence against women. WHO conducted an eight-country study on domestic violence against women, which revealed that between 23 percent and 69 percent of women have experienced physical or sexual violence by an intimate partner during their lifetime (the different percentages varied according to the site). WHO's efforts in this area include guidance on policies and strategies in response to violence against women, as well as building capacity on addressing gender and gender-based violence within countries.

• Rights of the child. WHO identified areas where immediate action is needed to safeguard children's right to health. One mechanism is the fulfilment of the obligation of states parties to the Convention on the Rights of the Child to diminish infant and child mortality. A major life-saving effort to this end is child immunization, and WHO's support of GAVI (Global Alliance for Vaccines and Immunization) is the major activity related to this goal.

According to WHO, one in four children throughout the world did not receive routine immunization with the six basic vaccines against polio, diphtheria, whooping cough, tetanus, measles, and tuberculosis in 1998. The proportion of children immunized each year against these six diseases declined between 1990 and 1998.[32] In addition, the gap between vaccinated children in industrialized countries and those in resource-poor countries has widened. Until a few years ago, children in Africa and in Europe received the same childhood vaccines. Today, children in industrialized countries typically receive eleven or twelve vaccines, whereas children in developing countries receive six or seven. This disparity is likely to continue to increase due to the higher costs of newly developed vaccines. This reversal of equity in the provision of childhood vaccines is nothing less than an exacerbation of the double standard regarding access to preventive health services that exists between the industrialized world and the poorest countries.

• HIV/AIDS. WHO and its sister organization, UNAIDS (Joint United Nations Programme on HIV/AIDS), have worked incessantly to combat the disease in the most severely affected settings. WHO notes that "No other disease has so dramatically highlighted the stark injustices and inequities in access to health care, economic opportunity, and the protection of basic human rights as HIV/AIDS."[33]

One of the core principles that have guided the response to HIV/AIDS from the beginning has been the need to respect human rights. As an example of WHO's ongoing efforts, in December 2002, along with other partners in the public and private sectors, it launched the new international coalition described in the previous chapter – the International HIV Treatment Access Coalition (ITAC). It is served by a small secretariat at the WHO headquarters in Geneva.[34]

- Science and environment. WHO noted the importance of new genetic knowledge for the prospect of improving world health. The link with human rights is the provision in the UN Covenant on Economic, Social, and Cultural Rights that recognizes the right of everyone to enjoy the benefits of scientific progress and its applications. This is one area where a close connection exists between human rights documents and research involving human beings. WHO observed that "the potential for new research on the human genome to improve health is clear. For this to be realized, societies throughout the world will need to be served by basic genetic services and research." WHO has already established a program to work jointly with the NIH Fogarty International Center to assist countries in building capacity to conduct research in genetics and genomics.

  Another scientific area that may hold great promise for improving health is stem cell research. WHO was more cautious in its comments to the Commission on Human Rights on this topic, noting that "there is a need for a full and open debate among a broad range of interested parties to enable conclusions to be reached on the utility, safety and desirability of scientific research involving stem cells."[35] This caution was without doubt prompted by the obvious need to destroy human embryos in order to derive the stem cells for research. Those member nations that recognize human embryos as possessing human rights could object to a ringing endorsement of stem cell research by WHO, and WHO is ever mindful of stances it could take that would offend the political or religious sensitivities of member nations.

- Effective functioning of human rights mechanisms. No commitment to human rights can be complete without a plan for implementation for activities seeking to fulfill those rights throughout the world. WHO reported that the key mechanism for this is its interaction with treaty monitoring bodies, the entities established to see whether and to what extent nations are carrying out their obligations under the treaties they have signed and ratified. WHO's activities have included making regular input into the work of the Committee on the Convention on the Rights of the Child and the Committee on the Convention on the Elimination of All Forms of Discrimination Against Women. In addition, WHO has collaborated with the UN Office of the High Commissioner for Human Rights "to ensure that reproductive and sexual health is taken up adequately by the various human rights committees."[36] WHO has engaged in similar activities with the UNFPA (United Nations Fund for Population Activities) in connection with the UN treaty monitoring bodies on sexual and reproductive health issues.

HIV/AIDS and the right to health

There is little doubt that the HIV/AIDS pandemic has been a significant factor in bringing human rights and public health together. A major development was the publication in 1998 of the International HIV/AIDS and Human Rights Guidelines.[37] According to the Office of the High Commissioner for Human Rights:

OHCHR and UNAIDS published the International Guidelines on HIV/AIDS and Human Rights in 1998 as a tool for States in designing, coordinating and implementing effective national HIV/AIDS policies and strategies. The Guidelines provide the framework for a rights-based response to the HIV/AIDS epidemic by outlining how human rights standards apply in the context of HIV/AIDS and translating them into practical measures that should be undertaken at the national level, based on three broad approaches:
- improvement of government capacity for multi-sectoral coordination and accountability;
- reform of laws and legal support services, with a focus on anti-discrimination, protection of public health, and improvement of the status of women, children and marginalised groups; and
- support and increased private sector and community participation to respond ethically and effectively to HIV/AIDS.[38]

As this statement of the purpose of the guidelines indicates, the focus of human rights with regard to HIV/AIDS is broad, going well beyond the concerns of research and provision of effective treatments. The guideline most directly related to the provision of medical care and treatment in the 1998 document was Guideline 6, entitled "Regulation of goods, services and information":

States should enact legislation to provide for the regulation of HIV-related goods, services and information, so as to ensure widespread availability of qualitative prevention measures and services, adequate HIV prevention and care information and safe and effective medication at an affordable price.

Specific items under this general guideline included the need to enact legislation to promote provision of information about HIV/AIDS through the mass media, laws and policies to ensure the quality and availability of HIV counselling and testing, legal quality control of condoms, and other legal and regulatory measures. Rapid developments – political as well as biomedical – since these guidelines were first published in 1998 prompted a revision of Guideline 6, emanating from the Third International Consultation on HIV/AIDS and Human Rights held in Geneva in July 2002. The updated Guideline 6 is now entitled "Access to prevention, treatment, care and support," and reads as follows:

States should enact legislation to provide for the regulation of HIV-related goods, services and information, so as to ensure widespread availability of quality prevention measures and services, adequate HIV prevention and cure information, and safe and effective medication at an affordable price. States should also take measures necessary to ensure for all persons, on a sustained and equal basis, the availability and accessibility of quality goods, services and information for HIV/AIDS prevention, treatment, care and support, including antiretroviral and other safe and effective medicines, diagnostics and related technologies for preventive, curative and palliative care of HIV/AIDS and related opportunistic infections and conditions. States should take such measures at both the domestic and international levels, with particular attention to vulnerable individuals and populations.[39]

This makes it abundantly clear that revised Guideline 6 is intended to promote greater accessibility of drugs and wider availability of prevention and treatment, especially in the developing world. According to a press release issued jointly by UNAIDS and the Office of the High Commissioner for Human Rights:

The revised guideline breaks new ground by calling for specific actions on the part of governments. For example, Guideline 6 asks governments to establish concrete national plans on HIV/AIDS-related treatment, with resources and timelines that progressively lead to equal and universal access to HIV/AIDS-related treatment, care and support . . . and strengthen international cooperation and assistance to HIV/AIDS-related prevention, treatment, care and support through contributions to the recently-established Global Fund to Fight AIDS, Tuberculosis, and Malaria.

The stipulation that the national plans "progressively lead to equal and universal access" recalls the way in which the provisions of the International Covenant on Economic, Social, and Cultural Rights are to be achieved: through their "progressive realization," and not all at once, as is the case for provisions of the International Covenant on Civil and Political Rights. The Committee on Economic, Social, and Cultural Rights, the body that monitors the ICESCR, declared that the right to health includes access to treatment for HIV disease, among other things.

Possibly the chief circumstance that prompted the revision of Guideline 6 was a recognition of the growing gap between industrialized and developing countries in their ability to provide treatment for people living with HIV/AIDS. The 2002 document explicating the revision of Guideline 6 notes that life-preserving antiretroviral treatments for AIDS still reached fewer than 5 percent of people in developing countries, despite major decreases since 2000 in the prices of the drugs.

Additional evidence of the role of HIV/AIDS in spurring new initiatives for access to treatment is the Declaration of Commitment on HIV/AIDS adopted by the United Nations in June 2001. In this, the first meeting of member states of the U.N. devoted to a public health issue, an unprecedented decision was taken to adopt a human rights framework in combating a disease, thus augmenting the United Nations' response to the HIV/AIDS pandemic.

Obviously, it is not sufficient to issue and reissue ethical and human rights guidelines. Monitoring activities are needed to ensure that implementation of provisions in these guidelines is taking place. To that end, Guideline 6 specifies a large array of actions that governments must take in order to fulfill their human rights obligations regarding HIV/AIDS and the right to health. These actions include setting benchmarks and targets for measuring progress; consulting with people living with HIV/AIDS, nongovernmental organizations, and international health organizations; enacting laws to ensure that an adequate supply of medicines is available in a timely manner; allocating funds for research, development, and promotion of therapies; and working with the private sector to achieve these goals; among many others.

One key recommendation for implementation of Guideline 6 implicitly acknowledges the double standard that exists between industrialized countries and all developing countries except Brazil regarding access to antiretroviral therapy. This recommendation says:

States and the private sector should pay special attention to supporting research and development that address the health needs of developing countries. In recognition of the human right to share in scientific advancement and its benefits, States should adopt laws and policies, at the domestic and international levels, ensuring that the outcomes of research and development are of national and global benefit, with particular attention to the needs of people in developing countries and people who are poor or otherwise marginalized.[40]

Human rights, access, and affordability of drugs

How does this array of developments in the sphere of human rights relate to other activities designed to make needed medicines accessible and affordable to people in resource-poor countries? The previous chapter described four such efforts:

1 differential pricing and financing of essential drugs;
2 negotiations followed by prior agreements before research is initiated;
3 collaborative efforts like those of the Global Fund to Fight AIDS, Tuberculosis, and Malaria and the Global Alliance for Vaccines and Immunization (GAVI);
4 manufacture of generic copies of patented drugs in developing countries and sale of such drugs to other poor countries.

These are in addition to donations of free drugs made by several manufacturers, usually on time-limited bases.

Drug companies have reduced prices and shifted their traditional stance on patent protections, albeit with some pressure from governments and international agencies. The Declaration on the TRIPS Agreement and Public Health, made at the World Trade Organization's Ministerial Conference on November 14, 2001, was an agreement reached by 142 member governments. For it to be implemented, however, it requires the cooperation of pharmaceutical companies, whether national or multinational. It is worth noting that human rights have not been mentioned in these discussions. Although the World Trade Organization is a member of the United Nations family of organizations, its commercial orientation appears to distance it from concerns about human rights. To analyze these developments using a human rights framework, we begin by noting a sequence of points in a background paper prepared for the CIOMS consultations that led to the revision of the international ethical guidelines:[41]

(a) governments of developing countries incur responsibilities under human rights instruments for the progressive realization of everyone's right to enjoy the benefits of scientific progress and its applications;
(b) the realization of this right exists independently of the increase in resources; it requires effective use of available resources;
(c) the international community incurs certain responsibilities to provide – through international cooperation and assistance – resources enabling developing countries to fulfill their obligations under the relevant human rights instruments;
(d) the above-mentioned responsibilities include the more equitable distribution of the benefits of science;
(e) the responsibilities of host country governments and those of the international community are clearly interrelated; and
(f) non-state agents (for example, non-state sponsoring agencies) incur certain responsibilities under existing international human rights instruments.[42]

The two key human rights provisions are Article 12 of the International Covenant on Economic, Social, and Cultural Rights: "the right of everyone to the highest attainable standard of physical and mental health," and Article 15 of the same Covenant. It is evident that the actions of pharmaceutical companies in giving away free drugs and lowering the prices of some drugs, however commendable, are insufficient to provide necessary medications for "everyone" in developing countries. These actions by drug companies are only a small step toward the "progressive realization of everyone's right to enjoy the benefits of scientific progress and its applications."

The establishment of the Global Fund to Fight AIDS, Tuberculosis, and Malaria is a much larger step toward fulfilling several of the responsibilities identified in the above-noted CIOMS background paper. With regard to point (a), it is worth recalling that relatively poor countries, such as Uganda and Zimbabwe, contributed a significant amount to the Global Fund. Similarly, regarding point (c), many industrialized countries made pledges to the Global Fund and fulfilled portions of those initial pledges (albeit more slowly than was hoped for). With regard to point (f), contributions to the Global Fund by private foundations and a few corporations were a step toward fulfilling the responsibility of non-state agents.

It is when we come to the World Trade Organization's Doha Declaration of November 14, 2001 that we see both a positive step toward respecting and fulfilling human rights provisions, and, at the same time, evidence that the TRIPS Agreement does not go far enough. In its clear statements articulated in paragraphs 4 and 5, the WTO Declaration is certainly an improvement over the previous version of the TRIPS Agreement in the way the earlier agreement had been interpreted by drug companies and their governmental allies, such as the United States.

However, the restrictions stated in paragraph 6, which limit the ability of developing countries without their own manufacturing capabilities to import generic drugs manufactured in other countries, fail to meet a key human rights test on two counts. First is the failure to take the necessary steps for the progressive realization of everyone's right to enjoy the benefits of scientific progress and its applications under the test stipulated in the CIOMS background paper: "the realization of this right exists independently of the increase in resources; it requires effective use of available resources." To deny to poor countries the opportunity to import inexpensive drugs from other countries does not meet the test of "effective use of available resources."

The second count on which the 2001 TRIPS Agreement fails a human rights test is the barrier erected for developing countries. If the opportunity to import cheaper medications is disallowed, developing countries cannot fulfill their own human rights responsibility noted in the CIOMS background paper: "governments of developing countries incur responsibilities under human rights instruments for the progressive real-ization of everyone's right to enjoy the benefits of scientific progress and its applications." And if the TRIPS Agreement hampers developing coun-tries in the fulfilment of their responsibilities, the result is a violation of Article 12 of the ICESCR – the right of everyone to the highest attainable standard of physical and mental health.

According to a report prepared for the World Health Organization's Department of Essential Drugs and Medicines Policy, the TRIPS Agree-ment may be in violation of human rights provisions:

The UN Sub-Commission for the Promotion and Protection of Human Rights also pointed out the "apparent conflicts between the intellectual property rights regime embodied in the TRIPS Agreement, on the one hand, and international human rights law, on the other", including human rights to food, health and self-determination.[43]

Numerous factors besides lack of money hinder access to drugs in many developing countries, although poverty is the single most important reason why people in developing countries cannot obtain the drugs they need.[44] These other factors include inefficiency and waste in healthcare delivery systems, inadequate systems for distribution of drugs within a country, lack of reliable scientific information and appropriate education and training of healthcare personnel, and local perceptions and beliefs about illness and medicine. The relatively poor healthcare infrastructure in many developing countries is a leading factor that inhibits access to drugs by large numbers of people. These diverse barriers to adequate access to much-needed drugs cannot readily be removed, even if cheaper medications are made available and the Global Fund provides financing for drugs to treat AIDS, malaria, and tuberculosis.

These background conditions underscore the salient responsibility of industrialized countries to contribute to capacity-building in developing countries. As already noted, the UN Declaration on the Use of Scientific and Technological Progress includes a provision that states this responsi-bility of governments to: "co-operate in the establishment, strengthening and development of the scientific and technological capacity of devel-oping countries with a view to accelerating the realization of the social and economic rights of the peoples of those countries."[45] Moreover, this responsibility is not confined to governments. The huge pharmaceutical companies that conduct drug trials in developing countries (and reap the financial rewards) have the same responsibility, as do individual biomed-ical researchers from industrialized countries, whether sponsored by the public or the private sector.

Conceptual, ethical, and policy questions regarding the interpretation of human rights provisions require further study and discussion. How can it be determined when the highest attainable standard of health has been reached? Against which measures is "highest attainable" to be defined? How should priorities be set among the competing health-related needs in developing countries, and what role, if any, should donor nations and international organizations play in promoting some priorities over others in working with ministries of health in developing countries? Making drugs more affordable to the populations in developing countries is only a first step toward realization of the human right to health, but it is a giant step.

Human rights, international guidelines, and ethical principles

Earlier chapters examined various aspects of the leading international ethical guidelines for biomedical research involving human subjects. None of those documents couch their guidelines or recommendations in the language of human rights. The front matter of the CIOMS international guidelines does reference pertinent human rights instruments discussed in this chapter: the Universal Declaration of Human Rights; the International Covenant on Civil and Political Rights, and the International Covenant on Economic, Social, and Cultural Rights, as well as the Convention on the Elimination of All Forms of Discrimination Against Women and the Convention on the Rights of the Child. Referring to those human rights instruments, CIOMS says: "All endorse in terms of human rights the general ethical principles that underlie the CIOMS International Ethical Guidelines."[46] What CIOMS has in mind by "general ethical principles" are the familiar (and sometimes unfairly maligned) trio: respect for persons, beneficence, and justice. CIOMS devotes two pages in the introductory material to a brief elucidation of this famous trio.

Based on the definitions and elucidation of these general ethical principles provided in the *Belmont Report*, CIOMS describes *respect for persons* as incorporating at least two fundamental ethical considerations:

a) respect for autonomy, which requires that those who are capable of deliberation about their personal choices should be treated with respect for their capacity for self-determination; and
b) protection of persons with impaired or diminished autonomy, which requires that those who are dependent or vulnerable be afforded security against harm or abuse.[47]

Although none of the international guidelines or human rights instruments refer to the *respect for persons* principle by name, its elements are nevertheless embodied in various provisions of all these documents.

Respect for autonomy

The requirement to obtain voluntary, informed consent from each potential subject is the core application of *respect for autonomy* in the context of research. Paragraphs 20 and 22 of the Declaration of Helsinki state the requirement that potential subjects of research provide freely given, properly informed consent. Paragraph 20 consists of one sentence only: "The subjects must be volunteers and informed participants in the research project." Paragraph 22 is more detailed regarding the information to be provided to potential subjects and the obligation of the researcher to ensure that the subject has understood the information.

In addition to these direct applications of respect for autonomy, other paragraphs in Helsinki embody a broader interpretation of *respect for persons*. Paragraph 8 states that "Medical research is subject to ethical standards that promote respect for all human beings and protect their health and rights." "Respect for all human beings" is simply another formulation of "respect for persons." Under the heading, "Basic principles for all medical research," paragraph 10 specifies the duty of physicians in medical research: "to protect the life, health, privacy, and dignity of the human subject." Respect for the privacy of research subjects is a component of *respect for persons* that is related to, yet distinct from, respect for autonomy. And as for the "dignity of the human subject," that is a concept still to be clarified.

Several guidelines in the CIOMS international guidelines address various aspects of the informed consent requirement, all of which are illustrative of respect for persons. Guideline 4 requires the investigator to obtain the voluntary, informed consent of the prospective subject; Guideline 5 specifies in great detail the essential information that is to be provided in the process; Guideline 6 mandates the duties of sponsors and investigators in the process of obtaining informed consent; and Guideline 7 addresses inducement to participate in research, a provision designed to ensure that consent to participate in research is fully voluntary, without undue inducement.

The definition of *respect for persons* provided by CIOMS notes that the principle incorporates "at least" two fundamental ethical considerations. The first of these is respect for autonomy, and the second is protection of persons with impaired or diminished autonomy. Other ethical considerations, beyond these two fundamental ones, might be included under *respect for persons*. As noted above, one paragraph in the Declaration of Helsinki mentions protection of the privacy of individuals. CIOMS Guideline 18 is entitled "Safeguarding confidentiality," and requires researchers to establish secure safeguards of the confidentiality of subjects' research data. The commentary pays special attention to genetics research because many people are concerned about the potential consequences of disclosure of genetic information. Since respect for the privacy of persons and protection of confidentiality are widely held to be ethical requirements in research, the principle of respect for persons can reasonably be interpreted to cover these considerations, as well as respect for autonomy.

The UNAIDS Guidance Document for HIV/AIDS vaccine research complies with *respect for autonomy* in Guidance Point 12, the requirement for voluntary, informed consent not only for participation in the research itself, but also for HIV testing conducted before, during, or after the research.

Both the International Covenant on Civil and Political Rights and the International Covenant on Economic, Social, and Cultural Rights begin with a general statement that implies a recognition of the autonomy of each individual. Article 1, paragraph 1 of each covenant states: "All peoples have the right of self-determination. By virtue of that right they freely determine their political status and freely pursue their economic, social and cultural development." Use of the term "peoples" makes it appear that the statement refers to groups or to collections of people within a state, rather than to individuals. However, one authority on human rights law contends that "There is little doubt that international human rights law was intended to endow individuals directly with basic rights."[48] A General Comment on the ICCPR, issued by the Human Rights Committee in 1984, adds:

The right of self-determination is of particular importance because its realization is an essential condition for the effective guarantee and observance of individual human rights and for the promotion and strengthening of those rights. It is for that reason that States set forth the right of self-determination in a provision of positive law in both Covenants and placed this provision as article 1 apart from and before all of the other rights in the two Covenants.[49]

This leaves no doubt that the human rights in question belong to individuals. Despite the existence of a considerable literature in philosophy and bioethics that makes fine distinctions and nuanced conceptual analyses of "autonomy," it is reasonable to construe the "right of self-determination" to be equivalent to the ethical requirement to respect the autonomy of individual persons.

As noted earlier, the human rights provision most directly relevant to research is Article 7 of the ICCPR: "In particular, no one shall be subjected without his free consent to medical or scientific experimentation." A General Comment that was issued in 1992 by the Human Rights Committee as a replacement for the original Article 7 said: "The aim of the provisions of article 7 of the International Covenant on Civil and Political Rights is to protect both the dignity and the physical and mental integrity of the individual," and went on to express concern about the monitoring and implementation of this provision:

Article 7 expressly prohibits *medical* or scientific *experimentation* without the free consent of the person concerned. The Committee [referring to the Human Rights Committee, the monitoring body for this treaty] notes that the reports of States parties generally contain little information on this point. More attention should be given to the need and means to ensure observance of this provision.[50]

This serves as a reminder that mechanisms exist for monitoring and implementing the human rights provisions in the various treaties. Such mechanisms are entirely absent for ethical guidelines such as the Declaration of Helsinki and the CIOMS international guidelines. Those documents exist as statements of ethical principles governing research and they also provide procedural details regarding how to implement the guidelines. But there is no body responsible for monitoring Helsinki or CIOMS and no mechanism for reporting violations or imposing sanctions for such violations.

The Office of the United Nations High Commissioner for Human Rights and UNAIDS jointly issued International Guidelines on HIV/AIDS and Human Rights in 1998. These guidelines have a status somewhere in between the provisions contained in the various international conventions that have been ratified by countries, on the one hand, and the Helsinki Declaration and CIOMS guidelines, on the other. As stated in the foreword to the HIV/AIDS and Human Rights Guidelines: "The challenge we face is to integrate efforts in the areas of HIV/AIDS and human rights . . . by encouraging United Nations human rights bodies and mechanisms to incorporate HIV/AIDS issues into their monitoring functions and general mandates."

Guideline 5 in the HIV/AIDS and Human Rights Guidelines calls upon states to enact protective laws "that will ensure privacy and confidentiality and ethics in research involving human subjects." The commentary under the guideline calls for the enactment or strengthening of protective laws governing the legal and ethical protection of human participation in research. Informed consent and confidentiality of personal information are among the specific items such laws must seek to protect.

Protection of vulnerable persons

As CIOMS describes *respect for persons* in the context of research, the principle incorporates a second fundamental ethical consideration in addition to respect for autonomy: "protection of persons with impaired or diminished autonomy, which requires that those who are dependent or vulnerable be afforded security against harm or abuse." This is one of the cardinal precepts of research ethics, arising out of a grim history of abuses and exploitation of vulnerable individuals or populations: poor, uneducated, African–American men in the rural South of the United States (the Tuskegee syphilis study); mentally retarded children housed in a squalid public institution (the Willowbrook hepatitis studies); demented, elderly persons (Jewish Chronic Disease Hospital); prisoners (vulnerable because they are incarcerated in an inherently coercive environment); sick hospitalized patients in whom researchers injected plutonium without their knowledge or consent (Cold War human radiation experiments); and numerous others, some known and others undocumented, in both industrialized and developing countries. All the international ethical guidelines and human rights provisions embody this requirement to protect dependent or vulnerable people against harm or abuse in biomedical research.

The Declaration of Helsinki states, in paragraph 8: "Some research populations are vulnerable and need special protection . . . Special attention is also required for those who cannot give or refuse consent for themselves." Paragraph 24 addresses the need to obtain consent from parents of minor children, and from legally authorized representatives of legally or mentally incompetent adults. In addition, "These groups should not be included in research unless the research is necessary to promote the health of the population represented and this research cannot instead be performed on legally competent persons." Paragraph 26 states further restrictions and conditions for the enrollment of individuals who are unable to give consent on their own behalf, including the requirement that the research protocol submitted to the research ethics committee provide the reasons for involving such subjects in the proposed research.

The CIOMS guidelines address vulnerable populations and individuals lacking capacity to grant informed consent on their own behalf in several guidelines: Guideline 4, individual informed consent, requiring permission of a legally authorized representative for subjects who lack the capacity to consent; Guideline 9, special limitations on risk when research involves individuals who are not capable of giving informed consent; Guideline 13, research involving vulnerable persons; Guideline 14, research involving children. Because CIOMS includes detailed commentaries following each guideline, it provides an opportunity to specify the different types of protection appropriate for different types of vulnerability.

The following comment issued by the Human Rights Committee addresses both individuals with diminished capacity and also those who are incarcerated or in other coercive environments:

Article 7 expressly prohibits medical or scientific experimentation without the free consent of the person concerned . . . The Committee [referring to the Human Rights Committee, the monitoring body for this treaty] . . . observes that special protection in regard to such experiments is necessary in the case of persons not capable of giving valid consent, and in particular those under any form of detention or imprisonment. Such persons should not be subjected to any medical or scientific experimentation that may be detrimental to their health.[51]

The prohibition stated in the final sentence would be problematic for some types of ethically defensible research carried out on persons not capable of giving valid consent. The prohibition would rule out research on individuals lacking decisional capacity that is designed to benefit them but could – because it is experimental – result in more harm than good. Any biomedical research *could be* detrimental to the health of subjects, even if a properly constituted ethical review committee made a favorable benefit–harm assessment based on the research proposal that it reviewed prospectively. Examples could include any drug research on young children (who, by definition, are not capable of giving valid consent), some drug research on severely psychotic or demented patients, and surgical or medical experiments on victims of accidents that impair their ability to grant valid consent. Although it is surely true that all of these individuals are vulnerable and require added protections (as stipulated in CIOMS Guideline 13, for example), to prohibit research altogether involving this category of persons would almost certainly preclude findings that would ultimately benefit these populations. Arguably, such research should be conducted only in those countries, communities, or institutions where the proper safeguards are securely in place.

Beneficence

The second in the famed trio of principles is *beneficence*, which CIOMS describes in these terms, again following the *Belmont Report*:

Beneficence refers to the ethical obligation to maximize benefit and to minimize harm. This principle gives rise to norms requiring that the risks of research be reasonable in the light of the expected benefits . . . Beneficence further proscribes the deliberate infliction of harm on persons; this aspect of beneficence is sometimes expressed as a separate principle, *nonmaleficence* (do no harm).[52]

Like *respect for persons*, this ethical principle is embodied in all international guidelines for research involving human subjects.

Paragraph 16 of the Declaration of Helsinki states: "Every medical research project involving human subjects should be preceded by careful assessment of predictable risks and burdens in comparison with foreseeable benefits to the subject or to others." Paragraph 17 says that physicians conducting research should be "confident that risks have been adequately assessed and can be satisfactorily managed." In a somewhat less direct expression of *beneficence*, paragraph 18 says: "Medical research involving human subjects should only be conducted if the importance of the objective outweighs the inherent risks and burdens to the subject." Even more indirect is the statement in paragraph 5: "In medical research on human subjects, considerations related to the well-being of the human subject should take precedence over the interests of science and society." Another relevant section is paragraph 11, which calls for adequate laboratory or animal experimentation before humans are placed at risk. It is abundantly clear that the main objective of the Declaration of Helsinki is to seek to ensure that the benefits of research – including benefits to science and society – outweigh the risks to the human participants in research.

The CIOMS document contains several guidelines expressing the letter or the spirit of the principle of beneficence. Guideline 8, benefits and risks of study participation, begins by stating: "For all biomedical research involving human subjects, the investigator must ensure that potential benefits and risks are reasonably balanced and risks are minimized." The guideline itself contains further elaboration of the balance between risks and potential benefits, and the commentary goes into even greater detail.

CIOMS Guideline 9, mentioned earlier in connection with *respect for persons*, pertains also to *beneficence*. This guideline (special limitations on risk when research involves individuals who are not capable of giving informed consent) addresses the level of risk that is acceptable when the research subjects lack the capacity to consent on their own behalf.

Guideline 11, which addresses what may (or must) be provided to a control group, including the acceptability of placebo controls, was at the center of controversy precisely because of sharply different perceptions of the risks to subjects versus potential benefits to science and society. The seven-page commentary that follows the guideline is clear testimony to the need for explanation, justification, and elaboration of the arguments pro and con that formed the controversy. Of the twenty-one CIOMS guidelines, Guideline 11 has the lengthiest commentary. Since this guideline was discussed extensively in earlier chapters, nothing further will be said here.

The various human rights declarations, treaties, and guidelines contain no explicit provisions that make reference to the need for a favorable balance of benefits over harms in research involving human subjects.

These instruments were not designed to address research, and with the exception of Article 7 of the ICCPR, the terms "experimentation" and "research" do not appear in the documents. Looked at from a much broader perspective, however, all of the instruments indirectly call for compliance with the principle of beneficence since the requirement to respect, protect, and fulfill human rights seeks to ensure a favorable balance of benefits over harms, regardless of the source of the potential harms and the nature of the benefits.

Moreover, the provisions that directly or indirectly establish the right to health as a human right can be construed as seeking to fulfill the principle of beneficence with regard to health. Article 27 of the UDHR says that "Everyone has the right freely . . . to share in scientific advancement and its benefits," which entails that benefits resulting from advances in the prevention, diagnosis, and treatment of disease are owed to everyone. The most direct and obvious statement of the obligation of states to provide health-related benefits exists in the correlative "right of everyone to the highest attainable standard of physical and mental health." The specific benefits that would accrue from steps the states are required to take include "the prevention, treatment and control of epidemic, endemic, occupational and other diseases" and "the creation of conditions which would assure to all medical service and medical attention in the event of sickness." A comparison between people having such medical benefits, even if they are only progressively realized, and people having little or no access to them, demonstrates that in complying with the human right to health, states would be fulfilling the ethical obligation to maximize benefit and minimize harm, as *beneficence* requires.

Justice

In elucidating the principle of justice, CIOMS says: "In the ethics of research involving human subjects, the principle refers primarily to *distributive justice*, which requires the equitable distribution of both the burdens and the benefits in research. Differences in distribution of burdens and benefits are justifiable only if they are based on morally relevant distinctions between persons."[53] Chapter 3 addressed in detail the concept of distributive justice in the context of international research, including an examination of how international ethical guidelines deal with questions of justice, and what the NBAC report and the Nuffield report have to say. It remains here to look at the relevant human rights instruments.

As already noted, with one basic exception the human rights instruments do not directly address research involving human subjects.

However, with regard to the fruits of research – the benefits of scientific advancement – several human rights provisions are directly relevant. Earlier in this chapter we examined the human rights provisions that constitute a basis for the right to health and the right to health care. As stated in the Preamble to both the ICCPR and the ICESCR, the articles in those covenants rest on: "recognition of the inherent dignity and of the equal and inalienable rights of all members of the human family is the foundation of freedom, justice and peace in the world." If everyone is granted equal rights to the benefits stated and implied in the ICESCR, and everyone deserves equal rights to avoid the burdens that the ICCPR seeks to prevent, this surely would amount to a just distribution of benefits and burdens.

As is true of the gap between the enunciation of ethical principles and their full realization, a gulf exists between the human rights stipulated in or derived from these instruments and their full realization. In developing countries generally, but especially in those that have the fewest economic and medical resources and the poorest health infrastructure, this gulf is the widest. A General Comment on the nature of states parties' obligations, issued by the Committee on Economic, Social, and Cultural Rights, addresses this problem of severe resource constraints:

[E]ven where the available resources are demonstrably inadequate, the obligation remains for a State party to strive to ensure the widest possible enjoyment of the relevant rights under the prevailing circumstances. Moreover, the obligations to monitor the extent of the realization, or more especially of the non-realization, of economic, social and cultural rights, and to devise strategies and programmes for their promotion, are not in any way eliminated as a result of resource constraints.[54]

If realization of the right to health were left entirely to the poorest countries, those nations might achieve a measure of distributive justice but only by leaving the majority of inhabitants with little or nothing in the way of health care. The distribution could be reasonably equitable yet minuscule in what is actually provided. Leaving everyone equally bereft of health-related goods and services does not go very far in fulfilling a human rights obligation. However, the fulfillment of that obligation does not rest on each state party alone. The Committee on Economic, Social, and Cultural Rights drew attention to the fact that:

the undertaking given by all States parties is "to take steps, individually and through international assistance and cooperation, especially economic and technical . . ." The Committee notes that the phrase "to the maximum of its available resources" was intended by the drafters of the Covenant to refer to both the resources existing within a State and those available from the international community through international cooperation and assistance.[55]

The Committee further emphasized that "international cooperation for development and thus for the realization of economic, social and cultural rights is an obligation of all States. It is particularly incumbent upon those States which are in a position to assist others in this regard."[56] The principle of justice and the principle of beneficence jointly impose obligations on governments to ensure that the distribution of health-related benefits are both equitable and, even in the poorest countries, adequate "to the maximum of its available resources." The Global Fund to fight AIDS, Tuberculosis, and Malaria, the Global Alliance for Vaccines and Immunization, and the other public–private partnerships discussed in chapter 6 are steps toward the progressive realization of the human right to health.

NOTES

Portions of this chapter are excerpted from my chapter entitled "Affordable and Accessible Drugs for Developing Countries: Recent Developments," to appear in (eds.) George Andreopoulos, Zehra Arat, and Peter Juviler, *Looking Beyond the State but not Ignoring It: Non-State Actors and Human Rights.* Excerpts reprinted with permission from the editors.

1. Lawrence O. Gostin, "Public Health, Ethics, and Human Rights: A Tribute to the Late Jonathan Mann," *Journal of Law, Medicine and Ethics*, 29:2 (2001), 121–130.
2. Others include the European Convention on Human Rights, American Convention on Human Rights, and African Charter on Human and Peoples' Rights.
3. I thank Bebe Loff for providing me with this information about the concept of human rights as understood by human rights lawyers, and for her many other helpful comments and corrections on an earlier draft of this chapter. I also benefited from Sofia Gruskin and Daniel Tarantola, "Health and Human Rights," in (eds.) R. Detels and R. Beaglehole, *Oxford Textbook on Public Health* (New York: Oxford University Press, 2001).
4. Available at http://www.un.org/Depts/dhl/resguide/spechr.htm#rights, accessed December 16, 2002.
5. CESR General Comment 3, The Nature Of States Parties' Obligations, December 14, 1990, fifth session, 1990.
6. Lawrence O. Gostin, "The Human Right to Health: A Right to the 'Highest Attainable Standard of Health'," *Hastings Center Report*, 31:2 (2001), 29–30; Gostin, "Tribute to the Late Jonathan Mann."
7. Stephen P. Marks, "Jonathan Mann's Legacy to the 21st Century: The Human Rights Imperative for Public Health," *Journal of Law, Medicine and Ethics*, 29:2 (2001), 131–138.
8. General Comment No. 14 (2000), Committee on Economic, Social, and Cultural Rights, Economic and Social Council, E/C.12/2000/4, August 11, 2000.

9. This committee is the treaty-based body responsible for monitoring the implementation of the ICESCR.

10. General Comment No. 14 (2000), 3.

11. Oviedo, 4.IV (1997).

12. Paris, 12.I (1998).

13. Bioethics Unit of UNESCO, undated.

14. Jonathan M. Mann, "Medicine and Public Health, Ethics and Human Rights," *Hastings Center Report*, 27:3 (1997), 6–13.

15. Marks, "Jonathan Mann's Legacy," 132.

16. NBAC, *Ethical and Policy Issues in International Research: Clinical Trials in Developing Countries* (Bethesda, MD, 2001), 10.

17. Ibid., 35.

18. *New York Times* (Sunday, January 12, 2003), 14.

19. Ibid.

20. Gruskin and Tarantola, "Health and Human Rights," 7.

21. The following are only a few of these scholars: George Andreopoulos, "Declarations and Covenants of Human Rights and International Codes of Research Ethics," in (eds.) Robert J. Levine and Samuel Gorovitz, with James Gallagher, *Biomedical Research Ethics: Updating International Guidelines: A Consultation* (Geneva: CIOMS, 2000), 181–203; Sofia Gruskin, "Ethics, Human Rights, and Public Health," *American Journal of Public Health*, 92:5 (2002), 698; Lawrence O. Gostin and Zita Lazzarini, *Human Rights and Public Health in the AIDS Pandemic* (New York: Oxford University Press, 1997); Gruskin and Tarantola, "Health and Human Rights"; Bebe Loff and Sofia Gruskin, "Getting Serious about the Right to Health," *Lancet*, 356:9239 (2000), 1435; Mann, "Medicine and Public Health."

22. Andreopoulos, "Declarations and Covenants," 191.

23. *Basic Documents*, 43rd edn (Geneva: World Health Organization, 2001).

24. UN Declaration on the Use of Scientific and Technological Progress, cited in Andreopoulos, "Declarations and Covenants,"193.

25. General Comment No. 14 (2000).

26. Ibid., 11.

27. Ibid., 11–12.

28. 58th session, Commission on Human Rights, United Nations Economic and Social Council, E/CN.4/2002/133, 31 (January 2002), 4.

29. World Conference Against Racism, Racial Discrimination, Xenophobia and Related Intolerance, Programme of Action, paragraph 154.

30. Commission on Human Rights, E/CN.4/2002/133, 5.

31. Ibid., 6.

32. WHO Vaccine Preventable Diseases Monitoring System, 1999 Global Summary.

33. Commission on Human Rights, E/CN.4/2002/133, 10.

34. Available at http://www.itacoalition.org/content.html?folder=4&envelope=5&page=13, accessed December 16, 2002.

35. Commission on Human Rights, E/CN.4/2002/133, 12.

36. Ibid., 13.

37. Office of the United Nations High Commissioner for Human Rights and the Joint United Nations Programme on HIV/AIDS, *HIV/AIDS and Human*

Rights: International Guidelines (New York and Geneva: United Nations, 1998).

38. Available at http://www.unhchr.ch/hiv/guidelines.htm, accessed January 20, 2003.
39. Office of the United Nations High Commissioner for Human Rights and the Joint United Nations Programme on HIV/AIDS, *HIV/AIDS and Human Rights: International Guidelines*, Revised Guideline 6 (New York and Geneva: United Nations, 2002).
40. Ibid.
41. Andreopoulos, "Declarations and Covenants."
42. Ibid., 196.
43. Carlos M. Correa, "Implications of the Doha Declaration on the TRIPS Agreement and Public Health," WHO, Essential Drugs and Medicines Policy, EDM Series No. 12, Annex 2 (Geneva: World Health Organization, 2002), citing the Commission on Human Rights, Sub-Commission on the Promotion and Protection of Human Rights, fifty-second session Agenda item 4, The Realization of Economic, Social and Cultural Rights, Intellectual Property Rights and Human Rights; 2, n. 15.
44. Richard Laing, "Improving Access to Essential Drugs," talk presented to the World Bank on February 28, 2000.
45. Cited in Andreopoulos, "Declarations and Covenants," 193.
46. Council for International Organizations of Medical Sciences, *International Ethical Guidelines for Biomedical Research Involving Human Subjects* (Geneva: CIOMS, 2002), 16.
47. Ibid., 19.
48. René Provost, *International Human Rights and Humanitarian Law* (Cambridge: Cambridge University Press, 2002), 18.
49. CCPR General Comment 12, The Right to Self-Determination of Peoples (Art. 1), March 13, 1984, twenty-first session, 1984. Available at http://www.unhchr.ch/tbs/doc.nsf/(symbol)/CCPR+General+comment +12.En?OpenDocument, accessed January 29, 2003.
50. Office of the High Commissioner for Human Rights, CCPR General Comment 20, replaces General Comment 7 concerning prohibition of torture and cruel treatment or punishment (Art. 7), March 10, 1992, forty-fourth session, 1992. Available at http://www.unhchr.ch/tbs/doc, accessed January 28, 2003.
51. Ibid.
52. CIOMS, *International Ethical Guidelines*, 16.
53. Ibid., 18.
54. CESR General Comment 3, The Nature of States Parties' Obligations, December 14, 1990, fifth session, 1990.
55. Ibid.
56. Ibid.

Discussing international ethical guidelines for biomedical research, a bioethicist from Africa wrote:

[W]e need, in particular, as far as biomedical research goes, to make appropriate distinctions between the ethics of developed world research in the developing world, collaborative or cooperative research between the developed and developing worlds, developed world research in the developed world and developing world research in the developing world.[1]

What is to be gained by making all these distinctions? One possibility is that making such distinctions would yield different ethical obligations, different rules, or different standards in these various contexts. However, the African bioethicist insisted that "the general moral principles that should guide correct moral action would be the same" at these different levels, and further: "while the use of double standards can never be morally justified, different standards are not only permissible but also inevitable."[2] The challenge, then, is to specify the criteria for distinguishing standards that are merely "different," and therefore allowable, from those that are "double," and hence unacceptable.

A bioethicist from the United States offered an analysis intended to show the possibility of accepting universal ethical standards for research while permitting differences in what is provided to research subjects in developed and developing countries.[3] The key to this analysis lies in distinguishing the ethical *principles* that apply to particular research endeavors from other aspects, such as the research design. The relevant ethical principles embody the well-known and widely accepted requirements of informed consent, reasonable risks in light of potential benefits, and minimization of risk. As long as those universal ethical principles are fulfilled, according to this account, the research can be judged ethically acceptable. What permits the research design to be different in an industrialized country and a resource-poor country is a difference in the local circumstances – in particular, the economic resources. As a result, "it does not follow that, if a research study is unethical in the United States, it is also unethical in Kenya."[4] On this view, the determination of whether a double standard exists depends on whether research in different countries adheres to the same ethical principles, and not whether a particular study could be conducted in one country but not in another.

This analysis has a certain appeal. The key to accepting it, however, lies in whether the different economic circumstances of industrialized and resource-poor countries should count as a morally relevant factor in assessing the ethics of a particular research design. If a study is designed and conducted by Kenyan researchers, funded only by available Kenyan resources, with no collaboration or sponsorship by the pharmaceutical industry or an industrialized country, then a good case can be made for accepting the moral relevance of the local economic circumstances. "Ought implies can": if the Kenyan researchers *cannot* provide expensive drugs or laboratory equipment to carry out a particular study design, then it makes no sense to say they *ought* to do so. Perhaps this is what the African bioethicist had in mind in referring to "developing world research in the developing world."

However, in the type of research most commonly carried out in developing countries, there is an external sponsor or industrialized country collaborator. These external sponsors or collaborators could surely supply the same costly drugs that the sponsor would provide for participants if the research were conducted in the industrialized country. If we reject the idea that different economic conditions in rich and poor countries can justify research in the poor country that could not ethically be conducted in the rich country, it closes a loophole that would otherwise permit withholding established, effective drugs from research subjects in developing countries on a routine basis. When that loophole remains open, a double standard still exists even if a study in the poor country adheres fully to the universal ethical principles of respect for persons and beneficence. Adherence to these universal ethical principles is a necessary but not a sufficient condition for a research study to be ethically acceptable. Also required is adherence to justice, the third fundamental ethical principle.

If there is something inherently unjust about allowing a double standard of ethics in research – one for industrialized countries, another for resource-poor countries – what are the options for arriving at a single standard, applicable wherever human beings are enrolled as research subjects? The views cited and described in this book show that some people justify a double standard based on the undeniable differences in wealth and other resources that exist in the world. Arguments in defense of this view point to the vast array of activities outside the sphere of human subjects research where inequalities exist. Further, they contend, rectifying these unfortunate inequalities among nations, or even subpopulations within countries, will not be accomplished by imposing obligations on the sponsors of biomedical research.

This argument begins with the true premise (1) that the world is filled with inequalities in resources; adds a second premise, also true (2) that striving for a single standard in research will do nothing to rectify the larger number of existing inequalities; inserts the implicit premise (3) that research involving human subjects should be treated no differently from all those other international endeavors; and concludes (4) that double standards in research are ethically acceptable. The validity of this argument turns on premise (3), which is not a factual statement but an "ought" statement. To accept it is to consider biomedical research and health care as just one more commodity in a market-driven world. However, if we view health care, medical benefits, and the research that yields these goods and services as a special sort of social good, we can readily reject the idea that research involving human subjects should be treated no differently from other activities driven by market forces.

One way of arriving at the same ethical standard for industrialized and developing countries has not (yet) been proposed. That would be deliberately to introduce a double standard of research in a developed country. This would require *lowering* the ethical standard for some studies conducted in industrialized countries, making them analogous to what typically exists in resource-poor countries. As bizarre as this sounds, how might it be accomplished?

One possibility is deliberately to seek out for research individuals who do not have access to the "best current treatments" and invite them to serve as subjects in a study on moderate-to-severe hypertension. A good pool of research subjects could probably be found among the 41 million uninsured people in the US. Another source of subjects could be users of public hospitals in poor, rural areas in the US, facilities with very limited resources and fewer technical capabilities than large urban hospitals. The research would adhere to the universal ethical principle of informed consent. Potential subjects would be told that by enrolling in the study, they would have a 50–50 chance of receiving an inexpensive, experimental medication for hypertension, and those randomized to the control group would receive a placebo. In fact, the information given to potential subjects would have at least one additional detail that is usually not told to participants in similar studies in developing countries: they would be informed that the researchers do not expect the experimental treatment to be as effective as the best current therapy available to people with health insurance, but better than no treatment at all for patients with moderate to severe hypertension.

The research would also adhere to the universal ethical principle of beneficence (a favorable benefit–risk ratio). Neither the experimental group nor the control group would be made worse off than they would be if they were not enrolled in research in the first place, and the subjects who receive the experimental treatment could potentially be much better off than if they received no treatment.

Some might contend that this is, in fact, the way some research is carried out in the United States. Although researchers do not deliberately seek out poor people without medical insurance to serve as subjects, it is widely perceived that people without access to the highest levels of medical care are over-represented among research subjects in some geographic areas and in some types of biomedical research. There appears to be no documentation of this perception, only the anecdotal experiences of academic researchers in medical schools located in neighborhoods where the majority of the population is relatively poor.

Nevertheless, there is a sharp difference between this hypothetical example and what occurs in settings in which many poor people are enrolled in research in the US. In the actual situation, it may well be true that people without access to the best current treatments are found in disproportionate numbers among research subjects. But for any serious or life-threatening medical condition – such as moderate to severe hypertension – an established, effective treatment would not be withheld regardless of whether the subjects would have access to the standard treatment outside the study. The research design would be an equivalency study, looking to see whether the cheaper, experimental treatment is as good as, or almost as good as, the best current treatment. The ethically problematic feature of the hypothetical example is obviously that of withholding an established, effective treatment from research subjects in a wealthy country where the majority does have access to the best current treatment, and where the subjects in the placebo group are likely to experience serious or irreversible harm.

There is an altogether different situation in which some people have invoked the notion of a double standard. This is the ironic twist in the comment made by critics of the CIOMS guideline that calls for making the successful products of research reasonably available to the population in resource-poor countries where the research is conducted. These critics maintain that no such obligation exists to provide successful products of research to the subjects in the US once their participation has ended, much less to others who were not subjects of the research. So, it is argued, to impose such an obligation on sponsors of research conducted in resource-poor countries would create a double standard.

The irony here lies in the reversal of the typical situation in which double standards are alleged. In this case, it is the population in the poor country who would benefit from the "higher" standard (the obligation to provide needed medications, free of charge or at much reduced cost) and the US population would be left with the "lower" standard of having no guaranteed medications following their participation in research.

These different scenarios clearly illustrate the lack of precision in referring simply to "single" or "double" standards. It is necessary to specify more precisely what the term "standard" refers to, and in what specific respects different standards are ethically acceptable or unacceptable. The first situation addresses the question of what should be provided to research subjects in a control group in a randomized, biomedical study. The second deals with what should be provided to research subjects and to others after a study in which an experimental product proves to be successful. These situations differ in a number of respects, and are the subject of separate and distinct guidelines and recommendations for multinational research.

A single standard for control groups

If it would not be unethical for subjects in a control group in Botswana to receive something other than the best current treatment, why would it not similarly be ethically acceptable for unemployed, uninsured subjects in Boston to receive a placebo or less-than-the-best existing treatment?

Replies to this question could take several different tacks. One approach is to acknowledge that what's right for poor Botswanians is similarly right for poor Bostonians. The uninsured Bostonians who are randomized to placebo are not made worse off in the research than they would be if they were not enrolled and remained untreated for their condition. The US government does not provide housing for the homeless, food for the hungry, or medicines for poor people who are uninsured, unemployed, and are not enrolled in Medicaid. So why should researchers or private sponsors be obligated to provide the best current treatment for subjects in research?

A quite different approach makes a sharp distinction between what is owed to poor people in one's own country and what is owed to poor people in a faraway land. Recall the viewpoint of the reviewer of a manuscript (discussed in chapter 3), who argued that the concept of distributive justice is applicable only within countries or to groups that have some interaction with one another. According to that conception of distributive justice, the benefits and burdens to be distributed fairly are only those that pertain to a group of people living together in a society. According to this view, US researchers would owe nothing to the Botswanians, but arguably, they would be obligated to treat the uninsured Bostonians differently because they live in the same society as the researchers, along with wealthier Americans who do have access to the best current treatment.

This same view was expressed in a letter to the Editor of the *New York Times*, responding to an article by the economist, Jeffrey Sachs, who has promoted a global approach to the AIDS crisis in Africa. The letter said:

[S]tates should not be expected to value the lives of noncitizens as much as citizens . . . [T]he fundamental purpose of any state institution is to further the well-being of its members. If this requires helping other nations for national security purposes . . . then foreign aid is a worthwhile endeavor. But if it is merely charity . . . then such aid is foolish.[5]

A third approach would argue that focusing only on what should be provided to a control group, in the absence of considering other contextual features, is a flawed way of looking at research that is intended to benefit a disadvantaged population. On this view, it is illegitimate to isolate a single factor in research – what a control group receives in a randomized, clinical trial. Instead, it is necessary to look at the larger context in which the research is conducted, including the infrastructure in resource-poor countries, what the country will be able to afford when the research is concluded, and whether the population would be left much worse off if a single standard were required because the research could not possibly be conducted. An article authored by four individuals at the National Institutes of Health makes a persuasive case for this point of view by imagining the following hypothetical study.[6]

"Early Versus Delayed Initiation of Antiretroviral Therapy"

The study is to take place in a country in sub-Saharan Africa committed to implementing antiretroviral therapy for the HIV-infected population. The country can afford a relatively inexpensive antiretroviral regimen based on generic drugs that could be used for a portion of the infected population but not for all infected individuals. The government and healthcare providers are seeking to maximize the number of people who could be treated, and to that end they have devised a study to determine whether a delay in beginning treatment would result in benefit comparable to that of starting treatment earlier in individuals who have not yet manifested symptoms of HIV infection. Here is where the question of "standards" enters in. In many industrialized countries, it is standard practice to begin highly active antiretroviral therapy in HIV-infected people who do not have clinical symptoms, but who have specified levels of CD4

T-cell counts. In the hypothetical study proposed for the African country, subjects would be randomized to one of two groups: one would receive antiretroviral therapy while they are still asymptomatic, and the other would receive treatment only when symptoms appear. A third group – HIV-infected individuals who are already symptomatic – would have treatment started immediately.

This research has a second objective, arising out of low resources and deficiencies in the healthcare infrastructure in the African country. The study requires sophisticated laboratory measurements in order to monitor progress, but the ones used in industrialized countries are not economically affordable or practically feasible in the developing country. Instead of the sophisticated measurements, the researchers propose to use a patient-management technique based on total lymphocyte count and various clinical factors to make decisions about when to initiate therapy and for the ongoing management of patients. In order to validate the new patient-management approach, the researchers will conduct more sophisticated tests for CD4 T-cell counts and viral loads on a subset of subjects in the trial. Thus only that subset will get the more sophisticated laboratory assessments commonly used in industrialized countries.

What is this hypothetical example designed to show? The authors seek to reject what they call the Uniform Care Requirement, which they describe as the minimal requirement that all participants in research "should receive the level of care they would receive in a developed country."[7] The authors reject the contention that studies conducted in developing countries are unethical if those same studies could not be conducted in the country that sponsors the trial. According to this article, those who consider such trials unethical claim that "to permit different levels of care in different clinical trials implies an ethical double-standard, one consequence of which is opening the door to exploitation of developing-country populations by researchers from resource-rich countries."[8] The authors attempt to show that the Uniform Care Requirement would not permit this hypothetical study, which is designed to bring benefits that would otherwise be unavailable to the population. The result would – paradoxically, they claim – increase the potential for exploitation of the poor country.

On its face, the argument is persuasive and the hypothetical example telling. Two different aspects of the trial depart from medical procedures commonly employed in the United States: provision of antiretroviral treatment to asymptomatic HIV-infected individuals with low CD-4 T-cell counts and high viral loads; and use of sophisticated laboratory measurements to guide clinical decision-making. If the trial were redesigned to incorporate these features, the research question could not be answered and the hoped-for benefits would not accrue to the developing country.

The authors contend that the hypothetical study with the features they describe "would probably be deemed unethical" in the United States because some asymptomatic people would be randomly assigned to delayed therapy, which is contrary to standard practice guidelines. In addition, the study does not employ the standard and widely used method of laboratory monitoring. A separate consideration, not relevant to the ethical argument, is that the study would probably fail to be carried out even if proposed in the US, because patients and physicians have strong opinions on when treatment should be initiated. That may well be true as a practical matter, but it is irrelevant to whether it would be unethical to propose such a study in the US.

It is not evident that a study designed to reach the first objective would be unethical in the United States. Only if it had already been demonstrated in a randomized, controlled trial that the majority of individuals in whom treatment is delayed regularly worsen and cannot be helped by later antiretroviral treatment would it be unethical to do such a study. But that is presumably what the study in the African country is designed to show. Whether a study of this design is ethical depends very much on what the current treatment guidelines are based. Here are but a few examples of past studies with basically the same research design.

When the first randomized trial for treatment of breast cancer was initiated in the United States, many physicians strongly objected that it was unethical because women who were randomized to the group that received lumpectomy and adjuvant radiation instead of radical mastectomy – then the "standard of care" – were being denied the best treatment medicine had to offer. By now, years of research – including randomized, controlled trials – have demonstrated that a variety of alternatives to radical mastectomy have equally good survival rates from breast cancer.

When a study was proposed to see whether premature newborns could survive by being given much less oxygen than was the standard of care in the 1940s and '50s, some pediatricians argued that babies would needlessly die if oxygen was withheld during the study. The problem was, however, that premature babies who received high doses of oxygen were becoming blind, and researchers sought to determine whether the high dose of oxygen was the cause. The research was done and the oxygen was discovered to contribute to the condition then known as retrolental fibroplasia (now called retinopathy of prematurity), resulting in blindness. As a result of the research, oxygen for premature newborns was drastically reduced and this terrible consequence was eliminated.

Studies that established the efficacy of oral contraceptives in preventing pregnancy and of RU-486 as a medical means of abortion initially began with high doses of the compounds. After these methods were put into general practice, with the experimentally proven regimen as a standard, research continued in an effort to see whether lower doses worked as well as the higher ones, with the likelihood of fewer unwanted side effects. The women in the later studies who were randomized to the lower doses were provided with something "less" than the standard of care. Yet the studies were not deemed unethical because of that, and they eventually demonstrated that the lower doses were efficacious.

These are only a few examples of a very common research design: comparing the standard treatment with an experimental regimen that might turn out to be less efficacious, but there have been no randomized, controlled trials. The trials are proposed precisely to see whether similar benefits could be achieved with the experimental treatment without the unacceptable side effects that accompanied the "best current treatment." Studies with this design and objective have long been conducted in the US and even under today's heightened scrutiny of research, are considered ethically acceptable. The same can be said for testing a new diagnostic or laboratory method. When a less complex, cheaper, or more efficient laboratory or diagnostic method is proposed, it must be tested against the current standard to see whether it is as good, or almost as good. This is the utility of an equivalency study, the research design described in the hypothetical study in the article that rejects the Uniform Care Requirement.

There are risks as well as benefits in early treatment of HIV infection, which the authors of the above-noted article know much better than I. Some HIV-infected individuals seek to delay treatment because they know of these risks and have seen friends or family members who would not or could not adhere to the complex treatment regimen. In making their case that the hypothetical study provides a lower care level of care than the "standard" in the US, the NIH authors cite current treatment guidelines proposed by the NIH. These current treatment guidelines identify the following risks of early therapy:

1. the adverse effects of the drugs on quality of life;
2. the inconvenience of most of the suppressive regimens currently available, leading to reduced adherence;
3. development of drug resistance over time because of sub-optimal suppression of viral replication;
4. limitation of future treatment options due to premature cycling of the patient through the available drugs;
5. the risk of transmission of virus resistant to antiretroviral drugs;

6. serious toxicities associated with some antiretroviral drugs (e.g., elevations in serum levels of cholesterol and triglycerides, alterations in the distribution of body fat, insulin resistance, and even frank diabetes mellitus); and
7. the unknown durability of effect of the currently available therapies.

The NIH guidelines also cite potential benefits of delayed therapy:

1. avoidance of treatment-related negative effects on quality of life and drug-related toxicities;
2. preservation of treatment options; and
3. delay in the development of drug resistance.[9]

These NIH guidelines also address the timing of initiating antiretroviral therapy for asymptomatic HIV-infected individuals with CD4 T-cell counts greater than 200 cells/mm^3. The guidelines explicitly state that there is an absence of data from randomized clinical trials on the optimal time to start treatment. The guidelines say that randomized clinical trials provide strong evidence for treating patients with a count of less than 200 CD4$^+$ T-cells/mm^3, but only observational data exist for the question of optimal time. It is evident that much is still to be learned about the optimal time to begin highly active antiretroviral treatment, a factor that could justify doing the hypothetical study in the US.

Could a study like the hypothetical one described in the article be approved in the US? The main ethical problem is not the inclusion of a group for whom therapy would be delayed – the primary objective of the study. Rather, the design leading to the secondary objective is ethically problematic. The study would use a patient-management technique based on total lymphocyte count and various clinical factors to make decisions about when to initiate therapy, rather than the sophisticated laboratory measurements used in industrialized countries. Would that aspect of the study be ethical, if subjects could be found who were willing to be randomized?

I think it would not be ethically acceptable to do a randomized trial that would include HIV-infected individuals who lack background knowledge about current standards for diagnosis and treatment, and who might choose to initiate therapy earlier if they knew about it. However, this is simply an issue for the informed consent process. As long as there are some HIV-infected individuals who are willing not to initiate therapy until they become symptomatic, because they are truly ambivalent about the potential side effects of antiretrovirals, then it would be ethically acceptable to enroll them in a randomized trial.

For the secondary objective of the study as hypothesized, however, some subjects would be randomized to a measurement technique that is known to be inferior to the method employed in the US. In that case, randomization would probably not be ethically acceptable, since the imperfect technique of measurement could lead to errors in providing appropriate treatment for the subjects. However, if this aspect of the study were not randomized – that is, if some subjects would be willing to self-select to receive the less rigorous measurement technique, it could arguably be ethically acceptable. Purists will immediately object that randomization is a necessary component of the gold standard in research design. To forgo that necessary feature would jeopardize the scientific results. This is another example of a conflict between the gold standard in research and the gold standard in ethics. Would a "silver standard" (allowing subjects to self-select for the comparison group) yield no valid results whatsoever?

Many studies using comparison groups for which the subjects have self-selected are being done all the time and are supported by international agencies. I have reviewed numerous such studies that researchers propose and scientific members of ethical review committees consider methodologically sound. One example is studies in which women choose a method of contraception – a daily oral pill, a long-acting injectable preparation, or a long-acting implant – and these methods are compared for patients' acceptance, rates of pregnancy, and other factors. Another group of studies compares the efficacy, side effects, and acceptability to women of medical abortion, using RU-486, versus the aspiration method. The women come to a reproductive health clinic having already chosen a method of abortion, and they are then invited into the comparative study on a non-randomized basis.

If a randomized study using the best current diagnostic method versus an inferior method could not be conducted ethically in the United States, could it still be ethically acceptable in the sub-Saharan African country? The NIH authors say "yes," I say "probably not." The goal is to be able to treat as many HIV-infected people as possible, given the limited resources of the country. The goal is laudable. But is there only one way to reach that goal, to wit, conducting the study as described in the article? A comparison study could be conducted using a non-randomized, self-selected group for those subjects for whom the less sophisticated measurement would be used.

Like most people who find a double standard ethically acceptable when justified by the public health goals of research in developing countries, the authors of this article have constructed an appealing argument. They may well be right that a *randomized* study with these same goals would not be acceptable in the United States. It is likely that researchers would not be willing to enroll subjects in a study that failed to provide what would otherwise be available outside the trial, even if willing subjects could be found. But there is another problem with the argument as presented by the NIH authors. They provide a formulation of the Uniform Care Requirement that nobody actually holds.

Once again, here is their definition: "[A]s a minimal requirement, all participants of clinical research, wherever it is conducted, should receive the level of care they would receive in a developed country." Adherence to this requirement would make it impossible to do research anywhere. As Robert J. Levine correctly observed with regard to the way the earlier (1996) version of the Declaration of Helsinki was formulated, the wording of the provision requiring the "best proven" method precluded any or all experimental treatments.

Here is what Levine said about the previous declaration:

Article II.3 states, "In any medical study, every patient – including those of a control group, if any – should be assured of the best proven diagnostic and therapeutic method. This does not exclude the use of inert placebo in studies where no proven diagnostic or therapeutic method exists." The requirement that all patients be assured of the best proven therapeutic method rules out the development of all new treatments except those for diseases for which there are no proven therapeutic methods . . . Progress in the treatment of hypertension would have ended with a demonstration of the efficacy of ganglion-blocking drugs.[10]

Levine proceeded to criticize and reject the placebo clause in that paragraph in the declaration, a mission he continued to pursue and eventually lost throughout the contentious process of revising the declaration. But with regard to the requirement that "every patient be assured of the best proven method" his criticism is sound. The revised declaration is more carefully worded to avoid that pitfall, but makes the same point that was intended in the original version: "The benefits, risks, burdens and effectiveness of a new method should be tested against those of the best current prophylactic, diagnostic, and therapeutic methods."

The NIH authors crafted a formulation of the Uniform Care Requirement that no one could reasonably believe. Had they chosen to cite paragraph 29 of the 2000 Declaration of Helsinki, they would have been on firmer ground. Even then, the hypothetical study they devised to illustrate their point differs significantly from the placebo-controlled, mother-to-child HIV transmission study that launched the controversies over research conducted in developing countries. In the placebo-controlled HIV trials, *no* "best current therapeutic method" was provided – either for the control group or for the experimental group. The experimental group received the short-course AZT, which was believed in advance to have some efficacy, and the control group got nothing. In the hypothetical delayed treatment study, the control group gets the "best current" therapy, and the experimental group gets delayed treatment, which is not expected to be as good as therapy initiated at an earlier time. But it could turn out to be almost as good – which is what the trial is trying to find out. A third group (the symptomatic individuals) gets the "best current method."

Critics of the placebo-controlled, maternal-to-child transmission studies argued that the control group in those studies *should have* received the best current treatment, the one pregnant women in the US routinely got. The critics did not argue that an equivalency trial would have been unethical because the experimental group would get something less than the "best current method." On the contrary, leading critics[11] endorsed the design of an equivalency trial to study more affordable and practically feasible methods to prevent maternal-to-child transmission of HIV/AIDS. I cannot say, of course, whether all of the alleged proponents of the Uniform Care Requirement cited in the NIH authors' article[12] would reject as unethical the hypothetical study described in the article, whether some or all would consider it ethically acceptable, or whether they might accept an altered version, as I have suggested. What is clear, however, is that precision is needed in formulating statements of principle, and accuracy is required in claiming that other people subscribe to such formulations.

Providing successful products after a trial is concluded

As described in chapters 3 and 4, there is a wide range of views on what is owed to research subjects or to an entire population when research yields successful products. At one end of the continuum is the position that failure to provide successful products to a country in which the product has been tested but it is unaffordable grossly exploits those who served as research subjects in the developing country.[13] This position not only endorses Guideline 10 of the CIOMS ethical guidelines, but goes considerably farther in claiming that failure to adhere to this guideline constitutes exploitation.

At the other extreme is the rejection of CIOMS Guideline 10, which states that researchers must make every effort to ensure that any product developed will be made reasonably available to that population or community. Recall Dr. Robert Temple's urging that the guideline should be deleted, and his comment that "Individual patients may also be given access to treatments otherwise unavailable to them (how can they possibly be 'exploited' by this?)." These two extreme positions are so far apart as to be irreconcilable.

Somewhere in between these extremes are the recommendations of the NBAC and Nuffield reports, both of which maintain that it would be a good thing if products were made available to populations in need in developing countries, but there is no moral obligation on anyone's part to ensure that outcome. These recommendations pose a major challenge: how to transform a judgment that something is ethically desirable into the much stronger claim that an ethical obligation exists to bring about the desired state of affairs?

A rather different intermediate position requires that some benefit accrue to the developing country when research is concluded, but the benefit need not be provision of the drug or other tangible product of the research. Here is one statement of this intermediate position:

> [I]f one is to talk in terms of distributive justice, then one has to include the whole package of benefits and burdens that are to be distributed when assessing whether the state of affairs is just or not. Hence it could be that it is perfectly just to conduct research on a population that will not get any direct benefit of that research so long as that population is compensated with some other important goods.[14]

On this view, other types of benefit should count, such as monetary payments or contributions to the country's infrastructure that are not health-related. Although it is surely true that monetary payments *could* be used for a public health purpose, a country's leaders could equally well decide to use the money to purchase arms from the United States in order to wage war against its neighbor. The sponsoring country could not dictate to the developing country how the money will be used.

This consideration leads to another point raised by those who favor allowing different kinds of benefit to the developing country: it would avoid the paternalism of imposing on the developing country a single view regarding what may count as a benefit. To deny the option of different kinds of benefit "might wrongly tie the developing country's values to the values of the developed country."[15] This is surely a matter of concern, especially because of the history of colonialism and the now-rejected doctrine of "the white man's burden." Nevertheless, the ethical acceptability of this intermediate position relies fundamentally on what the money is used for. If the payments are used to develop effective preventive measures for a disease or other public health interventions, that could be considered a proportionate benefit to the host country. But if the country's leaders took the royalties or fixed payments and used them to purchase military weapons, there would likely be no benefit to the population and there might even be harm.

A key consideration in assessing the ethics of different kinds of benefits is the procedural matter of who determines what is to count as a benefit. If, for example, a robust community consultation is conducted before, during, and after the research – a process recommended in several international guidelines and reports – then there is much greater likelihood that the population will benefit from externally sponsored research in ways appropriate to their needs. Consultation with the community from which research subjects are drawn has not been a feature of research in the United States, with the exception of research conducted by the HIV Vaccine Trials Network (HVTN), an organization with a global reach, established in 1999 by the Division of AIDS in the NIH. The mission of the HVTN is to develop and test preventive HIV vaccines in US and international sites.[16] A central feature of its operation has been the creation of Community Advisory Boards in connection with the studies that it sponsors.

Increasingly, international guidelines and recommendations call for the involvement of the community at all stages of research. For example, Guidance Point 5 of the UNAIDS Guidance Document states that "community representatives should be involved in an early and sustained manner in the design, development, implementation and distribution of results of HIV vaccine research."[17] Recommendation 2.3 of the NBAC report states that

Researchers and sponsors should involve representatives of the community of potential participants throughout the design and implementation of research projects. Researchers should describe in their proposed protocol how this will be done, and ethics review committees should review the appropriateness of this process. When community representatives will not be involved, the protocol presented to the ethics committee should justify why such involvement was not possible or relevant.[18]

To date, however, except for the HVTN studies, there is not much in the way of hard evidence that these recommendations are being implemented.

We are left, then, with conflicting positions on the question of what should count as benefits to developing countries where studies are sponsored by industrialized countries. Some people argue that it is sufficient for the sponsoring country or industry to provide something to the developing country: a share in the profits from products developed during research, intellectual property rights, assisting in building capacity for conducting research, construction of laboratories, or even roads in rural areas.

Others contend, however, that something is owed more directly to the population in which the research is carried out. It is from that population that the research subjects were drawn, and they are the people in need of the health-related benefits that result from successful research. On this latter view, if health-related benefits derived from the research accrue only to the population in industrialized countries, the arrangement is unjust. Since the burdens of serving as research subjects (exposure to risks, discomforts, inconveniences) fall upon the developing countries, the population in those countries or regions deserves the same type of benefits that will flow to the wealthier or insured population in countries that sponsor research. These two fundamentally different positions on post-trial benefits to the host country do not appear to be amenable to easy resolution or compromise.

Irreconcilable differences

The draft of the CIOMS guidelines that was initially posted on the CIOMS website contained one guideline that had to be abandoned because of irreconcilable differences expressed by commentators who responded to the website posting. The guideline dealt with research involving "the products of conception," a euphemism the medical profession uses to refer to embryos and fetuses. Few topics are likely to engender more debate than that of research involving human embryos. This remains one of the most controversial topics worldwide, regardless of the purpose of the research and the goals it strives to achieve. The committee responsible for drafting the 1993 CIOMS guidelines had deliberately avoided including any guidelines on this contentious topic, and avoided, as well, the somewhat less controversial issue of research involving pregnant women. The CIOMS group that began work in 2000 was less timid and decided to include guidelines in these heretofore neglected areas. Accordingly, CIOMS commissioned a background paper, "Reproductive Biology and Technology,"[19] for discussion at its consultation in March 2000.

As could have been anticipated, at the March 2000 consultation debate erupted over this topic, in addition to the fundamental questions about obligations to research subjects and to the community or country. Participants in the CIOMS meeting from some countries in which there is an absolute prohibition of embryo research saw no possibility of even a partial acceptance of a guideline dealing with this issue. As a next step, CIOMS appointed interested participants at the consultation to form subcommittees to explore various topics covered in the draft guidelines and to report back with findings and recommendations for guidelines on those topics. The individuals who volunteered to work on the topic of reproductive biology and technology submitted material for a guideline on embryonic research, and the resulting item was posted on the CIOMS website as proposed Guideline 18:

Embryos should not be created specifically for the purpose of research, whether or not there are cultural or legal barriers to research involving products of conception. Research using tissue or germ cells from aborted fetuses may be carried out where there is no legal or cultural barrier, provided the researcher obtains the informed consent of the woman after the abortion has occurred or been performed. No products of conception used for research purposes may be bought or sold. The researcher has a duty:

- to obtain the informed consent of both parents for use of their embryos for research;
- if they cannot agree, researchers should not use their embryos in research;
- for research involving fetal tissue or fetal germ cells, to obtain the informed consent of the woman after she has undergone abortion.

Responses to the proposed guideline ran the gamut from full endorsement to total rejection.

The US Centers for Disease Control and Prevention observed:

This is an extremely controversial issue in the United States right now and the ethics of this practice is under discussion.

A Danish group acknowledged disagreement among its own ranks:

Some Council members believe it is unethical to produce embryos for research purposes. Others question this view if it precludes development of treatment methods that build on embryo cloning.

The Swiss Academy of Medical Sciences pointed out that

14 days after fertilization [is] applicable only for some countries, e.g. England, Denmark, Israel. In most other countries, at least in Europe, research on embryos left over from IVF is forbidden.

Another European group said:

The statement that "Embryos should not be created specifically for the purpose of research" should become a Law for the World. How can CIOMS get consensus on that?

From the British Medical Association:

We recognize that the creation of embryos for research is a subject that attracts controversy. Nevertheless, our national legislation and BMA policy allows the production of embryos for research within a tight ethical and legal framework. Certain types of important research, such as that on infertility, necessarily requires the creation of embryos.

Two other organizations in the UK said that they could not accept the sentence in the guideline that prohibits the creation of embryos for research. One organization replied:

In the UK we could not accept the first sentence. Whether or not embryos may be created specifically for research purposes is a subject on which strong and deeply divided views are held, both between individuals and between nations. After nearly 10 years of extensive public and Parliamentary debate, the UK finally decided in . . . 1990 that embryos may be created for specified research purposes under strict safeguards.

Moreover, this group added:

The inclusion of embryo research within these guidelines, given the lack of agreement on this topic, may limit the acceptability of the guidelines . . . It would be preferable to delete references to embryos entirely and if necessary cover these in another instrument.

The National Committee of Medical Research Ethics of Norway concurred that this guideline should not be included at all:

Advise delete. Not desirable to have a guideline on a very narrow and specific area in which there is substantial disagreement ethically, legally and culturally.

Other comments addressed different features of the guideline. One questioned the requirement that consent from the woman must be obtained after the abortion occurs; another questioned the need for both parents to consent to research involving their embryos, saying that only the woman's consent should be required. On this last point, one commentator wrote, in addition:

I don't see what founds [the husband's] right to a veto. On the other hand, I cannot see why the woman should not have a veto, over the request by the husband to use the embryo in research.

After deliberating the wisdom of including a guideline on embryo research, the informal drafting committee concluded that it would be better to omit reference to this controversial topic. Because these are international guidelines, and given the wide disparity among nations in laws, as well as cultural and religious views, consensus could never be achieved. If the guidelines were to include any statement about embryo research, the document as a whole might suffer from a loss of credibility. Although it was possible to omit a guideline on embryo research in order to avoid a loss of credibility, it would not have been credible for CIOMS to omit a guideline on the controversial issue raised by the use of placebo controls in clinical trials.

Soon after the informal writing group was appointed to work on a draft of the revised CIOMS guidelines, members of the group wondered what would happen if they disagreed among themselves about the substance of any of the guidelines. The group was not concerned about small differences that might arise on editorial or stylistic matters. Rather, they were concerned about the possibility of a disagreement, in principle, over the content of any of the guidelines.

Fortunately, major disagreements did not arise among the members of the informal writing group, with the one chief exception discussed in chapter 2: Guideline 11, "Choice of control in clinical trial." As recounted in that chapter, a few members of the group adopted sharply opposite positions on the acceptability of placebo controls, with one or two members occupying a somewhat noncommittal neutral ground. Faced with inability to come to a resolution, some members of the group suggested that the only solution would be to omit a guideline on this topic. It soon became clear, however, that this could not possibly be a satisfactory solution. The issue was too important, the controversy had already been brought to light in the process of revising the Declaration of Helsinki, and there was a widely perceived link between the Declaration of Helsinki and the CIOMS international ethical guidelines.

The same sharp disagreement that arose among several members of the informal writing group was expressed in the comments CIOMS received from the many individuals and organizations responding to the call for comments when the draft was posted on the CIOMS website, and yet again by those who attended the final consultation in February 2002. In the end, something of a compromise was reached that undoubtedly left some individuals unhappy, especially those who stood for the polar opposite positions on the issue of placebo controls. But achieving a compromise was still a far better solution than to have omitted altogether a guideline on this topic.

Any differences that existed among the commissioners who participated in the deliberations leading to the NBAC report were also resolved by a compromise. In the case of the controversial recommendation on placebo controls and the one on making products available following successful research, the resolution took the form of creating loopholes. A general presumption in favor of providing established, effective treatments to members of a control group could be overridden if researchers provided a good enough justification to the IRB or research ethics committee. Similarly, on the matter of providing post-trial benefits to the community or country, NBAC's recommendation allows the researcher to override the presumption:

In cases in which investigators do not believe that successful interventions will become available to the host country population, they should explain to the relevant ethics review committee(s) why the research is nonetheless responsive to the health needs of the country and presents a reasonable risk/benefit ratio.[20]

The need to be open to compromise is a necessary feature of serving on commissions charged with making recommendations for public policies of any sort. There is bound to be some disagreement between members of groups engaged in this process, so if there is to be a reasonable and timely outcome of the effort, people must be prepared to compromise, at least to some extent. A dilemma confronts any individual involved in the process for whom compromise would result in a loss of moral integrity. Refusal to sign on to a report is one option, writing a dissenting piece is another possibility, and appending a "personal statement" is a somewhat weaker option. However, since dissenting opinions and refusals of group members to endorse a report result in diminished credibility for the entire report, committee chairpersons typically try to arrive at a consensus, even if it means watering down recommendations to make them acceptable to all members. Of course, too much watering down has the effect of making policy recommendations so weak that they are meaningless.

Building capacity and assessing ethics in ongoing research

Of the many research proposals submitted for funding each year to the World Health Organization's Department of Reproductive Health and Research, most make an explicit acknowledgment that the research will be conducted in accordance with the Declaration of Helsinki. A much smaller number refer to the CIOMS International Ethical Guidelines for Biomedical Research. The great majority of these studies take place in developing countries. As a member of the Scientific and Ethical Review Group of the Human Reproduction Programme since 1989, I have had the opportunity to read all of these research proposals. This has enabled me to assess the extent to which the contents of the submission comply with the requirements of Helsinki and CIOMS.

In several respects it is considerably easier to comply with the Declaration of Helsinki. For one thing, there are fewer details in the provisions of Helsinki than in CIOMS. For another, CIOMS includes topics that Helsinki does not mention, such as what must be provided to the community or country when trials are over, research involving pregnant women, and research in populations and communities with limited resources. Yet even with respect to the simpler requirements of the Helsinki Declaration, virtually all the protocols I have reviewed fall short in one way or another.

This state of affairs is not particularly surprising. The research proposals I review as a member of my own institution's IRB in the United States are typically less than perfect in their adherence to the totality of ethical requirements. Of course, biomedical research in the United States must comply with the US Code of Federal Regulations and the FDA regulations for drug studies. As noted in earlier chapters, the US regulations say nothing about placebo controls in clinical trials or about what must be provided to research subjects and others at the conclusion of the research. So, while there are many detailed provisions in the federal regulations, some of the more controversial items in the international guidelines are absent. Still, informed consent documents continue to be too long, too complex, and too technical. And conspicuously absent from the majority of proposals are any details about the process and personnel involved in recruiting subjects.

Another reason it is not surprising to find shortcomings in ethical aspects of proposals submitted to WHO is the rather recent entry into the field of many developing country researchers and local institutions. It takes time to get up to speed in both the scientific and ethical aspects of biomedical research, and one would expect to see improvement over time. The Human Reproduction Programme sends to all potential applicants a copy of a booklet (called "the orange book" because of the color of its cover) containing detailed instructions for completing the research application. The booklet enumerates the items that must be addressed in each section of the protocol, and describes under the heading "Ethical considerations" what the proposal must include regarding risks and benefits, informed consent, protection of confidentiality, recruitment procedures, gender considerations, and more. The orange book also contains a copy of the latest version of the Declaration of Helsinki. Despite the distribution of this detailed information about ethical requirements for protocols submitted to the Programme, the learning curve rises ever so slowly.

Both the Human Reproduction Programme at WHO and the HIV/AIDS vaccine initiative sponsored jointly by WHO and UNAIDS have done a great job in launching programs to build capacity in ethics among researchers and members of ethical review committees in developing countries. By the end of 2002, the WHO program had conducted five training workshops in the major regions in which the organization has offices, and it plans additional ones in subregions in the near future. The HIV/AIDS vaccine program held a similar series of workshops, and has sponsored other capacity-building efforts, in addition. One such effort is sponsorship of a comprehensive vaccine network on the African continent, a component of which is devoted to ethical, legal, and human rights aspects of vaccine research and development.

A quite different activity facilitated by the WHO/UNAIDS vaccine initiative was not so much an exercise in capacity-building as an ethical assessment of an ongoing vaccine trial. This came about in response to a request from the Thai head of a phase III preventive vaccine trial being conducted in Thailand. The vaccine research was a joint effort undertaken by the industrial sponsor, VaxGen, the Bangkok Vaccine Evaluation Group, and the US Centers for Disease Control and Prevention (CDC). As this was the first phase III trial of a preventive vaccine for HIV/AIDS and was being carried out in a developing country (a simultaneous study was being conducted in the US), it was inevitable that the media and watchdog groups would be paying close attention. The Thai researcher sought assistance from the head of the vaccine program (then located within UNAIDS) to conduct an independent evaluation of the vaccine trial while it was still ongoing.

The head of the UNAIDS vaccine program, Dr. José Esparza, assembled a five-person team to communicate with the investigators and make a site visit to Bangkok. The team comprised a Thai physician-researcher unaffiliated with the trial, a Thai health advocate who works at the community level, a member of the UNAIDS vaccine program in Geneva, an internationally renowned European bioethicist with expertise in research ethics, and me. Since neither my European bioethics colleague nor I had ever done an ethical assessment of an ongoing clinical trial, we had to invent the entire process in consultation with the three other members of the assessment team. This took approximately four months of advance preparation – reviewing documents we requested of the sponsors, communicating amongst ourselves, and drawing up a plan for the five-day site visit to Bangkok.

The documents we requested included the original research protocol and later revisions; the informed consent documents, along with a test of comprehension that was used to evaluate potential subjects' understanding of the research; ancillary protocols for implementing the study that were developed after the initial protocol; reports of the four research ethics committees that reviewed the research protocol and its revisions; correspondence from the National AIDS Commission of Thailand; and additional items of correspondence relevant to approval and implementation of the study. During our five-day site visit, we met on more than one occasion with the principal investigator and project coordinator, other members of the Bangkok Vaccine Evaluation Group, and the CDC official working with the research team. We visited four different sites in Bangkok where the study was being conducted, including a prison where some of the volunteers had been incarcerated following their enrollment and having received some injections of the vaccine. At those sites we interviewed counselors and nurses (our Thai colleagues conducted these and translated for the other three of us) and several research subjects.

The Thai health advocate on our assessment team was also able to arrange an informal discussion with several individuals in the community who had volunteered for the study but ended up not being enrolled. The Thai volunteers in this vaccine trial were all intravenous drug users, a group that was selected because the subjects in a preventive vaccine trial have to be people who are at high risk of becoming infected through their behavior (the cohort for the simultaneous US vaccine trial were gay men). Despite formidable barriers in being able to locate intravenous drug users and invite them to a meeting, thanks to our Thai colleague we were able to do so. She had gained the trust of these drug injectors as a result of her work at the community level.

Our assessment team began with several initial ethical concerns: the enrollment of a marginalized group as subjects in a five-year vaccine trial; the knowledge that at some point during the trial, a predictable number of the volunteers would be incarcerated and would have to be located by the researchers and visited for injections or examinations during their incarceration; the literacy level of this population; what would be provided by way of medical treatment for any volunteers who became infected (as a result of their behavior, not the vaccine) during the trial; and what would be made available to the group that received placebo, as well as to the wider Thai community, if the vaccine proved to be efficacious.

The final report submitted by our assessment team is not a public document, as it was prepared at the request of the Thai principal investigator, facilitated by the UNAIDS secretariat, and handed over to the Thai and CDC co-sponsors. However, I am able to say that the assessment team found no major departures from international ethical guidelines and judged the study to be carried out at a high level of ethical and scientific conduct. We did raise a number of questions of clarification in our initial report and made several recommendations for changes we believed would further improve the ethical aspects of the trial. This was a valuable exercise for us on the assessment team and appeared to have been appreciated by the group conducting the study and the co-sponsors. This experience could serve as a model for future assessments if any researchers or sponsors seek an independent ethical evaluation of a trial in progress.

Dilemmas in future HIV/AIDS preventive vaccine trials

The results of the first phase III efficacy trial for an AIDS vaccine were announced in early 2003. The industrial sponsor, VaxGen Inc., said that the initial results of this three-year study in the United States showed that the AIDSVAX vaccine did not protect most volunteers against HIV infection, although it may have offered some protection to African-American and Asian-American volunteers.[21] Nevertheless, the trial revealed valuable scientific information that can be useful for subsequent preventive vaccine trials. At the time of this writing, the results of the parallel VaxGen study taking place in Thailand are not yet available. If the AIDSVAX vaccine had been much more successful, a potential dilemma would have arisen immediately for researchers and sponsors planning the next phase III vaccine trial. Since phases I and II vaccine trials are ongoing in various sites in the world, this dilemma will eventually loom on the horizon, once a preventive HIV/AIDS vaccine is demonstrated to be efficacious.

The dilemma has two parts, by now familiar from the earlier discussions on "standard of care": (1) What should be provided to control groups in vaccine trials scheduled to begin after the results of a successful vaccine trial are announced? and (2) What type and level of treatment should be provided to subjects who become infected (as a result of their behavior, not the vaccine) during these new trials? This second question is not limited to future trials, but applies as well to preventive HIV/AIDS trials already initiated.

The control group in vaccine trials

In the VaxGen phase III trials in the US and Thailand, the control group received placebos and subjects in the experimental arm received the active vaccine. As noted in chapter 2, the UNAIDS Guidance Document for vaccine trials has this to say: "Participants in the control arm of a future phase III HIV preventive vaccine trial should receive an HIV vaccine known to be safe and effective when such is available, unless there are compelling scientific reasons which justify the use of a placebo."[22] The other familiar guidelines are the relevant paragraph in the Declaration of Helsinki and the CIOMS guideline, both of which permit the use of placebos in a control group when there is no "best current" or "established, effective" preventive method. This remains the case following the announcement of the disappointing results of the VaxGen product. But what if the AIDSVAX vaccine had proven to be efficacious? The dilemma that would have arisen for the very next trial will have to be faced at some future time for a different vaccine.

As the VaxGen trials neared completion in 2003, another phase III trial was scheduled to begin in Thailand. In that trial, the VaxGen product was to be given in conjunction with another product manufactured by the French company, Aventis-Pasteur.[23] The experimental group would get both the VaxGen and Aventis-Pasteur products in combination, but the control arm would get the Aventis-Pasteur vaccine along with a placebo. It follows from Guidance Point 11 in the UNAIDS Guidance Document that if the VaxGen product was demonstrated to be safe and effective, it should be used – instead of a placebo – in the control arm of the pending trial in Thailand.

Recall also, however, that the guidance document mentions "compelling scientific reasons" that would permit a research design that includes a placebo for the control group: if "the effective HIV vaccine is not believed to be effective against the virus that is prevalent in the research population"; or "the biological conditions that prevailed during the initial trial demonstrating efficacy were so different from the conditions in the proposed research population that the results of the initial trial cannot be directly applied to the research population under consideration." There was little reason to believe that either of these two factors pertained to the new trial scheduled for 2003 in Thailand, since the virus in the research population was the same as in the earlier VaxGen trial and the Thai population was basically the same.

What, then, would be the problem in determining whether the VaxGen vaccine, rather than a placebo, should be used for the control group in the new trial? The key issue was the degree of efficacy that would be demonstrated in the VaxGen trial then nearing completion. If the VaxGen product demonstrated no, or very low efficacy in the trials nearing completion, it would have been ethically justifiable to use placebos in the control group of the Aventis-Pasteur Thai trial. Even a low-efficacy vaccine is unlikely to be licensed by the FDA, and therefore would be available to no one, anywhere, outside future vaccine trials.

Alternatively, if the VaxGen vaccine had demonstrated high efficacy, it would have been unethical to withhold it from the control group in the subsequent Thai trial. CIOMS Guideline 11 does allow a placebo control in the following circumstance: "when withholding an established effective intervention would expose subjects to, at most, temporary discomfort or delay in relief of symptoms." Clearly, this does not apply to a preventive method for HIV/AIDS, since withholding an effective prevention could expose subjects to a great deal more than "temporary discomfort."

The problem, then, is one of drawing the line: how low must the efficacy be of a preventive vaccine as demonstrated in one trial, in order to permit the use of placebo in the control arm of a subsequent vaccine trial? Put the other way around: how high must the proven efficacy of one vaccine be, in order to conclude that it would be unethical to use a placebo control in the next vaccine trial? I confess, I do not have a ready answer to this question. At 60 percent or higher efficacy, it would appear to be ethically necessary to have required the VaxGen vaccine rather than placebo for the control group in the Aventis-Pasteur Thai trial. At 30 percent efficacy or lower, a placebo control seems to be ethically acceptable. But somewhere in between it is just not clear.

One possible criterion for arriving at an answer is whether the sponsoring company applies to the FDA for a license for its product. In that case, the vaccine would be deemed sufficiently efficacious for the company to make application for a license; but the license would almost certainly not be granted prior to the time that a proposed new trial is scheduled to begin. It would be months before the FDA could approve a license for a vaccine that showed sufficient efficacy. In this situation, the vaccine could be considered "effective" but not "established" because it is not yet licensed. In that case, it would still be unethical to withhold the vaccine from a control group, since it is only a matter of time before the license would be granted.

An additional consideration arises if the established, effective vaccine is not available to provide to the control group at the time the new trial commences. What could be the reasons for lack of availability? One possibility is that the product used in the initial trial was not manufactured in sufficient quantities for use in the control group in a new trial. This possibility would be unfortunate but not remediable, given the time it takes to put in place manufacturing facilities for making much larger batches of the vaccine. Lack of a sufficient amount of vaccine for a control group in the next trial illustrates the "ought implies can" maxim: it is pointless to say something ought to be done when it simply cannot be done.

There is still another possibility: the vaccine demonstrated to be effective in an earlier trial is manufactured in sufficient quantities, but is claimed not to be affordable in the country where the next trial is about to begin. But here it is necessary to ask: affordable to whom? To the researchers conducting the new trial? Surely not, because it is not they, but industry that always supplies the product needed for the research to be carried out. Affordable to the participants in the control group in the new trial? Again, obviously not, because the majority of people in developing countries cannot afford these products. Affordable to the Ministry of Health in the developing country or the local health authorities responsible for making a licensed product widely available in the country or community? It is this last possibility that leads some people to say there is no obligation to provide the effective vaccine to the control group if they would not readily have access to it outside the study. There is a more than faint resemblance to the placebo-controlled, maternal-to-child HIV transmission studies that resulted in a worldwide controversy.

My own conclusions are: (1) it would be ethically acceptable to have a placebo control in a subsequent vaccine trial if the only vaccines tested in earlier trials showed no efficacy or very low efficacy; (2) a placebo control would require a strong justification if a previously tested vaccine has demonstrated some efficacy but is judged insufficiently efficacious to apply for licensing; (3) a placebo control is ethically unacceptable if the previously tested vaccine shows moderate to high efficacy, even if it is not yet licensed.

Those who would defend the CIOMS "ethically exceptional use of placebo" could come to a different conclusion. The CIOMS commentary on Guideline 11 describes the circumstance:

> An exception to the general rule is applicable in some studies designed to develop a therapeutic, preventive or diagnostic intervention for use in a country or community in which an established effective intervention is not available and unlikely in the foreseeable future to become available, usually for economic or logistic reasons.[24]

As argued at length in chapter 2, this circumstance cannot serve to justify withholding an established, effective intervention from a control group when failure to provide the product could result in serious or irreversible harm, including death.

Treatment for subjects who become infected

As for the second "standard of care" question – what level of treatment should be provided to participants in future vaccine trials if they acquire HIV infection during the trial – the familiar debate about double standards looms large. The author of the *New Yorker* article cited in chapter 1 asserts the simplistic view that the only way to think about this question is in terms of what poor countries can afford:

> No country in Africa, and few countries elsewhere in the developing world, can afford Western levels of treatment. So the principal question for researchers and public-health officials is both simple and harsh: Will scientific objectives drive the search for an AIDS vaccine, or will a series of ethical imperatives imposed by the West take precedence? Because that question has gone unanswered, fear of exploitation and abuse hangs over the trials, threatening not only to impede their progress but to prevent them altogether.[25]

The simplistic view that what can be provided to participants in a vaccine trial is limited by the economies of poor countries is demonstrably false, as illustrated by the various efforts going forward to make drugs more affordable and accessible for people living in those countries. Furthermore, given the relatively small numbers of individuals who are participants in preventive HIV/AIDS vaccine trials, and the much smaller number that will become infected during the trial, it is also a gross overestimate to think that the cost of providing antiretroviral treatment to this group would be exorbitant. Informal estimates indicate that the cost would be affordable, even if required for the lifetime of that group.

What is more, the suggestion that the alleged "ethical imperatives" are imposed by the West is also wrong. Who or what in the West is seeking to impose this requirement? Both of the reports and recommendations[26] issued by the Western countries that conduct the preponderance of research in developing countries – the US and UK – leave plenty of room for research to go forward even if research subjects and others do not receive the same care and treatment as that provided to subjects in industrialized countries.

The only spokespersons for the alleged "Western ethics" cited in the article are Peter Lurie and Marcia Angell – two of the individuals who have been among the strongest defenders of a single ethical standard. But Lurie and Angell are outnumbered by others from the US – including the NIH and the FDA – whose comments are cited in previous chapters in defense of allowing different standards for rich and poor countries. The *New Yorker* article characterizes the views of African scientists, saying that they see the matter differently and implying that all Africans speak with one voice in opposition to "Western ethics." This, too, is an overgeneralization, apparently based on the two or three African scientists the author interviewed for the article.

My own experience at conferences and workshops in South Africa, Uganda, and Zimbabwe, and at meetings in Geneva, Washington, DC, and New York, has been decidedly different. Some Africans are adamantly in favor of a single ethical standard in multinational research. One group in South Africa strongly advocates providing antiretroviral treatment to subjects in preventive vaccine trials who acquire HIV infection.[27] Others from the continent hold the view that the *New Yorker* article construes as the "African position." An honest assessment must acknowledge the existence of a profound disagreement among Africans, Asians, Europeans, and North and South Americans on the question of what level of care and treatment is owed to research subjects in resource-poor countries.

It is neither accurate nor helpful to characterize the different viewpoints on this issue as "Western ethical imperatives" versus "non-Western ethics." A more appropriate way of describing the opposing positions is with reference to their adherence to the two conceptions of justice outlined in chapter 2: justice as *equity* and justice as *equality*. We noted there that both principles of justice are legitimate and are potentially applicable to a variety of situations, and that it requires further argument and analysis to determine which is more applicable in a particular context.

Those who defend justice as equity as the more appropriate principle would have to point to the background economic conditions in rich and poor countries as a basis for saying that justice does not require treating everyone, everywhere in the same way. Equitable treatment in what is provided to research subjects who become HIV-infected during vaccine trials is based on what the subjects themselves or their governments can afford. On this analysis, research ethics is a function of economics.

In contrast, those who defend justice as equality as the more appropriate principle in this context deny that economic differences among research subjects or their governments justifies treating them differently. Instead, the justification lies partly in another principle of research ethics: maximize benefits and minimize harms to subjects. Granted, that principle is usually interpreted to refer to the benefits and harms that flow directly from the research maneuvers themselves. But there is no reason why the principle of beneficence cannot also apply more broadly to care and treatment provided to research subjects. Beyond that, justice as equality rejects both geographical location and economic status as a basis for determining what justice requires. Since research in today's world is a global enterprise, justice in international research calls for treating subjects equally whether they live in Boston or Botswana, Utah or Uganda. I find this analysis to be more persuasive than the defense of justice as equity. It leads to a more robust conception of justice.

What the guidelines say

With regard to the international guidelines, nothing in any of the major documents would prevent vaccine research from going forward unless host-country governments or sponsors of research provide the best treatment anywhere in the world to volunteers who acquire HIV infection while enrolled in a vaccine trial. The Declaration of Helsinki is silent on this point. Paragraph 29 deals only with what should be provided to control groups, not with the more general question of the level of care and treatment of subjects who become sick during a trial. CIOMS Guideline 21 states that external sponsors are ethically obliged to ensure the availability of healthcare services that are essential to the safe conduct of the research and treatment for subjects who suffer injury as a consequence of research interventions. The commentary on this guideline says that sponsors' obligations in particular studies should be clarified in advance of the research, but notes also that obligations to provide healthcare services will vary with the circumstances of particular studies and the needs of host countries.[28] The only one of the international documents that says anything directly about treatment of subjects in vaccine trials is the UNAIDS Guidance Document. But even that guidance point does not require anyone to provide the best HIV/AIDS treatment anywhere in the world or else forgo conducting a vaccine trial altogether.

In the VaxGen vaccine trials conducted in the US and Thailand, the company sponsor did not take responsibility for providing any antiretroviral treatment for HIV/AIDS. The informed consent document for the Thai trial made that abundantly clear. Presumably, the North American volunteers could gain access to antiretroviral therapy that is readily available outside the trial. The Thai volunteers who became infected were eligible for treatment under the Bangkok Metropolitan Administration Guidelines for the Clinical Care of HIV-infected Patients. These guidelines have been updated periodically, and by the end of the VaxGen trial they prescribed different treatment regimens from those available when the trial began in 1999. The Thai participants who became infected during the trial did, therefore, receive some treatment, though not at the level likely to have been provided to the North American volunteers.

Whatever treatment infected Thai subjects received was not "ideal," but may have been reasonably close to what the UNAIDS Guidance Document says: "the 'ideal' is to provide 'the best proven therapy,' and the minimum is to provide 'the highest level of care attainable in the host country.'" It is simply a factual matter to discover what level of treatment Thai subjects actually received. The difficult conceptual problem is to determine just what constitutes "the highest attainable" at any time or place.

But suppose some or all participants in the Thai vaccine trial who became HIV-infected did receive a level of treatment equivalent to that available to North American participants. Then a different question arises about the fairness of double standards. Subjects in the trial in Bangkok would be receiving a level of treatment for HIV that is higher than that generally available to HIV-infected individuals who are not in the vaccine trial. Except for wealthy Thais, who are able to afford the best current treatment anywhere in the world, the trial participants would be made better off than their family members or neighbors, who could receive only the level of treatment affordable to the public health authorities in the city or country. Is this double standard not as ethically problematic as the double standard of providing different levels of treatment for Thai volunteers and those in North America? Either situation produces what may termed "the dilemma of double standards."

At one UNAIDS consultation, which took place several years ago when the discussion of ethics in vaccine trials was just beginning, a participant from one developing country was adamant in rejecting the suggestion that antiretroviral drugs should be provided for subjects who become infected during the trial. This individual argued that vaccine trial subjects who become infected during the research do not deserve treatment any more than anyone else in the society who acquires HIV infection. In fact, he argued, research subjects are *less* deserving of treatment since they have been carefully counseled, before and during the trial, to avoid behaviors that would put them at risk of becoming infected. Expressing a somewhat exaggerated fear, he said there would be rioting in the streets of his country if some people received treatment for AIDS while almost everyone else lacked access.

As an abstract exercise, there is no easy answer to this dilemma. One approach is to insist that being a research subject puts one in a category distinct from one's neighbors who are not research subjects. The potential risks, discomforts, and inconveniences justify treating research subjects differently from their fellow citizens. This approach, although promising, is less persuasive when the research carries relatively low risks. In the case of the VaxGen vaccine, there is abundant evidence that it is safe. Not only did the vaccine succeed in passing through the first two phases, in which safety and toxicity were evaluated, but there have been very few serious adverse events reported in the carefully monitored phase III trial.

Another approach to the dilemma of double standards is to look, once again, at the international guidelines. The Declaration of Helsinki does not contain any paragraphs that directly relate to this concern. Guideline 3 of the 2002 CIOMS international guidelines, which deals with externally sponsored research, is a revised version of Guideline 15 from the 1993 CIOMS document (see chapter 2 for a brief discussion of the earlier guideline). Guideline 3 of 2002 CIOMS says:

An external sponsoring organization and individual investigators should submit the research protocol for ethical and scientific review in the country of the sponsoring organization, and the ethical standards applied should be no less stringent than they would be for research carried out in that country.[29]

Unfortunately, this is of little help. It all depends on what are to count as "ethical standards." Does the level of treatment provided to research participants who acquire a disease in the course of a trial constitute an "ethical standard"? As discussed at length in chapter 2, the ambiguity of the term "standard" and the various interpretations of the expression "standard of care" are sufficiently problematic to warrant abandoning them as a practical guide in the context of research.

The only one of the international guidelines that is directly on point is UNAIDS Guidance Point 16, designed specifically for the situation at hand: care and treatment for HIV/AIDS and its associated complications for participants in preventive vaccine trials who become infected. As noted earlier, this guidance point stipulates an ideal – "the best proven therapy" – and the minimum – "the highest level of care attainable in the host country" – in light of several circumstances that are listed in the guidance point. The UNAIDS vaccine guidance document combines the quest to attain an ideal ethical situation with the pragmatic need to pursue vaccine trials even if it is not possible to provide the best known treatment to research subjects.

As the price of antiretroviral drugs continues to drop, and as access is improved through the Global Fund and the other avenues discussed in chapter 6, the highest attainable level of treatment may come close to, if not match, the best proven treatment in some developing countries where vaccine trials are conducted. In addition, there are hopeful signs as a group of NIH researchers has begun to argue in favor of providing treatment to infected vaccine trial participants. The HIV Vaccine Trials Network (HVTN), which sponsors trials in developing countries as well as in the US, has suggested that on economic and ethical grounds, the best current antiviral treatments can and should be provided for HIV-infected vaccine trial participants.

What about post-trial benefits? On the assumption that the AIDSVAX vaccine would turn out to be sufficiently efficacious, VaxGen promised to make it available to the Thai volunteers who received placebo. This commitment is in strict fulfillment of the Declaration of Helsinki's paragraph 30: "At the conclusion of the study, every patient entered into the study should be assured of access to the best proven prophylactic, diagnostic, or therapeutic methods identified by the study." VaxGen also agreed to tiered pricing of the vaccine, thereby increasing the likelihood that a successful product could eventually be made more widely available in Thailand. Even in that circumstance, in order to make the vaccine much more widely available Thailand might have had to receive additional financing from the Global Fund to Fight AIDS, Tuberculosis, and Malaria or the Vaccine Fund. As more vaccine trials are initiated in Thailand and the other developing countries for which they are planned, these challenges will have to be faced.

Harmonizing international guidelines

As described throughout this book, there exists a large and still growing array of international ethical guidelines and recommendations from detailed reports on ethics in multinational research. These are in addition to the laws, regulations, and guidelines adopted in different countries, and the International Conference on Harmonisation (ICH) Tripartite Guideline, providing detailed technical requirements for product registration in the applicable countries – the United States, Japan, and regulatory authorities in Europe. One possible approach in seeking to arrive at a single ethical standard would be to harmonize the existing guidelines. Is that possible, would it be desirable, and could it achieve the aim of providing a single ethical standard for research? Would doing so make it easier or more difficult for developing countries to build their capacity for conducting biomedical research and for ethical and scientific review of proposed research?

One view maintains that the guidelines have to be harmonized, or else researchers and sponsors can simply pick and choose the ones that suit them best. A quite different view holds that where sharp disagreements persist over the features of an ethical guideline, it is a mistake to insist on retaining the guideline because it will inevitably be violated by some researchers and thereby fail to command respect. Still another position observes that it will take some time for developing countries to reach the sophistication of industrialized countries, so it would be a mistake to impose the most rigorous form of guidelines for ethical review of research on countries that have only recently begun to develop their own capacity.

I take a pessimistic view regarding the feasibility of any real harmonization. The controversy over the contents of paragraph 29 of the Declaration of Helsinki remains, and the World Medical Association itself appears ambivalent, given the murky and ambiguous clarification it issued in 2001. Among the strongest opponents of the clause mandating "the best current diagnostic, prophylactic, and therapeutic method" for control groups in randomized clinical trials are the most powerful US governmental organizations related to biomedical research: the NIH and the FDA. Members of the Working Party that issued the report of the Nuffield Council on Bioethics represented several of the leading research institutions in the UK, including the Medical Research Council, the London School of Hygiene and Tropical Medicine, and Oxford and Cambridge Universities. The comments individuals and organizations submitted on the CIOMS guideline on this same topic included sharply opposing views (see chapter 2), with some demanding the strictest limitation on placebos, others endorsing a slight weakening of Helsinki's paragraph 29 (minus the "clarification"), and others arguing for abandoning the Helsinki presumption altogether.

The same array of disagreements persists with respect to providing post-trial benefits to research subjects and to the community or country. Many commentators are skeptical about the feasibility or wisdom of establishing a requirement that there be a prior agreement to make products demonstrated to be successful widely available after a study is completed. Helsinki's paragraph 30 seeks to ensure access to successful products on the part of individuals who were in enrolled in a trial; CIOMS goes farther, presuming that products should be made "reasonably available" to the population or community; and the UNAIDS vaccine guidance document states the strongest presumption for availability as soon as possible. Some people argue that there is no obligation whatsoever to provide any post-research benefits; others say there should be benefits but they need not be medical or health-related benefits; still others contend that if the population in developing countries does not have access to products developed during research conducted there, it amounts to exploitation.

Even if opponents in these controversies were to come closer together, a huge problem remains. These guidelines and declarations have no binding force on anyone and no sanctions are in place for violations. Helsinki is a mere "declaration," despite the somewhat lofty reputation it has enjoyed. The CIOMS guidelines, for all their details and helpful explanatory commentary, are issued by a nongovernmental organization that is much less prominent than the World Medical Association. The UNAIDS guidance points for preventive HIV/AIDS vaccine research are somewhat narrow, as they apply to one area of research for a single disease.

At bottom, I believe that harmonization of ethical guidelines for research is not feasible. My reason for drawing this conclusion is that parties to these disagreements have radically different interests at stake. The pharmaceutical and biotechnology industries are business enterprises that seek to make the greatest profit from research and development of new products. It is in their interest to conduct clinical trials as quickly and as efficiently as possible, with the fewest commitments to provide products at lower cost to resource-poor countries. The US FDA is a strong ally of the pharmaceutical industry and has no independent interest in seeing that research subjects or communities in developing countries receive direct benefits equivalent to what people in the US normally receive.

The NIH and the MRC have as their mission the conduct of research, not the provision of health benefits to research subjects or the developing countries from which they are drawn. It is in the interest of these governmental sponsors to conduct research efficiently and effectively, and that can be done only by sticking to their narrow mission. Ministries of health and researchers in developing countries gain by having external sponsors foot the bill of research in their countries. With a new emphasis on the obligation of sponsors to assist in building scientific capacity and capacity for scientific and ethical review of research, developing countries receive benefits beyond the immediate flow of research money, scientists, and equipment in the service of a particular research effort.

Those on the other side of these disagreements also have interests. Researchers, ethicists, and other spokespersons from developing countries seek treatment of research subjects and benefits for inhabitants of their countries equivalent to those that are provided to research subjects and inhabitants of sponsoring, industrialized countries. They have an interest in avoiding both the reality and the appearance of being exploited for gains realized by others. As for the other proponents of a single global standard for research – the health advocates, bioethicists, human rights activists, and scholars throughout the world – their interest lies in securing justice and equal rights for all.

The future

Probably the best hope for the future lies in an approach to making health-related goods and services available to resource-poor countries through the efforts of public–private partnerships. This approach should be informed by a human rights analysis. The implementation of findings from analysis can apply to non-state actors as well as to states parties to the various human rights instruments. A tangible mark of success would be the abandonment of the World Trade Organization's barriers to the importation of generic copies of patented drugs, thereby enabling the poorest countries to take some responsibility for providing needed medications to their own people.

The purpose of biomedical research is to contribute to scientific knowledge that can be used to provide better clinical care and introduce better public health measures for all people, not just the inhabitants of wealthy countries or the wealthy inhabitants of poor countries. In the service of that goal, the conduct of research should conform to universal ethical principles governing research, despite the political factors that prevent a universal, harmonized set of ethical guidelines. It is ludicrous to hold that there are Western ethical imperatives that apply only to the West, African ethical imperatives that apply only to Africa, and Asian ethical principles that apply only to that part of the world. Maintaining the same ethical standards for research will not thwart the research enterprise, but can help to ensure that judgments made at some future time will not condemn the current era as one that accepted and even endorsed double standards of research ethics.

NOTES

1. Godfrey B. Tangwa, "International Regulations and Medical Research in Developing Countries: Double Standards or Differing Standards?" *Notizie di Politeia*, 18:67 (2002), 46–50 at 47.
2. Ibid.
3. David Orentlicher, "Universality and its Limits: When Research Ethics Can Reflect Local Circumstances," *Journal of Law, Medicine and Ethics*, 30 (2002), 403–410.
4. Ibid.
5. Greg Patterson, Letter to the Editor, *New York Times* (February 15, 2001).
6. Jack Killen, Christine Grady, Gregory K. Folkers, and Anthony S. Fauci, "Ethics of Clinical Research in the Developing World," *Nature Reviews/Immunology*, 2 (March 2002), 210–215.
7. Ibid., 212.
8. Ibid.
9. Available at http://www.aidsinfo.nih.gov/guidelines/adult/AA_071403.html PrevNoTreat, accessed October 10, 2003.
10. Robert J. Levine, "The Need to Revise the Declaration of Helsinki," NEJM, 341 (1999), 531–534 at 532.
11. Peter Lurie and Sidney Wolfe, "Unethical Trials of Interventions to Reduce Perinatal Transmission of the Human Immunodeficiency Virus in Developing Countries," NEJM, 337 (1997), 853–856.
12. Citations included Lurie and Wolfe, "Unethical Trials", Marcia Angell, "The Ethics of Clinical Research in the Third World," NEJM, 337 (1997), 847–849; Marcia Angell, "Investigators' Responsibilities for Human Subjects in Developing Countries," NEJM, 342 (2000), 967–969; David J. Rothman, "The Shame of Medical Research," *New York Review of Books* (November 30, 2000), available at http://www.nybooks.com/nyre/WWWfeatdisplay.cgi?20001130060F; George J. Annas, "Prominent Opinion: The Ethics of International Research Trials in the Developing World," *Journal of Medical Ethics*, 2 (2001), 7–10.
13. Leonard H. Glantz, George J. Annas, Michael A. Grodin, and Wendy K. Mariner, "Research in Developing Countries: Taking 'Benefit' Seriously," *Hastings Center Report*, 28:6 (1998), 38–42 at 39.
14. Unnamed reviewer of manuscript submitted to journal by a colleague, cited in chapter 3, note 4.
15. Ibid.
16. http://www.hvtn.org/trials, accessed May 2, 2003.
17. Joint United Nations Programme on HIV/AIDS (UNAIDS), *Ethical Considerations in HIV Preventive Vaccine Research* (2000), 19.
18. National Bioethics Advisory Commission, *Ethical and Policy Issues in International Research: Clinical Trials in Developing Countries* (Bethesda, MD, 2001), 30–31.
19. I authored this paper, which appears in Robert J. Levine and Samuel Gorovitz, with James Gallagher, *Biomedical Research Ethics: Updating International Guidelines: A Consultation* (Geneva: CIOMS, 2000), 208–224.
20. NBAC, *Ethical and Policy Issues*, Recommendation 4.2; 74.

21. http://www.aidsmeds.com/news/20030224drgd001.html, accessed May 2, 2003.
22. UNAIDS, *Vaccine Research*, 31.
23. The design is called a "prime boost trial": canarypox-HIV vector + gp120 BE (the VaxGen product used in the Thai trial).
24. CIOMS, *International Ethical Guidelines for Biomedical Research Involving Human Subjects* (Geneva: CIOMS, 2002), 57.
25. Michael Specter, "The Vaccine: Has the Race to Save Africa from AIDS Put Western Science at Odds with Western Ethics?" *The New Yorker* (February 3, 2003), 54–65 at 56–57.
26. NBAC, *Ethical and Policy Issues*, and Nuffield Council on Bioethics, *The Ethics of Research Related to Healthcare in Developing Countries* (London: Nuffield Council on Bioethics, 2002).
27. The position of this group was presented in a preliminary report on June 9, 2003, at a conference I attended in Durban, South Africa.
28. CIOMS, *International Ethical Guidelines*, 81.
29. Ibid., 30.

Index

justice
  CIOMS, 221
  compensatory, 81
  distributive *see* distributive justice
  double standards, 227
  equal treatment, 37, 79, 80, 117
  exploitation, 68
  global justice, 68, 71
  health policy, 75–77
  human rights, 221–223
  norms, 69, 76
  occupational/environmental health,
    76–77
  parity of respect, 58, 116
  past wrongs redressed, 81
  reciprocity, 80
  research, 68–95
  socioeconomic inequality, 76
  treat like cases alike, 44, 58, 116
  vulnerability, 69, 76
  see also equity

Kazakhstan, 181
Kenya, 10

Laos, 11
least developed countries (LDCs), 9
Levine, Robert J., 28, 29, 237
local population
  health benefits, 2
  health needs, 24
  obligations towards *see* obligations
  vulnerability, 1, 3, 24
losses, 80, 103
Lurie, Peter, 18
Lutheran World Federation, 180

Madagascar, 180
malaria
  Africa, 9, 26, 73
  biomedical research, 9
  developing countries, 73
  drug trials, 26
  Global Fund to Fight AIDS,
    Tuberculosis, and Malaria, 72, 79,
    175, 179–182, 211, 212, 223
  insecticides, 73
  Malaria Vaccine Initiative, 175
  Medicines for Malaria Venture (MMV),
    175, 177, 178
  mortality, 73
  prevalence, 9, 12, 73
  public–private partnerships, 177–179
  research and development, 178
  resistance, 73, 178

Riamet, 169
Roll Back Malaria, 178
United States, 9, 26, 73
malariotherapy, 151
Malawi, 13, 180
Mann, Jonathan, 198, 201
market forces
  affordability, 164, 175
  market distortion, 168
  pricing, 164, 167
  vaccine gap, 176
market system, 68, 164, 167
Marxism, 78, 102
Medicaid, 168, 230
medical authority, 4, 7, 141
Medical Research Council (MRC), 16, 70,
  89, 92, 172, 259
medical treatment
  benefits denied, 1, 3, 124
  best therapy *see* best proven method
  biomedical research distinguished, 142
  control groups, 21, 36
  Declaration of Helsinki, 21
  facilities *see* infrastructure
  resource-poor countries, 26, 28
  short-course regimen, 26
  standards *see* standard of care
medical treatment withheld
  context, 45
  harm–benefit ratios, 45
  HIV/AIDS, infection during trial, 5, 6, 36
  placebos *see* placebo-controlled studies
Medicare, 168
Medicines for Malaria Venture (MMV),
  175, 177, 178
meningitis, 99, 119, 133
Merck, 168, 169
method of tenacity, 44
Mexico, 187
military expenditure, 75
Mill, John Stuart, 170
Mitsuishi, Tadahiro, 90
monetary payments
  compensation, 122, 123
  corruption, 138
  out-of-pocket expenses, 166
  physicians, 122, 135, 138
Mongolia, 181
moral agency, 165
moral development, 11, 30
Morocco, 180
mortality
  HIV/AIDS, 12, 72
  malaria, 73
  maternal mortality, 74